An Explanation of the History of the Suffering and Death of our Lord Jesus Christ

Erklärung

der

Historie des Leidens und Sterbens

unsers HErrn Christi JEsu

nach den vier Evangelisten also angestellet

daß wir dadurch zur Erkenntnis der Liebe Christi erwecket werden
und am innerlichen Menschen seliglich zunehmen mögen.

Verfasset durch

Johann Gerhard

weil. Doctor der Heiligen Schrift und Professor an der Universität Jena.

Nach der Ausgabe von 1663.

Berlin 1868.
Verlag von Gustav Schlawitz.

An Explanation of the History of the Suffering and Death of our Lord Jesus Christ

according to the four evangelists,

presented so that we may be awakened in the knowledge of the love of Christ and may blessedly grow according to the inner man.

composed by

JOHANN GERHARD,
Doctor of the Sacred Scriptures and Professor at the University of Jena.

Translated from the German by Elmer M. Hohle

Edited by David O. Berger
Director of Library Services
Concordia Seminary, St. Louis

From the 1663 edition
Second Printing

Repristination Press
Malone, Texas

Copyright 1998 by Elmer Hohle. Published by permission of the translator. No part of this publication may be reproduced, stored in a retrieval system, or transmitted, in any form or by any means, electronic, mechanical, photocopying or otherwise without the prior written permission of Repristination Press.
Hardcover edition published in 1999;
Paperback edition published 2019

REPRISTINATION PRESS
716 HCR 3424 E
MALONE, TEXAS 76660

E-mail: HUNNIUS@AOL.COM

ISBN 1-891469-30-4

Table of Contents

Abbreviations vii
Prefatory Note ix
Foreword to the Christian Reader 1
On the Suffering of Christ in General (1 Pet. 2) 17
How Christ was anointed in the home of Simon (Mt. 26) 29
The Sections of the History 43

> **THE FIRST ACT:** The history of the matters which took place in the garden of the Mount of Olives.

The First Sermon: Christ goes out from the city of Jerusalem to the Mount of Olives and announces to His disciples how they will forsake Him. 45

The Second Sermon: The inward suffering and passionate prayer of Christ in the garden on the Mount of Olives. 55

The Third Sermon: Christ is taken captive in the garden through the betrayer Judas. 73

The Fourth Sermon: Since Christ won't allow Himself to be defended with the sword, He is, on that account, forsaken by His disciples. 85

> **THE SECOND ACT:** Comprising the history of the matters which have to do with Jesus before the ecclesiastical council in the house of the high priest Caiaphas.

The First Sermon: Christ was bound, was led first before Annas and next before the high priest Caiaphas; He was examined regarding His disciples and about His teaching and was struck in the face. 97

The Second Sermon: Concerning the fall and reclamation of Peter .. 109

The Third Sermon: Christ is accused by false witnesses and is condemned to death by the high priests as a blasphemer. ... 124

> **THE THIRD ACT:** Which encompasses the history of the affairs that have to do with Christ before Governor Pilate in the judgment hall.

The First Sermon: Christ is led before Governor Pilate, which, when observed by the betrayer Judas, causes him to fall into despair .. 139

The Second Sermon: How Christ was accused before Pilate and gave a good witness about His kingdom. 152

The Third Sermon: How Christ was adjudged to be innocent before Pilate and was sent to Herod...163

The Fourth Sermon: How Pilate recommended that Christ be scourged and was warned by his wife about shedding innocent blood; Barabbas is given preference over Christ..............................176

The Fifth Sermon: How Christ was scourged by Pilate, clothed with purple by the soldiers, crowned with thorns, and mocked..188

The Sixth Sermon: How the high priests and the leaders of the Jews unrelentingly demanded that Pilate condemn Christ to death on the cross. 198

The Seventh Sermon: Pilate acknowledges Christ as the King of the Jews, and as he demonstrates His innocence by the washing of the hands, he condemns Him to death on the cross................209

THE FOURTH ACT
Encompassing the history of the crucifixion of Christ.

The First Sermon: Christ is led out from the city of Jerusalem to be crucified and preaches to the sorrowing women about future misfortune..221

The Second Sermon: As He first tastes the bitter wine denatured with myrrh, Christ is crucified, and prays for those who crucify Him. 233

The Third Sermon: Pilate honors Christ's cross with a glorious superscription; the soldiers divide Christ's garments. 245

The Fourth Sermon: How Christ commanded John to take care of His mother, and how He was defamed on the cross. 257

The Fifth Sermon: Heaven is opened to the converted criminal; the sun becomes darkened; Christ laments His being forsaken by God. 267

The Sixth Sermon: Christ complains of His thirst, declares that everything has been accomplished, commends His soul into the hands of His heavenly Father, and thereupon falls calmly asleep. 277

The Seventh Sermon: The miracles that took place after Christ's death. 290

THE FIFTH AND FINAL ACT: Containing within it the history of the burial of Christ..305

Translator's Epilogue...319

Index of Citations from the Sacred Scriptures and Apocrypha...........323

Abbreviations

Genesis	Gen.	Haggai	Hag.
Exodus	Exo.	Zechariah	Zec.
Leviticus	Lev.	Malachi	Mal.
Numbers	Num.		
Deuteronomy	Deu.	Matthew	Mat.
Joshua	Jos.	Romans	Rom.
Judges	Jud.	1 Corinthians	1 Cor.
1 Samuel	1 Sam.	2 Corinthians	2 Cor.
2 Samuel	2 Sam.	Galatians	Gal.
1 Kings	1 Kin.	Ephesians	Eph.
2 Kings	2 Kin.	Philippians	Phi.
1 Chronicles	1 Chr.	Colossians	Col.
2 Chronicles	2 Chr.	1 Thessalonians	1 The.
Nehemiah	Neh.	2 Thessalonians	2 The.
Esther	Est.	1 Timothy	1 Tim.
Psalms	Psa.	2 Timothy	2 Tim.
Proverbs	Pro.	Titus	Tit.
Ecclesiastes	Ecc.	Philemon	Phm.
Song of Solomon	SSo.	Hebrews	Heb.
Isaiah	Isa.	James	Jam.
Jeremiah	Jer.	1 Peter	1 Ptr.
Lamentations	Lam.	2 Peter	2 Ptr.
Ezekiel	Eze.	Revelation	Rev.
Daniel	Dan.		
Hosea	Hos.		
Obadiah	Oba.		
Jonah	Jon.		
Micah	Mic.		
Nahum	Nah.		
Habakkuk	Hab.		
Zephaniah	Zep.		

Prefatory Note

Johann Gerhard views the Passion of Christ with Old Testament eyes. Anyone seeking a clear definition of the old German compound *Heilsgeschichte* will appreciate the unabridged functional definition furnished here. The events, people, and prophecies of the Old Testament are seamlessly connected with their culmination in the suffering, death, burial, and resurrection of Christ. Gerhard's method is the epitome of the typological approach (not to be understood as precluding rectilinear prophecy). He doesn't miss a single detail. Obviously steeped in the writings of the Church fathers, as well as in the Scriptures (cf. the Translator's Epilogue), Gerhard finds broader and deeper significance in almost every event and aspect of the Passion account. Not only does he see the intimate relationship between God's actions and promises in the Old Testament and their fulfillment in the life, death, and resurrection of Christ, but he also sees in the Passion story a pre-figuring of the life of the Church and the lives of Christians after the resurrection. Thus, Gerhard's *Heilsgeschichte* extends gloriously from the Fall through the present to the Last Day.

And lest the reader view this volume as "just another book of sermons," be forewarned: Gerhard does not speak (write) down to his audience; no popularizer, he. These sermons, prepared for a fortunate congregation and readership of early Lutherans some time before 1622, are a thorough exegetical and devotional account of Christ's Passion. In fact, the work might better be characterized as a "devotional commentary."

For reasons more pragmatic than scholarly, the present translation is based on a 19th century edition (see fascimile of title page in the forepart). The primary differences between the early 17th century edition and the 1868 edition are in orthography and in some substitutions for archaic words and grammatical forms. Also missing from the 19th century printing of this work on the Passion are a number of Latin quotations from the early Church fathers. In general, however, the substance of these quotations is also in the German text, and the loss of content is minimal.

—David O. Berger,
October 1998

Foreword to the Christian Reader.

In the Song of Solomon [chapter] 7, the spiritual Bride of Christ (that is, the true Christian Church and each particular true member of the same—each individual believing soul) is described as follows: that the hair on her head is bound in folds like the purple [gown] of the King. Luther explains it this way: that for the true Christian it serves as a constant meditation on the salvific suffering of her King and Bridegroom, Christ, during which He was clothed with a purple mantle, [stained] with His crimson-colored blood. Such meditation does not justly occur only because of their indebted thankfulness and love for Christ, but also on account of the great benefit which they receive and possess from a proper contemplation of Christ's suffering, even as there is in circulation a saying attributed to Albert that an unpretentious, simple contemplation of the suffering and passion of Christ benefits a person more than if he fasted on bread and water for an entire year, or if he daily flogged himself bloody, or if he read through the entire Psalter. Dr. Luther in his Church Postille also recalls this saying in his sermon on contemplating the passion of Christ—that's why at all times the history of the suffering (passion) of Christ has been considered precious and held in high regard, just as Ireneus, who is one of the most ancient of all teachers of the Church, testifies that in his time it was actually the practice to include a number of weeks for the comprehensive exposition and contemplation of the entire Passion History. In this regard we especially have the noteworthy example of the apostle, St. Paul, who in 1 Cor. 2 writes of himself: **I regarded myself as knowing nothing among you except solely Jesus Christ, the Crucified One.** And in the Epistle to the Galatians [ch.] 3 he testifies that he so avidly promoted this history among them, that Christ pictured Himself, as it were, before his eyes, as if He were crucified in their midst and he [Paul] himself took his place under the cross of Christ. For here, in his language [Greek], he uses a glorious simile which is taken from those who artistically portray a person's likeness with living colors.

Such a contemplation of Christ's suffering should be presented in a two-fold manner: 1. historically, [and] 2. practically. The first, historical contemplation of Christ's suffering, consists of a person's accurately and in an orderly manner seizing upon and pondering all the events of the suffering, cross, and death of Christ as described in exhaustive detail by the holy evangelists. But just as this historical contemplation is incomplete without the second, spiritual contemplation (which we want to describe later), and would be of little benefit, it nevertheless must begin with the first. And just as with other spiritual contemplations (which the holy prophets and apostles prominently promote in their writings), they are based upon the [historical events].

This historical consideration may be presented and composed in three different styles and manners. First, by dividing the entire history into five distinct acts or chief parts: as to what Christ experienced first in the garden on Mt. Olive; secondly, in the high priests' palace; thirdly, what befell Him in Pilate's hall of justice; then fourthly, the history of the crucifixion; and fifthly, the burial which then followed. These five acts are encompassed in this old verselet:

Hortus, Pontifices, Praeses, Crux atque Sepulchrum
[Garden, Priests, Governor, Cross and also Sepulcher].

That the story of Christ's sufferings [presented] in such a manner is regarded as similar to a comedy* is not unreason-

---

* i.e., in the classical sense of including a happy ending, Ed.

able, because to our reason it at first appears as wonderful and strange. But thereupon follows a gloriously decisive turn, a blessed and joyful result: namely, His resurrection, ascension into heaven, and His sitting at the right hand of God. However, as pertains to the Devil and his agents (namely, Judas, the high priests, the scribes, Pilate and the soldiers, etc.), to them it is a horrible tragedy, because at the beginning things appear to go happily and well for them, but ultimately turn out for the worst. That's why the foremost teacher of the Church, Gregory of Nasianzus* composed the sufferings of Christ into a tragedy which he entitled "The Suffering Christ." We, too, have employed this kind of division in our explanation [exegesis], and each individual act has been divided and arranged into its particular part, as the diligent reader will perceive from it after a while.

In the second place, the history of the passion may be conveniently arranged according to the time each event occurred, for which that excellent teacher, Dr. Chemnitz, provides fine guidance, which we can briefly summarize [as follows]:

The Jews began their day in the evening and ended it with the setting of the sun or evening of the following day. They thus count in a natural day the remainder of the night and the next day until the setting of the sun. The entire history of Christ's suffering was carried out within the framework of such a Jewish day. It began on Green [Maundy] Thursday, lasted through the same night and throughout the ensuing Good Friday, and ended shortly before the setting of the sun.

Furthermore, the Jews divided the night into four parts or night-watches, just as the day [was also divided] into four equal parts. The first part of the night or the first night-watch began after the setting of the sun and lasted until 9 p.m. on our clock, the next one until 12 midnight, the third until 3 a.m., the fourth until the morning as the sun arose and daylight began.

---

* Fourth century bishop of Constantinople and champion of Nicene orthodoxy, Tr.

14

The first part of the day began from morning at sunrise until half-way to noon, or 9:00 a.m. our time. The next part lasted until 12:00 noon, the third until 3:00 p.m., the fourth until the setting of the sun. Since the passion of the Lord indeed occurred in accordance with this order [time system], the history [of Christ's passion] can thus be rightly divided in the same way, so that one may observe what took place with Christ in four such night watches and the four parts of Good Friday.

On the evening of Maundy Thursday, Christ traveled with His disciples up to Jerusalem. He ate the Passover lamb with them in keeping with God's command. With this He concluded the Old Testament, and He immediately established His Holy Supper, the worthy sacrament of the New Testament. He washed the disciples' feet, spoke to them in a friendly manner, comforted them against future misfortune, warned Judas, and offered to God His fervent prayer as the sole High Priest of the New Testament. Afterwards, He and His disciples went out of the city, over the brook of Kidron, through the valley of Jehosaphat, to the Mount of Olives. On the way He proclaimed to them His suffering and their flight, [although] Peter with great steadfastness misses the point. He hereupon came with them into a garden and left eight of His disciples to sit down near the entrance [to the garden], but three of them He took with Him closer to the place where then began His inner suffering in prayer. Meanwhile, Judas, the betrayer, came and with a kiss betrayed [Jesus] over to His enemies. And as the disciple wanted to defend Him with the sword, Christ restrained him and allowed Himself to be bound willingly. All this occurred during the first night watch, from evening until 9 o'clock. In the second watch, from 9 o'clock until midnight, the following happened to Christ: He was taken bound through the sheepfold gate first to Ananias, then next was led to Caiaphas the high priest, where the other high priests, elders and scribes had assembled themselves, before whom He was falsely accused as being a heretic and a rabble-rouser. Here He was slapped in the face by the high priest's servant and denied by Peter, His disciple. Thereupon false witness was brought against Him again. And since He, upon a prior oath, had confessed before the high priest that He was God's Son, He was on this account maligned and condemned. During the third and fourth watch—that is, from midnight until morning—the following occurred: after the entire counsel adjourned and went to rest, Christ was mocked, despised, and terribly treated for the remainder of the night by the servants who guarded Him. During the first part of Good Friday, from the rising of the sun until 9:00 a.m., the following took place with Christ: the entire council assembled early and asked Him one more time whether He still wanted to abide by His previous statements, thereupon condemned Him, and led Him away to the Roman governor, Pilate. When Judas the betrayer saw [what was occurring], it caused him to despair.

    The high priests began their dealings before Pilate in this way. From the start they demanded that Christ should be condemned to death without a hearing on the charges. Since they could not prove their case, they accused Him of treason and sedition. Thereupon, Pilate asked Christ about His Kingdom and testified that He was not guilty. In the second watch of the day, from nine until noon, the following occurred: Christ was sent to Herod, who scorned Him, dressed Him in a white robe, and sent Him back to Pilate, who placed Him beside the murderer Barabbas, intending that the people would plead for Christ's release. But the offer by Pilate failed, and even though his wife warned him, he allowed Christ to be innocently and pitifully scourged. In this scourging Christ was crowned with thorns, dressed in a purple mantle, and in mockery a reed was placed into His hand instead of a scepter. Despite Pilate's intentions thereby to move the Jews to sympathy and secure Christ's release, he achieved neither. Consequently, as they threatened him with Caesar's disfavor, Pilate condemned Christ to death, even as he first acknowledged Christ's innocence with the washing of his hands. Thereupon, Christ was led from the city to the place of crucifixion, was wept over by many women, and had the cross carried behind Him by Simon. He was crucified between two murderers on Golgatha's hill. At the same time, He achieved a glorious testimony to His innocence with the inscription on the cross. The soldiers divided His clothes, and the crowds mocked Him. All this took place from 9 o'clock until noon. After that Christ further prayed for His crucifiers, promised paradise to the murderer, and directed John to take care of His mother. As He became aware of the unnatural darkness of the sun, He lamented being forsaken by God. Then, as He quenched His thirst with vinegar, He affirmed that everything now had been fulfilled. And, after commending His spirit into the hands of His Father, He quietly and willingly gave it up. In the fourth and last part of the day, from 3 until 6 p.m., the miraculous deeds after Christ's death occurred: the curtain in the temple ripped apart, the earth quaked, the boulders split, the graves opened up, and the captain confessed Him as God's Son. Thereupon, finally, follows the history of the burial.

In the third place, the passion history can be rightly and conveniently divided according to the persons who are remembered in it. Thus, one may reflect on: **1.** The Lord Christ, who is here the foremost Person, noting especially how He sweats blood, is tied up, falsely accused and condemned, innocently beaten, mocked, despised, whipped, crowned with thorns, crucified and killed; **2.** how the disciples flee from Christ, [especially] Peter, who denies Him, and Judas, who betrays Him and despairs over it; **3.** how the high priests, the Scripture-learned [scribes], and elders set up false witnesses against Christ in their council, how they condemn Him in spite of His innocence, and how their servants hit Him and despise Him; **4.** how Pilate was reluctantly brought to the point that he, at the urgent persistence of the Jews, finally condemned Christ to death against his own conscience; **5.** how Herod mocked and jeered at Christ; **6.** how the soldiers scourged Christ, crowned Him with thorns, clothed Him in purple, made fun of Him, finally led Him out of the city with violence, gave Him to drink of vinegar and myrrh, and divided His garments; 7. how the good-hearted women cried over Him, stood with Him under the cross, and how Simon carried the cross after Him; [and] **8.** how Nicodemus and Joseph finally gloriously buried Him with honor.

These, then, are three distinctive ways and modes according to which the entire passion history may be neatly and properly arranged, prepared, and considered, "so that the purple robe of the King might be neatly folded"—as the pertinent saying mentioned above thus describes the orderly, diligent contemplation of the sufferings of Christ.

Also appropriate to the historical contemplation of Christ's suffering is the diligent examination of the prophecies and types of the Old Testament which point, in general, to the history of the sufferings, or point especially to specific portions of it, and then compare them with the [passion] history. For since St. Paul testifies in 1 Cor. 15 that Christ died "according to the Scriptures," it undeniably follows that in the Scriptures of the Old Testament there had to have been a prior proclamation of the suffering and death of Christ. St. Peter even more clearly verifies this in the first chapter of his first epistle: the Spirit of Christ, which was in the prophets, had previously testified to the sufferings which Christ went through. Thus, in the first Gospel promise about the woman's Seed in Gen. 3, it is announced that the hellish snake would sting Him in the heel. This heel-prick is none other than the sufferings of Christ. Psalm 16 says of the Messiah: I must suffer on behalf of you. This Psalm is applied to Christ. In Acts 2 and 13 [and] in Psa. 22 are described the abusive words which the Jews poured out against Christ. Judas' betrayal is prophesied in Psa. 41 and 55, and in Psa. 69 it is announced how Christ was given to drink of gall and vinegar in His great thirst. In Isa. 50 are prophesied the beating and insulting of

Christ with which He was blasphemed. The fifty-third chapter of Isaiah looks at the whole passion of Christ. In Zec. 11 are mentioned the 30 pieces of silver for which Christ was sold; in Zec. 12, the opening [piercing] of His side. There are similar glorious types of the suffering of Christ in the Old Testament, as, for example, in Joseph, who was sold by his own brothers (Gen. 37); in the fetters of Samson (Jdg. 16); in the offering up of Isaac, who himself carried the wood (Gen. 22); in the previous lifting up of the serpent (Num. 21); in the Levitical sacrifices; in Jonah, who was in the belly of the whale-fish for three days and three nights (Jonah 2); in the opening of Adam's side as he slept (Gen. 2); in the Passover lamb (Exo. 12)—even as the Scriptures of the New Testament refer to certain of these same prophecies and types with clear words, [cf.] Mat. 12, John 3 and 19, Heb. 9. As opportunity arises, these prophecies and types will be pointed out in subsequent explanations. However, the comprehensive account and explanation of all the prophecies and types of the Old Testament that point to Christ should follow at another place, namely, in the comprehensive Scriptural explanation of the articles on Christ, provided that God will grant life and grace to this purpose, so that these and other articles may also be explained, even as the two articles about Holy Baptism and the Holy Supper have been completed and already are available in the public press.

As to what then pertains to the second—namely, the spiritual contemplation of Christ's suffering—this has to be given the utmost consideration, since the preceding historical consideration is incomplete and would be of little benefit without the spiritual one. However, we would conceive of these spiritual contemplations in the following six parts:

First, St. Paul writes in Rom. 5, how through the disobedience of one many became sinners; also how through the obedience of One many become righteous. Here we have a proper key to understanding the divine. With this key we can fathom many mysteries in the passion history; namely, if we view the profound obedience of Christ—the second heavenly Adam—as in His suffering He became obedient to His heavenly Father unto death (Phi. 2) as a payment and satisfaction for the disobedience and the sin of the first Adam. With this key, journey through the entire history [of the passion]. Adam had sinned in a garden. To atone for it, Christ began His suffering in a garden. Adam wanted to be like God. To atone for such haughty arrogance, Christ humbled Himself to the very depths. **Even though He was in divine form, He did not regard it as a thing to rob [seize] to be equal with God; instead He emptied Himself, taking on the form of a servant**, Phi. 2. Adam was a blasphemer of God; because he wanted to be like God, he tried to snatch His Creator's crown. To atone for [Adam's sin], Christ allowed Himself to be condemned as a blasphemer for confessing to be God's Son—which He actually was in deed and truth. Adam leaned himself up against God his Creator, becoming a rebellious perjurer. To atone for such, Christ in an innocent manner was accused and condemned as a seditious rabble-rouser. After his fall into sin, Adam still wanted to excuse himself for his crimes. To atone for such sin, Christ kept His silence before false accusations and became dumb like a sheep before its shearer, Isa. 53. Adam was a genuine murderer and a"Barabbas"; he brought death upon himself and over all his descendants—a greater murderer there never was. To atone for this, Christ was presented side by side next to an arch-murderer. Yes indeed, Barabbas was released; Christ, however, was condemned to death. Adam was dressed by God with the beautiful garment of innocence and righteousness; but that hellish robber, the Devil, undressed him of it through sin, and on this account the Devil still wounds all natural powers of body and soul, Luke 10. To atone for this and to divert it, Christ allowed Himself to be stripped naked and be wounded in all his members. Adam stretched out his hand to the forbidden tree and permitted the forbidden fruit to please him, thereby bringing sin and death into the world, Rom. 5. To atone for this and stave it off, Christ stretched out His hands on the tree of the cross and was given to drink vinegar and myrrh in order to win righteousness and life for us men. Through sin, Adam locked himself and us out from the gate to Paradise, Gen. 3. Christ promises entrance into the heavenly paradise to the converted criminal, Luke 23, thereby to indicate that through cross and death He has once more opened to us the way to eternal life, Psa. 16.

Secondly, the prophet Isaiah [in chapter] 53 testifies that Christ was wounded for the sake of our transgressions and was beaten on account of our sin. Here we again have another key with which to unlock the mystery of Christ's suffering; namely, if we view this as a payment and sacrifice for our manifold sin, since Christ took upon Himself such sin of ours and the justly earned punishment for it. Once again, journey through the entire [passion] history with this key. Christ crosses the brook of Kidron, into which flowed all the filth from the city of Jerusalem, for God had laid all our sins upon Him—which sins flowed and poured upon Him with heaping accumulation, just as the prophet himself states in the holy language [of Scripture]. Christ became sorrowfully distressed unto death, sweated bloody sweat, for we had deserved eternal, hellish anxiety and sadness. Christ was bound so that He might release us from our sin and the bonds of the Devil and death. False witnesses stood up against Christ. He suffered that for our sake so that we might stand before God's judgment when our sin, the divine Law, our conscience, and all creation correctly and truthfully accuse us. Christ is condemned in an innocent fashion so that we might be pronounced absolved. Christ kept silent so that we, as worthless servants, will not have to be dumb before God's judgment, Mat. 22. Christ was chastised and scourged so that Satan does not eternally beat us with his fists, 2 Cor. 12. Christ was cloaked with purple so that He might win for us the beautiful, white cloak of righteousness, Rev. 19 [:8].

Christ was crowned with a crown of thorns so that we might be crowned with grace and mercy, Psa. 103. Christ was disgraced with humiliation and shame to His face so that we would not come to shame before God. Christ became a curse for us on the tree trunk of the cross so that we may become recipients of divine blessings, Gal. 3. Christ was maligned and slandered so that we would not have to listen to the Devil's slander forever. Christ complained that He was forsaken by God so that we will nevermore be forsaken by God. Christ died so that we may live forever. In conclusion, our evil thoughts are the crown of thorns which pricked and stuck Christ; our sinful words are the spit which splattered on Christ's face; our evil deeds are the whips with which Christ was scourged.

Thirdly, in Acts 4 the apostles say the following in their prayer to God the heavenly Father: Herod and Pontius Pilate did what the hand and counsel of God had deliberated on in advance that it should take place. Here again we have another key of knowledge with which to open up the mystery of the passion history; namely, so that we should view everything that happened to Christ in His suffering as if God Himself has done it, just as He says in Zec. 13: "Sword, put yourself on the man who is close to me; strike the shepherd." Accordingly, whenever we look back on how Christ was bound, scourged, and crucified, we should look upon this as if God's hand is doing this. But why so? Is Christ's heavenly Father in His Person that antagonistic and grudging? Not so, for Christ is God's only-born, most beloved Son in His personhood. Why then does the heavenly Father deal with Him in such a manner? This is why: He took upon Himself our sin and stepped before God's judgment in our stead. That's why God in His judgment and wrath deals with Him like He would with the greatest sinner. He sees Him as being so black that Christ on that account cries out: My God, My God, why have you forsaken Me? As a result, the sufferings of Christ most clearly mirror divine wrath against sin. The fact that Christ shakes and quivers in the garden and is anguished to the point that He sweats blood...all that is a result of the burden of divine wrath which pressed down upon Him on account of our sin. That Christ, as He pleaded for the removal of the cup, obtained nothing, occurred because God set before Christ a beaker brim-full of His wrath for Him to drink. It occurred because Christ wanted to pay for our sin. That the sun in the heavens was darkened came about because the heavenly Father wrathfully viewed Christ as being black from all our sins which at that time lay upon Him. This we must take and ponder in the depths of our heart so that we fully recognize the gruesomeness of our sin and God's horrible wrath against it.

In the fourth place, St. Paul says in Gal. 2: Christ loved me, and gave Himself up for Me. Here we have another key of knowledge with which we may open up the mysteries of the passion history; namely, that we view the suffering of Christ as a clear reflector of His heartfelt, burning love towards us. John 15: No one has a greater love than this, that one give his life for his friends. Therefore, praise God for His love towards us, in that Christ died for us while we were still sinners and were His enemies, Rom. 5. Journey once more through the entire history with this key. Christ goes willingly to the place of suffering because His heartfelt love to suffer for us drove Him there. As He realized in the garden that humanity could not be helped in any other way than that He accept the cup [lit., the chalice of the cross], He did not waver for a moment. Sweet love made everything sweet to Him. As the disciples to a man fled from Him, He did not hesitate for a moment, as He well could have done. For His love had, as it were, taken Him captive, drawn Him down from heaven, [and] fastened Him upon the martyr's post and the cross. He bows His head on the timber-trunk of the cross to kiss us in love. He stretches out His arms in order to embrace us in love. He prays for His crucifiers because He suffered out of love for them. His side is opened up with a spear so that the flame of heartfelt love might break forth from it, "so that we through the wound's opening may behold the mystery of the heart." In love He longs for us, and thus He said: I thirst [that is,] for your salvation. On the timber-trunk of the cross [as on an altar] He roasted in hot love as the innocent Lamb of God. Yes indeed, be the outward love ever so great, His inner love is yet even greater. Had [His suffering] not been sufficient, out of love He would have suffered even more for our sake. Such fiery flame of Christ's love should now rightly also ignite our hearts.

Fifthly, St. Paul says in Col. 1 [v. 24] **I compensate in my flesh for what still is deficient regarding tribulations of Christ for His body, which is the congregational fellowship.** Here, then, the apostle himself explains that he is speaking of the spiritual Body of Christ, that is, of the true Church. Herewith we are given another key of knowledge with which to open up the mystery of the passion story; namely, that we should remember what happened to Christ, the Head of the Church, [for] that is also what the members of this Body also have to be prepared for. Gal. 6: **I carry on my body the scars of Christ.** Journey once more through the passion history with this key: Christ was betrayed by His own disciple; thus, human enemies are members of His own household, Mat. 10. Christ was cast aside and condemned by the high priests, scribes and elders—who regarded themselves as pillars of the Church. Thus also is the little flock of Christ most often betrayed by those who want to sit in positions of high authority in the Church. The high priests instigate (stir up) the worldly authority against Christ; so it also goes with Christ's members. Christ's teaching is accused of being heretical and misleading; so also is the same meted out to the confessors of divine truth. Pilate knew very well that Christ was innocent, yet at the same time he condemned Him to death so that he [Pilate] would not fall into Caesar's bad graces. How often is not this same [chicanery] practiced against Christ's members? Pilate and Herod became friends on account of Christ. Even though the Church suffers, the most intense enemies become reconciled. Christ is stripped of His clothes; thus is the Church robbed of its goods [blessings] such that Christ must suffer need through His members. And without a doubt, there is still much contained in the passion story which will yet be fulfilled within the spiritual Body of Christ before the end of the world.

In the sixth and last place, St. Peter states in his first epistle [ch. 2:21]: **Christ offered up Himself for our sins in His own body on the tree, and He has left us a type in that we are to follow in His footsteps.** Here we once again have a key of knowledge, namely that we should see the passion history as a reflection of Christ's glorious virtues; that we see these virtues as a prescribed model and formula; that we also direct and pattern our life and sojourn after it. Here we see Christ's obedience, Phi. 2; His heartfelt love, Gal. 2; His extreme humility, His patience, Isa. 53; His gentleness, 1 Peter 2. He speaks kindly to His betrayer, submits to God's will, restrains vengeance with self-imposed restriction, remains silent in the face of false, worthless accusations, gives good confession before Pilate, prays for His crucifiers, provides care for His own, [and] commends His spirit into the hands of the heavenly Father—all as an example for us to follow. Although we indeed will never be able to attain the same perfection of love, humility, patience, meekness and the like in this life, we nevertheless should still learn from Him, Mat. 11, and long for perfection and follow Christ as His disciples—just as Peter in the verse considered [above] uses a beautiful word in the original Greek* which actually means a *Vorschrift* [a prior writing, a prescription, instruction, direction or rule]: Just as the lads must always take note of their teacher's

---

*   Gerhard is obviously referring to v. 21 in which St. Peter uses the word υπογραμμος, translated as "example" in English language Bibles, although my Greek lexicon defines the word as a piece of calligraphy, a copy, (for children to imitate); hence a model or type which has to be followed. Tr.

Vorschrift [i.e., writings on a black board] and copy them, even though they are not able to write after him as neatly and beautifully as the teacher, so also should Christ's example hover before the eyes of our heart so that we follow it, even though we are unable to bring it to that kind of perfection.

These, then, are the six parts of the spiritual consideration of Christ's suffering. Blessed and holy is he who steadfastly practices himself therein. He will learn more from the Book of Life and the sufferings of Christ than from all the volumes of worldly wisdom. God the Lord through His Spirit grant us to know this, for the sake of His only-begotten Son, Jesus Christ. Amen.

> **The Lord [Master] dies instead of the servant;**
> **In place of the debtors, the Faithful One;**
> **The Physician dies for the good of the patient;**
> **The Shepherd rescues His sheep;**
> **The King dies for the sins of His subjects;**
> **The Peace-maker for the warriors;**
> **The Creator dies for His creation;**
> **God Himself wins man's salvation!**
> **What now should the servant, the debtor,**
> **The sick one, the sheep, the nation, the multitude do?**
> **What should the creatures, mankind, do?**
> **In love extol his Redeemer!**
>
> D. J. G.

26

Of the Suffering of Christ in General.

1 Peter 2

Christ sacrificed Himself in His own body on the tree for our sins, so that we, who have died to sin, live in righteousness; through His wounds you were healed.

Just as the love of Christ towards us manifests itself most intensely in His bitter suffering and in His wounds, so also each one of us who has a true love for Christ should frequently think about [ponder] His suffering and His wounds. For that reason Song of Solomon 1 says to the Christian Church and to each individual believing soul: **My friend is for me a cluster of myrrh that hangs between my breasts.** This Friend and beloved Bridegroom of the Church is Christ the Lord. It calls Him a cluster of myrrh because He suffered so many different afflictions and endured bitter pains on their account, and thereby He healed all their soul-wounds; that is, all their sin, just as myrrh, which is usually bitter, heals the wounds of the body. This cluster of myrrh, i.e., everything that Christ the Lord had to endure in bitter suffering (such as bonds, scourging, the crown of thorns, nails, spear, and the wooden cross), each individual believing soul has hanging between the breasts; that is, [these bitter sufferings] lie deeply within the heart, which oft thinks on them and can never, ever forget about them. Consequently, when one of the fathers was once asked what kind of book he studied most frequently, he answered that he daily read in one book which had three pages—one red, one white, and one black. The red page reminded him of the sufferings of Christ in which He shed His crimson-colored blood. By the white page he was reminded of the joy of the elect, who would be dressed with white garments. The black page put him in mind of the pain of the damned, who would be heaved into the black sink-hole which burns with fire and brimstone. If then, indeed, all believers should at all times remember Jesus Christ, who died on the cross, such remembrance should occur above all else at this particular time when the proper time of year demands that it should be dealt with and considered. Therefore, we would first of all comment briefly about what is to be remembered regarding:

I. **Who suffered?**
II. **What did He suffer?**
III. **Why did He suffer?**
IV. **What did He gain with His suffering?**
V. **How are we to present ourselves in regard to (as a result of) such suffering?**

I. **Who suffered?** Concerning this, our text shows us that it is Christ, whose name includes the entire Person and not just one nature in Christ, especially since Christ is called an Anointed One. Accordingly, with this name is comprehended not only the humanity of Christ (which was anointed by God with the Oil of Joy, the Holy Spirit, without measure, Psalm 45, John 3) but also the divinity of Christ, which has anointed His human nature. Therefore, it firmly stands that not only an ordinary man suffered, but the true God, which changes it into a special, marvelous suffering. Therefore, Paul says in Acts 20: **that God has with His own blood purchased His fellowship of believers**, and in 1 Cor. 2: **the Lord of glory was crucified**. And it most certainly remains true that God suffered, God shed His blood, and [God] died. Do you then say: "God is indeed an unchangeable, spiritual, immortal Essence. How can it be that God suffered, shed His blood and died?" To this Vigilius answers in opposition to Eutyches (2): God did not suffer according to

His own nature, but rather in His divine-human Personhood. The divine nature of Christ could not have suffered on its own; therefore, God's Son assumed a human nature and personally united Himself with it so that through it He could suffer and thereby achieve a perfect (complete) sacrifice for all the sin of the world.

Although it is true that the divine nature of Christ was not subject to any suffering and death, yet, because the self-same divine nature is personally united with the assumed human nature so that the human nature and all its attributes are taken on by the Son of God through the personal union; the suffering, the shedding of blood, and death—which Christ endured in His human nature—actually and most certainly are ascribed to God's Son and to the entire Person, as if He accomplished all this through His divine nature. We can take an example from [human experience]. If a person's body is wounded, one does not then say: Only the body is wounded. Instead, one says: The person was wounded and receives [the wound] as if it happened to the soul itself—even though the soul as a spiritual essence cannot become wounded. Thus a person can say concerning the deep union of the body and the soul, that for the body's sake the soul takes upon itself everything that happens to the body, [both] good and evil. The same also occurs with Christ's suffering. His divinity may not suffer or die, nor shed blood. At the same time, because this very same human nature which suffers, dies, and sheds blood is personally united with Christ's Godhood [divinity], this personal union makes for a much closer relationship between the divine and human natures in Christ than the body and soul of a person can ever be tied together [united]. Therefore, one states correctly—and it is thus portrayed in the truth—that God died, God suffered, God shed blood. Yet it remains true into all eternity that the divine nature of itself is immortal and is not subject to any suffering.

Since so very much depends on this [truth], we must explain it more thoroughly. As Saul persecuted the true Christians, Acts 9, Christ says to him: **Saul, Saul, why do you persecute Me?** Here we are made aware that when true Christians are persecuted, then Christ is also persecuted; if they suffer, then Christ suffers—simply because they are members of that spiritual Body of which Christ is the head, Eph. 1. If, however, one states concerning Christ's suffering that God suffered therein, that [statement] encompasses something further; for one [makes that statement] concerning the personal union between the self-same human nature, which suffers, and the divine nature. At the same time, it is certain that in this life we will never fully understand this mystery, for just as surely and certainly that God's Son unites Himself with the human nature, so surely and certainly He assumed to Himself the sufferings of the human nature. However, we are unable to fully understand in this life exactly how God's Son unites Himself with the human nature, for it is an especially great mystery, 1 Tim. 3. Therefore, we are also unable to understand exactly how this suffering of the human nature is assumed by the Son of God. This aspect of Christ's suffering must now receive maximum attention. It is indeed noteworthy that such great and manifold sufferings come together here, but that is still not the most important aspect. However, that this Person who suffers is not merely true man, but also true God, actually makes His suffering far surpass the sufferings of all the saints and martyrs and far more worthy and greater than heaven and earth. Yes, indeed, this true, perfect suffering provides the power to be an adequate payment for the sin of the entire world. Luther explains it this way: "If one were to lay our sin and God's wrath—which is the consequence of our sin—on one side of a balance scale, and on the other side only a man or a person's natural death, the one side would be far too heavy. On account of our sin and the burdensome weight of divine wrath, we would sink into hell. But if you laid God's suffering, God's blood, God's death onto the scale, then it would be far more weighty than all the world's sin and all the burden of God's wrath."

Thus, even though the divine nature of Christ does not suffer like the human nature, it is not superfluous to the suffering; instead, it remains at the same time personally united with the suffering human nature so that as a result of such a union, one may say that God suffers. Accordingly, it was also the counsel and good pleasure [of the divine nature] that this human nature suffer in this way so that it [the divine nature] would not shun such suffering for itself—as it well could have; it did not allow its light and glory to shine through with full brightness. Thirdly, it strengthened and upheld the human nature in such suffering so that the human nature would not sink (founder) under the immeasurable burden of sin and divine wrath. Finally, it thus gave to this suffering the kind of power that would be precious before God and salutary for the entire world, in order to be a satisfactory payment for all the world's sin.

II. What, then, did the Lord Christ suffer? Our text states [that] He offered Himself upon the tree. Understand by this the final act of the suffering, namely the crucifixion, in which Christ presented Himself before His heavenly Father as a sacrifice. But, if one wants to remember the entire suffering of Christ, one will find that it was a great and manifold suffering.

First of all, we must remember: from whom does He receive suffering? He is given into death by His heavenly Father; He is accused by the Jews; He is condemned to death by the Gentiles; He is tortured by enemies; He is forsaken by His best friends, the disciples. He suffers before men who take Him captive, whip Him and crucify Him. He suffers before a woman who motivates Peter's falling away. He suffers before rulers, the high priests, and their servants; before the learned Pharisees and the uneducated folks.

Next, He suffers not only for just one sin, also not for just one man's sin, also not for just the sins of a nation, also not just for the sin of the elect from every nation; rather, [He suffers] for the sin of all mankind which had been committed from the beginning of the world, and for all the sin that would be committed up to the end of the world.

Thirdly, He also suffers in His entire body and in every member of His body. His head is crowned with thorns and struck with a rod; His face is disfigured with spit; His cheeks feel slaps; His back is wounded and beaten with whips; His shoulders must carry the weight of the heavy tree of the cross; His hands and feet are pierced with nails; His side is opened with a spear; His entire body is stripped to the skin and filled with stripes and welts; His bones are pitifully stretched out on the cross so that one could count every one; His arteries gently pour out His blood; all His members dry up like a potsherd; His tongue sticks to the roof of His mouth; His heart becomes like melted wax in His body; His eyes shed tears and darken into death. With great pain He sees His beloved mother standing under the cross; His ears hear false testimony, slander, and scorn; His mouth is given to drink of vinegar and bitter gall.

Fourthly, He suffered in all His undertakings. If He spoke, He was contradicted; if He taught, [His teaching] was perverted; if He performed miracles, He was maligned; if He practiced compassion, He was chided as a companion of sinners; if He ate or drank, He had to be labeled a wine-guzzler; if He admonished, He was laughed at.

Fifthly, He also suffered in various places. In Bethlehem He was laid into a hard crib; in Egypt He had to travel in misery; in the wilderness He suffered hunger and anguish from the Devil; in the temple they picked up stones in opposition to Him; in the places of lodging they lay in wait for Him; on journeys He became exhausted and tired; at Nazareth they pushed Him out of the city and wanted to shove Him off the cliff; in the garden

He sweated bloody sweat; in [the garden] also He was taken captive, bound, and betrayed by His own disciple. In the palace of the high priest, He was struck in the face, falsely accused and despised. In the judgment hall, He was scourged, crowned with thorns, and sentenced to death. In Herod's palace, He was laughed at. At the place of the skull, He was stripped naked and crucified.

    In the sixth place, He suffered throughout His entire life. In His childhood He was born in a stall. He was circumcised, betrayed by Herod, and fled to Egypt. In His youth He suffered poverty and labor. In His adult life He suffered hunger and thirst in the wilderness for forty days and nights, was led by the Devil upon the temple pinnacle and to a high mountain, frequently prayed the entire night, and wore Himself out with many sermons and by journeying over land and sea. At the time of His death, as He arose from the evening meal, He began to shiver and shake [with fear]. His soul became sorrowful unto death, and His blood flowed from Him in anxiety. He was captured in the night, bound like a murderer; and dragged off to the high priests Ananias and Caiaphas. At dawn, at the first hour, He was accused before Pilate; in the third hour He was scourged, crowned with thorns, and cloaked with a purple mantel; in the ninth hour He suffered thirst on the cross, and with a loud cry gave up His spirit. In the evening hour He was pierced in the side, and later He was taken off the cross and laid in the grave.

    In the seventh place, His holy soul also suffered in many ways. He felt the burden of divine wrath, which weighed so heavily upon Him that He cried out: **My God, My God, why have you forsaken Me?** He no doubt also felt the huge burden of all the sin which lay upon Him. He felt the agony of hell and saw also how His precious suffering would be lost upon so many thousands of individuals [in that they would reject it].

III. **Why, then, did Christ suffer all this?** He Himself was innocent, as is shown completely throughout the entire passion history in the testimony to Christ's innocence by friend and foe alike. However, He endured all this for the sake of our sin, as our text indicates: **Christ offered Himself in His own body for our sins.** That is why the sufferings of Christ are the clearest reflection of divine wrath over sin that a person can ever obtain from any source. When the first man, Adam, fell—and through the Fall plunged all his descendants into eternal death—God's Son presented a petition before the throne of His heavenly Father and volunteered to pay for [the redemption of] the human race, thus burdening Himself down with foreign guilt. Thereupon, God the Lord most pitiably smote and tormented His only-begotten Son. He let Him struggle and flounder in the agony of death and hell for a long time so that one might behold His [the Father's] zealous, burning wrath against sin and [also] see that the satisfaction of His righteousness had been accomplished. Therefore, we all must view what Christ endured in His suffering as blows and agonizing torture against God the Lord Himself. He presents Himself so lamentably and pitiably when the suffering begins in the garden and cries out so pitifully on the cross so that, as a result of His suffering now coming to an end, other martyrs may consequently go to their death with a joyful courage. All of this came about because Christ, along with His outward sufferings, also inwardly felt the wrath of God, which descended upon Christ not on account of His own Personhood, but rather because He stepped into our place. Christ Himself speaks of this as He is led out to be crucified, when He says: **You daughters of Jerusalem, don't cry on account of Me; [rather] cry on account of yourselves, for if one does this to a green timber, what's to become of the dry one?** He is saying this to all of us, for we are all by nature dry timbers and unfruitful trees. Christ alone is the green and fruitful Tree of Life. If God the Lord then dealt with this green Timber—with Christ—in this manner simply because He had laid our sin on Him, how might He have rightly dealt with us unfruitful timbers on account of our sin had not Christ stepped in in our stead? How shall He then not also zealously punish all unfruitful timbers who are not implanted into this Tree of Life; that is, all people who do not seize this precious suffering of Christ for themselves through faith?

IV. What, then, has Christ acquired with His suffering?
Our text also points this out to us, in that it announces that through Christ's wounds we were healed (made whole). Therefore, St. Bernard correctly states that Christ's suffering is of the greatest consequence; for just as the death of the saints is precious to the Lord, Psa. 116, how much more will not the death of this most holy, innocent Son of God be precious to Him. This element must be drawn (threaded) through the entire passion [history], for the kernel and beneficial contemplation [of the passion] is embodied in it. Thus, Christ's soul was grieved unto death so that we might rejoice forever. Christ sweated bloody sweat and struggled in the throes of death so that we need never despair in the agony of death. Christ was led in captivity so that we would not have to be eternally captive to the Devil. Christ was bound so that He could rescue us from the bonds of sin and hell. Christ was forsaken by all the disciples so that He could reconcile us with God, from whom we had become disgracefully alienated in disloyal apostasy. Christ was struck in the face so that we would not be eternally battered with the fists of Satan's angels. Christ was falsely accused so that the Law could not accuse us before God's judgment. Christ kept His silence when He was falsely accused so that we would not have to be struck dumb before God's judgment. Christ was despised so that we would not end up in eternal, humiliating disgrace. Christ's countenance was concealed so that He might take away from us [our] sin—which sin is nothing other than covering up our heart so that we do not

recognize (see) God. Christ was stripped of His clothes so that He could win for us the garment of [His] righteousness. Christ was stabbed with thorns in order to heal every sticker and thorn of our hearts. Christ was sentenced and condemned to death so that we do not end up in eternal death. Christ carried the burden of the cross so that He could lift the burden of eternal punishment from us. Christ felt nothing less than that He was [actually] forsaken by God, so that we would not be eternally forsaken and rejected by God. Christ suffered thirst on the cross so that we did not end up in eternal thirst. Christ gave up His spirit with a great cry so that we would not have to fall into the eternal wailing and gnashing of teeth. Christ became for us a curse upon the timber-trunk of the cross so that we would not be eternally cursed by God. Christ was pierced in the side to atone for the sin which was brought into the world by Eve, who was crafted from the side of Adam. Christ died so that we might live forever. From this we see that the suffering of Christ is the clearest reflector of comfort in the face of sin.

V. How should we, on account of this suffering, show our gratitude towards Christ? Our text shows us this also, in as much as it admonishes **that we, having died to sin, should live righteously.** How dare we have an affection towards sin when it inflicted so much suffering on Christ? Why would we not serve Christ with a godly life, in as much as He purchased us at such great expense? If the sad picture of the crucified Christ constantly hovers before our hearts, all evil lusts are easily extinguished. Thus, then, Christ's sufferings should keep us from sinning in two ways: For one, because it is such a horrible example of the wrath of God against sin; we are not to awaken this wrath against ourselves with deliberate sins, even though this burden should become so very heavy for us. Secondly, because this suffering is such an excellent proof of Christ's love towards us. Therefore, we should indeed once again show our thankfulness to this our best Friend—who has expended (bestowed) so much upon us—with all kinds of good works. Christ suffered in all of His members; thus, we should serve Him, in turn, with our every member. To that end, God help us through Christ. Amen.

O Lord Jesus Christ, who was wounded for our transgressions, help [us] that we are healed through Your wounds. You who sacrificed Your own body for our sins, help [us] that we may die to sin and live in righteousness. Amen.

38

How Christ was anointed in the home of Simon.

Matthew 26.

As Jesus was setting out for Bethany to the home of Simon, a woman stepped up to Him with a glass of expensive perfume, while He was sitting at a table, and poured it over His head. As His disciples saw this, they became indignant and said: What purpose does this rubbish serve? This [perfume] could have been sold at a dear price and [the proceeds] given to the poor. As Jesus took note of this, He said to them: Why are you concerned about this woman? She has done a good work in respect to Me. You continually have the poor with you, but Me you do not always have with you. That she poured out this [perfume] on to My body, she did for My burial. Truly I say to you: Wherever this Gospel will be preached in the entire world, there one will relate in her memory what she has done here.

Among all of the other salutary contemplations which lead to the knowledge and love of God, none can be found that is more beneficial and appropriate than the contemplation of the sufferings and death of Christ. For in this life we may come to know God in no other way than through His works. Among all of God's works, the foremost one is the humanity of Christ. He is the singular holy Man who is called the "Door," through which we enter into the Godhead. Among all the works of the Man Christ, there is none more prominent and more marvelous than His holy suffering. For that reason, then, the contemplation of the suffering and death of our Lord Jesus Christ is properly regarded as most fitting for obtaining a knowledge of God and to awaken a godly love within us. Such holy suffering is portrayed through many metaphors in the Old Testament. You have an excellent type in Joseph, who was sold by his own brothers, Gen. 31, even as Christ the Lord was sold by His own disciple. In Noah, who was mocked by his own son, Gen. 9, you have an excellent type of how Christ would be stripped of His clothes and mocked by His own people. In Job, you have a type of how Christ would be despised, who also complained, chapter 16, **My friends are my mockers.** In all the Levitical sacrifices, you have a type of how [Christ] would be beaten and tortured. You have a type of how Christ was to be bound in Samson, who was bound by the Philistines, Jdg. 16. You have a type of how Christ was to carry His cross in Isaac, who on his back carried the wood upon which he was to be slaughtered as a burnt-offering, Gen. 22. In the brass snake which Moses raised up in the wilderness at the command of God, Num. 21, you have a type of how Christ was to be hammered onto the cross. You have a type of how the Lord Christ was to have His side opened up by a spear in Adam, who had his side opened by God, and from the rib which was taken from him was crafted a woman. Thus, as Christ fell into death's sleep on the cross, from His opened side flowed blood and water—the two Holy Sacraments—from which the Church, Christ's Bride, was built up. A type of how Christ was to be killed you have in Abel, who was murdered by Cain, his own brother, Gen. 4, just as Christ was murdered by His own people. You have a type of how Jesus was to be buried in [the experience of] Jonah, who was in the belly of the fish for three days, even as Christ rested in the earth for three days, Mat. 12.

 Even though all believing Christians should daily contemplate the suffering and death of Christ, we should, nevertheless, during this forthcoming time [the season of Lent] especially take to heart such costly suffering. Since the proper season [of the Church year] calls this to our attention, we should do so with even greater intensity. For this reason we want to begin such a historical contemplation here. Also, at this time we want to examine the story read above as to what took place in the house of Simon at Bethany as a preparation or preview, as it were. Hence, we will explain it in two parts.

I. The performance by the woman.
II. How she was talked about by the disciples, but defended by the Lord.

I. As the designated time for the suffering of Christ drew near, behold, the Lord also wanted to draw near to the place of the suffering. For that reason, He arose and went with His disciples towards Bethany, a little town located a mere fifteen 'field-paths' from Jerusalem. Here He had also awakened Lazarus from the dead; as it is described by John in chapter 11 of his Gospel. Here He called on Simon the leper, whom He had previously cleansed from leprosy. And look, a woman who had a bottle with expensive perfume stepped up to Him. (In Mark 14 it is recorded that it was genuine and expensive nard-water.) She poured it over His head while He was sitting at the table. Even though it was the custom with the Jewish people that one living in luxury would be in the habit of using good, expensive balsam, nard-water, and other [costly] things, yet this happened by the special prompting of the Holy Spirit, as subsequently is understood from the statements of Jesus.

1. The Lord now goes willingly to the place of His suffering. With this we have to consider His entire willing obedience to [the point of] suffering and death. About this He himself testifies in Psa. 40: **Sacrifice and food offerings do not please You. But You have opened my ears; You desire neither burnt-offerings nor sin-offerings. Then I said: Behold, I come; in the book it is written of Me; Your will, My God, I do**

gladly, and Your Law I have in My heart. In Gen. 22 we have an excellent type of this in Isaac. Isaac carried the wood upon which he was to be slaughtered as a burnt-offering, and, as they were coming to the place where God had told them, Abraham himself built an altar and laid the wood on it and he tied his son upon it. Nor indeed did the son refuse, for by the best of Hebrew reckoning he was at that time in his thirty-seventh year and might easily have fled. However, he let himself be bound so that in the slaughtering the wood designated for the sacrifice would not be rejected. This then, is the greatest and foremost [feature] of the sufferings of Christ: that He willingly suffered out of great love, which love He bore for the poor human race.* From this comes a holy saying: Out of the wounds of Christ shines forth the inward fire of passionate love, out of which He cries from the cross: **I thirst.** Understand by this [that He thirsts] for our salvation. For the inward fire of true love made Him thirsty for our salvation and for accomplishing the sacrifice, since in the Old Testament all sacrifices had to be consumed with fire which had fallen from heaven. So then, this holy sacrifice of Christ was consumed by the inward fire of heavenly love. Since Christ willingly suffered, [note that] His torture and death is not just a plain, simple suffering. Rather, it is a great and high work, just as His actions in life were not merely simple works, but instead were at the same time a deep, severe suffering. This holy obedience of Christ should give us a powerful comfort against our disobedience against God's commandment; for what the first Adam has spoiled and destroyed with his disobedience, behold, this other Adam, Christ, with His obedience has put right again. If indeed a faithful mother takes a bitter medicine in order to help her nursing baby, how should not the bitter death of

---

* Thus the parallel between Christ's willing sacrifice on the wood of the cross and Isaac's willingness to be bound to the wood intended for his sacrifice is preserved. Ed.

Christ, which Isa. 49 likens to a mother's love, benefit us for our soul's health? Why, if a physician at times cures the illness of a [bodily] member by giving a medicine into the patient's head [i.e., orally], how should not then the action and suffering of Christ, who is the Head of His believers, turn out for the best for us, His members? If someone accepts payment for your debt from someone other than you—just so it is completely paid—why should God the Lord not accept the entire, complete payment which Christ accomplished and provided for our sin? Behold, let this obedience of Christ comfort you at all times, especially in your last hour, when you will tremble before the judgment of God. And you will then say, Lord, I will not come into judgment, for you have set between me and You the obedience of Christ, my Lord.

2. This obedience of Christ should also be an example for us to follow. It is written, that, **just as Christ entered into glory through suffering**, Luke 24, so also, **we must through much suffering and tribulation enter into the kingdom of God**, Acts 14. Thus, the Lord says: **Whoever wants to be My disciple, he is to take upon himself his cross daily**, Mat. 16. That is to say, such a one must carry his cross willingly with an obedient heart. If you want to be God's child, you must not desire anything better in this world than what the true, natural Son of God had. If you want to be an heir of God, you have to take the entire inheritance. However, God did not only ordain eternal salvation for His heirs; rather, He also ordained cross and suffering in this world. If, as a result of your inheritance, you want to have eternal joy, you must not despise the inheritance of the cross in this world. And indeed there will be no cross or suffering so burdensome and bitter that you will not willingly endure it if you contemplate and ponder the great suffering of Christ the Lord. The bitterest thing in our suffering, namely the wrath of God, Christ has taken upon Himself. Our suffering does not come from a wrathful judge, but from a dear, loving Father. For

that reason one holy man calls our suffering, "bitter arrows from the sweet hand of God," love taps and Fatherly chastisements. As Christ the Lord has borne the greater burden for your sake, why would you not carry the little burden and suffer for His sake? "Sweet Jesus makes everything sweet." Behold, the loving Lord is with you in your cross. How can it be heavy and bitter for you from now on? We read in Exo.15 that the children of Israel came to Mara, and because they had been in the wilderness for three days without water, they were thirsty. But, they were unable to drink of the waters of Mara, in as much as they were completely bitter. However, God directed Moses to a tree, which was placed into the water, which then became sweet. That is a picture of how the cross and suffering of the Lord Jesus Christ, which He endured for us on the tree, take away all the bitterness of the water of our tribulation and even make it sweet and lovely for us. For that reason the Lord says of the cross which He lays upon His own, Mat. 11: **My yoke is gentle**; but it also states there that we should learn of Him how to carry the yoke properly; namely, in gentleness and humility. And why would we not willingly and patiently carry our suffering, in as much as we surely would not in our impatience [try to] remove our cross and instead thereby make it much more burdensome to us?

3. In the same manner as this kind-hearted woman, we should also anoint Christ. You ask: How can that take place, since the Lord testifies that we will not always have Him beside us? Indeed, in a visible, spatial manner we no longer have Him beside us so that we might honor Him with bodily ointment and fine-smelling perfume. However, He is still with us in an invisible, heavenly and inscrutable manner, and we may still pay our respects to Him with spiritual ointment. Therefore, go to Bethany; that is, to the home of pain and sorrow. There you will find Him, for He Himself testifies in Isa. 66: **Heaven is My throne, and the earth is My footstool. What kind of house is it that you wish to build for Me? Or which is the place where**

I should rest? **My hand has made everything that is, says the Lord. But I watch over the person who is in distress and of a broken spirit, and who fears My Word.** As the Lord would say: I don't live in a temple made with hands; rather, My resting place and residence are in a heart that is contrite and sorrowfully repentant over its sin. When you find Him in the little chamber of your heart, see to it that you take for yourself: **1.** *the ointment of bitter repentance.* This preparation is thus prescribed for us by a spiritual, well-tested [totally reliable] Physician, that thereto be taken the huge bundles and burdens of our sins which you at all times are able to gather up in overflowing abundance in the garden of your conscience. With [the pestle of] genuine repentance and inner sorrow you are to pulverize these various weeds of your many sins in the mortar of your heart, and with the heat of sorrow cook it up into a precious ointment. Then, like Mary Magdalene, anoint the feet of your Lord with it. These two feet are righteousness and mercy. You first must set before your eyes the strict righteousness of God, which by nature is an enemy of sin and the sinner. This strict righteousness will inflict eternal fire upon all the unrepentant sinners and their sin. However, you must not remain stuck on this foot, but must also seize the mercy (compassion) of the other foot and comfort yourself with the fact that Christ has paid for all your sin, and that He has won eternal redemption for every believer. **2.** Thus, there is yet another—*the ointment of thankful devotion and sacrifice*—as you especially remember all the benefits and gifts which God the Lord has granted you. And, as you then, by inward contemplation, warm to this little heavenly blossom within the vase of your heart, pour the spiritual oil of joy over it and, with the fiery flame of God's passionate love, prepare it also as a spiritual ointment. Behold, you may then anoint the head of the Lord with it—just as this woman did here. This ointment is of a much higher and greater worth than the first one, especially since the little plants and blossoms which hereto arise are not to be found in the garden of our heart; rather, they originate from the heavenly Paradise. 3. The third is the ointment of godly compassion, of which we have a portrayal in the three women who went forth to anoint the body of the Lord. As then with the first ointment the feet of the Lord [were anointed] [and] with the second one the head, so also one may anoint the entire body of the Lord with this [ointment]. To this anointing must be taken all the shortcomings, all the distress and misery, and all the faults of our neighbor. They must be collected in the mortar of our compassion and sympathy, then with heartfelt contemplation and with the oil of love be poured (basted) and warmed with the fire of true brotherly attachment. Behold, out of all this you will have prepared a precious ointment with which you will be able to anoint the entire body of Christ—which is the Christian Church!

II. Now then, the disciples (understand by this the betrayer, Judas) saw this and were displeased—meaning that they thought a great indecency and injury had taken place. **This perfume, they said, could have well been sold at a high price and [the proceeds] given to the poor.** But Judas was not concerned about the poor here. Instead, as John testifies in chapter 12: **Judas said this because he held the money-bag and carried around all the donations.** That's really why he wished that this had been given to the Lord in cash—as if Judas may have hoped to skim off a portion of this stately sum for himself! However, as the Lord took note of all this, He received this good-hearted young woman and said: **She has done a good work for Me.** Herewith He praised this deed. **Why do you trouble this woman? 2. You have the poor with you at all times; and if you wanted to, you could do good things for them. Me, however, you do not always have with you.** Understand by this: You may certainly show Me such loving service. In essence, He wants to say: From now on you will never lack for opportunity to perform good deeds for the poor. However, since I will soon enter into glory through My resurrection and sit Myself at the right hand of God, from now on you will never again have such opportunity to show Me such service. 3. He says, **The fact that she has poured this perfume upon My body, she did because I am going to be interred.** Learn from this that one is not to view this deed solely as a common service of love, as was the custom with the Jews; namely that they washed the feet of a guest and took care to anoint his head with ointment. Rather, it is a deed accomplished by a special motivation of the Holy Spirit, and it is a testimony to Christ's approaching death. Just as one usually anoints the deceased corpse with expensive spices so that it is for a long time preserved from decay, so also she wished to anoint Me while still alive, as well as for My approaching death and burial. 4. He prophesies that this would later be repeated to the eternal praise of this young lady. **Truly, I say to you, wherever this Gospel will be preached in the entire world, there also will be talked about to her remembrance what she did.**

1. Here we see that human reason is unable to comprehend of what true, God-pleasing works consist. It regards the true Christian life as foolishness. What is more foolish and idiotic to the eyes of man than that true Christians despise earthly glory, flee fleshly lusts, are kindly disposed to destitution, don't mind scorn, crucify their flesh, and shed their blood for the sake of their Christian faith? Human reason regards all this as foolishness. However, the inner, spiritual man understands that this is the noblest and best life; just as **Moses by faith no longer wanted to be called the son of Pharaoh's daughter; and he much rather chose to suffer hardships with the people of God than to possess the temporal delights of sin; and, he regarded the scorn of Christ as greater riches than the perks of Egypt**, Heb. 11. All true Christians follow [this precept]. And indeed, it is not surprising that human reason is unable to distinguish and recognize a true God-pleasing life and genuine good works. For

the life and works of a true Christian go forth and flow together in divine light. However, human reason seeks after its own natural light, which is, to the contrary, darkness and error. We have a type of this with the Israelites in Exo. 10. In all of Egypt there was such a thick darkness that no one could see anyone else nor go out from his place for three days. However, with all the children of Israel there was light in their homes, and that's how it still is with the true Israelites. The true heavenly light is with the godly, spiritual people; by it they recognize right living and right works. But with the people of this world, behold, there is darkness. Thus, David says in Psalm 36: **Lord, with You is the living Source, and by Your light we see the light.** Whatever is truly alive, whatever is spirit and life, that has to flow forth out of You; and, whatever is to be light, that has to be made known from Your light and must exist in the light of Your countenance. And the Lord said to the people, John 12: **Walk while you have the light, so that the darkness does not overcome you.** The holy life and godly life of Christ was such a light; anything that does not agree (match up) with it is darkness.

2. Christ advocates and praises the works of [those who are] His own. Note, that it happens this way: In this world He gives them the Holy Spirit, who inwardly gives witness that they are the children of God and that their works are performed in God. You have a portrayal of this in Simeon, Luke 2. The Holy Spirit dwelled in him, and Simeon had received an answer from the Holy Spirit that he would not see death until he first had seen the Christ of God. Thus the Holy Spirit still resides in all believers. He inwardly comforts them against all accusations and slanders and gives them proof that their actions and living are pleasing to God. At all times, the inward is more powerful than the outward. That's why this inward advocacy and witness of the Spirit is able rightly and well to sustain the believer and strengthen him against every outward accusation. Furthermore, this witness of the Spirit draws upon the Word. He leads us

into all truth—but by means of the Word, as the Lord testifies in John 17: **Your Word is truth.** When believers then see to it that they conduct their lives in keeping with the divine Word, behold, they can follow this inward witness with certainty, as it is written in 1 John 3: **You beloved ones, since our heart does not condemn, we thus have a joyfulness towards God.** If, however, our heart ever did condemn us in the midst of anxiety and inner trials, God is still greater than our heart, and knows all things. Take note, the works of God's own thus defend and praise God in this world; but on that Day He Himself will extol and praise them before all the angels and all people, even as He testifies in Mat. 10: **Whoever confesses Me before men, him I will confess before My heavenly Father.** And, in Mat. 25 He says that on that Day He will say to the elect: **Come here, you blessed of My Father,** etc. In the light of that, gladly let your works and life be despised in this world; behold, Christ will praise you on that Day. St. Paul comforts himself with this [promise] in 1 Cor. 4: **It is of little consequence to me that I am judged by you, or by any human** [judge]**. Do not judge prematurely, until the Lord comes. The Lord also will bring to light what is hidden in darkness and will reveal the counsel of the heart, since at that time each person will experience praise from God.** Look for such praise in your works, and not in human praise; otherwise your praise is lost.

3. The fact that Christ states that we do not have Him with us at all times is undoubtedly not to be understood to mean that Christ is no longer beside us, for He Himself testifies in Mat. 18: **Where two or three are gathered in My Name, there I am among them;** and, in Mat. 28: **I am with you each and every day until the end of the world.** Instead, in a manner of speaking, we no longer have Him with us; namely, as He was in His state of humiliation, [in which] He allowed Himself to be seen and handled and traveled about and permitted Himself to be made known in bodily service during the days of His fleshly

existence. In such a manner He is no longer with us. Nevertheless, we still find Him **1. in His Word,** as He says in Luke 10: **Whoever hears you, hears Me.** Even as the heavenly Father portrayed Himself in this self-contained Word, He also at the same time enveloped Himself once more in the same Word which He allowed to be recorded through His prophets and apostles. Such a Word is the diaper and cradle in which He still wants to be found. Yes indeed, the more you hear, read, and contemplate the Word, the closer you come to Christ. Yes, you will ultimately come so far through faith in this Word that you become Christ's brother or sister—just as He states in Luke 8: **My mother and the brother are these who hear and do** [act on] **God's Word.** You have a type of this in the Old Testament in that the Lord took great care to appear in the Ark of the Covenant within a cloud: thus He still is present in His Church—but enveloped in the Word. **2.** [We find Him] **in the Holy Supper,** where He distributes His true body and blood under bread and wine. You cannot see [fathom] how such a huge tree can lie hidden in such a tiny little seed; however, He lies therein through God's Word, which in the creation story reads: **Be fruitful and increase yourselves.** In the same way, you cannot know how the body and blood of Christ can be present under the bread and wine, but that also occurs through the power of the Word, which also states concerning this: **This is My body, this is My blood.** In this holy body You will find life, for He was given into death for the life of the world. In this holy blood you will find forgiveness of sin, for it was shed for the forgiveness of sin.

Ponder especially here the wisdom of God. The Lord Christ took upon Himself flesh and blood from our nature. He exalted and embellished it in His personal union with divine, incomprehensible attributes. He now gives that back to us again in the Holy Supper so that our nature no longer need be distanced from Him; but, on the contrary, through this eating and drinking of the Supper we again have restored to us that which Adam had lost with his forbidden eating. **3.** [We find Him] **in His reign.** So also Christ is beside us in keeping with His sitting at the divine right hand [of the Father]. He was raised up to this position and set over all principalities and rulers so that He now rules and reigns over all and within all—also according to His human nature. He mightily defends His Church against all foes and will ultimately receive us to Himself in His Kingdom. God through Christ, help us to that end! Amen.

O Lord Jesus Christ, You who were anointed with the fullness of the Holy Spirit, give me grace so that I may sprinkle Your feet with penitent tears and may thus be enabled to anoint the members of Your spiritual body—especially the needy and suffering ones—with the oil of compassion and gentle kindness. Amen.

THE SECTIONS OF THE HISTORY
Concerning the suffering and death of our Lord Jesus Christ as it is described by the four evangelists.

The history of the passion may be properly divided into five distinctive acts or chief events.

Act I: The history of the matters which occurred with Christ in the garden on Mt. Olive.
Act II: The historical account of the matters which have to do with Christ in the religious consistory in the house of Caiaphas.
Act III: The history of those matters carried out before the gentile judge, Pilate, in the judgment hall.
Act IV: The history of Christ's crucifixion.
Act V: The history of His burial.

Of these five acts it is stated:
Hortus, Pontifices, Praeses, Crux atque Sepulchrum.

Each individual act, each individual chief part, will (for the sake of greater accuracy and better recall) later be further divided and included in specific chapters, as we wish to provide a good introduction to this [subject].

THE FIRST ACT

*The history of the matters
which took place in the garden of Mt. Olive.*

The First Sermon

Christ goes out from the city of Jerusalem to the Mount of Olives and announces to His disciples how they will forsake Him.

After Jesus had sung a hymn of praise with His disciples, He (in keeping with His custom) went out with them over the brook of Kidron to the Mt. of Olives and said to them: During this night all of you will be offended because of Me, for it is written: I will strike the Shepherd, and the sheep of the herd will scatter; but after I have arisen, I will go before you into Galilee. But Peter answered and said to Him: Even though all are offended over you, I will never be offended. Jesus said to him: Truly I say to you, today in this night, before the rooster crows twice, you will deny (disown) Me three times. But [Peter] stated further: Indeed, even though I have to die with You, I still will never deny You. The other disciples also said the same thing.

In 2 Samuel 15, it is recorded that David, as he was fleeing from his son Absalom, left Jerusalem, crossed over the brook of Kidron and went up the Mount of Olives with weeping and sadness. This sad departure by David was a type of the departure which the Son of David, Jesus Christ, with similar sadness and trembling, would one day take across the brook of Kidron [and] up the Mount of Olives as the time of His suffering finally arrived, His spoiled children running from Him for their lives.

With this departure Christ's holy suffering is begun. Thus it is also called a departure in Luke 9. There the evangelist records that Moses and Elijah spoke with Christ about His departure; that is, about His suffering and dying, which was to be fulfilled in Jerusalem.

This same history is described in the lection just read in two parts:

> **In the first part is recorded the nature of this departure.**
>
> **In the second part [is recorded] what Christ said to His disciples on the way, and what they, in turn, offered to do for Him.**

I. First of all, the evangelist records that prior to His departure, Christ spoke [sang] a song of praise with His disciples. Prior to this He had eaten the Easter (Passover) Lamb with them, and herewith gave leave to the Levitical ceremonies of the Old Testament. In their place He instituted His evening meal—the Sacrament of the New Testament. He concluded this action with a hymn of praise, as was customary at that time among the Jews—in which, with their paschal lamb, they employed a song of praise consisting of eight Psalms, namely, from Psalm 111 through 119. (They called it the Great Hallelujah.) Even as Christ, the Son of God, here spoke [sang] a hymn of praise with His disciples, how much more is it not incumbent upon us that the praise of God be constantly in our mouths, Psalm 34? [Because] **Christ is Lord over everything**, Acts 10, He rightly has authority and power over all creatures; we, however, lost our rule over the creatures by our sin through Adam. Consequently, if the use of creatures for food and other benefits is to redound to our good, then prayer and thanksgiving are a necessary part—as it is written in 1 Tim. 4: **Every creature of God is good, and nothing that is received with thanksgiving is to be rejected, for it becomes sanctified through the Word of God and prayer.** Just as Christ here also sang the hymn of praise, thus it is written of the angels in Isa. 6 that they praised God with unceasing voice and sang: **Holy, holy, holy is the LORD of Sabaoth.** If we, accordingly, want to follow [the example of] Christ and the angels, then we must lift our voices to the praise of God with them; and, whoever thus praises God with the angels, such a person by all rights already becomes a member of the angelic, triumphant Church in this life. And, what he intones and begins already here, that he will bring to completion there in eternity with the more lofty choir. Such glorification and praise of God is also a sure indication of the indwelling by the Holy Spirit. Thus St. Paul says in Eph. 5: **Become filled with the Spirit, and speak among one another from Psalms and hymns of praise and spiritual songs. Sing and play to the Lord in your hearts.** With His example, Christ here particularly wanted to teach that one should praise God the Lord for His grace by the celebration of the Holy Supper and thank Him for the merits of His Son. For that reason, St. Paul admonishes in 1 Cor. 11: **As often as you eat of this bread and drink from this chalice, you are to proclaim the Lord's death until the time He comes.** That is, with the practice of this Supper you should remember the death of Christ and thank Him for it from your hearts. What Christ has instituted with a hymn of praise, that one should also practice with a hymn of praise.

    Secondly, the evangelists record that the Lord went out of Jerusalem over the brook of Kidron on to the Mount of Olives, which was located a little over a quarter of a mile distance from

Jerusalem. Between it and the city there was a deep valley, which was called the valley of Jehosaphat, since Jehosaphat's burial took place there. Also, the idolatrous god Moloch [at one time] stood there, an image made from brass. [The idolatrous worshipers] made it red hot and placed their children in its arms, intending it to be a pleasing sacrifice to such a god. Yet it was earnestly and frequently forbidden by God. [Moloch] also was the worst of all idols. For that reason, Christ referred to this place as the abyss of hell in Mat. 5. Through this valley flows the brook Kidron, in which [at this time] flowed all the filth from the city, especially also the water from the temple. (The water [of the brook] was piped through the temple, and together with it the blood of the sacrifices was washed away.) Therefore it was an unclean [polluted] brook, and on account of the fat-laden black dirt, it was called the black brook.

    The fact that Christ crossed over this brook near Mount Olive symbolizes the fruit of His suffering; namely, that He would drink from the brook along the way, Psa. 110 [v.7]. That is to say, He would not take a small drink; instead, He was going to drink up the entire brook of God's wrath, in which the filth of our sin flows together from every direction. And thereby He would bring us to Mount Olive; that is, He would win for us God's mercy, which is symbolized by [olive] oil. Had not Christ drunk from this brook, we would never have come to the Mount Olive of God's grace. Since Christ also had such a sad journey through this deep, dark valley, behold, we too now can say with joy: **Even though I wander in the dark valley, I fear no misfortune**, Psa. 23. Finally, that this valley, through which Christ went, was a valley cursed by God, indicates that Christ in His anticipated suffering wanted to become a curse for us, so that He could obtain for us the divine blessings, Gal. 3.

    Thirdly, the evangelists state that it was the habit of Christ in the evening that He used to go out from Jerusalem to Mount Olive both to pray and to renew His strength for His work. For in times of peace the gates to Jerusalem were left open day and night. Thus, Christ frequently went out in the evening to Mount Olive, and sometimes He would pray there all night, Luke 6. There He reminded Himself and set before His own eyes what kind of a difficult struggle He was going to have to endure at this very place, the report of which is recorded in the lection which follows.

The evangelists report this so that one may know that this very place was well known to the betrayer, Judas, and further, to conclude from this account that Christ suffered willingly. Just as Christ then gladly lingered at the place at which He knew that He would have to endure an oppressive situation—and in contemplation of it spoke many eager, passionate prayers—so also we should often and gladly remember what kind of battle we have before us in the anxiety of death. Thus will our hearts be moved to become warm and fervent in prayer; for it is very dangerous if one is overcome with unforeseen anxiety of death and did not in advance earnestly pray for support and help from God.

Fourthly, the evangelists report that Christ had His disciples following beside Him. Just as they had seen His divine wonder and transfiguration on Mount Tabor in the past, so now they were to see His suffering here. Christ did this to show that He does not constantly give to His own [i.e., believers] joy in the Spirit and peace of heart in this life. Instead, oftentimes He allows them to be overcome with spiritual sadness and gives them a sip from the chalice of the cross. And such changes (variations) occur throughout life, more often and severe with one [person] than with another. Also, before God everything is the same—be the heart grounded in the joy of the Spirit or in spiritual sadness. The one to whom God gives joy in the Spirit is not worth more before Him. Nor is the one to whom He gives spiritual sadness of any less importance to God—just so long as in both cases the heart steadfastly clings to God in faith and love.

That is the first part, namely, concerning the nature of this departure of Christ from Jerusalem over the brook of Kidron up to Mount Olive.

II. Secondly, now follow the conversations Christ had with His traveling companions. As they traveled together through the valley, Christ conversed with His disciples and proclaimed beforehand to them that on this very night they would all be offended because of Him; that is, they would be taken aback and be perplexed when they saw how Christ was going to be captured and bound. Christ told them this in advance and substantiated it with the passage from Zechariah 13, where it is recorded: **That the Shepherd was going to be struck down and the sheep would be scattered.** Yet Christ appends to this the comfort that He would not cast them aside because of such an offense. Rather, He would go before them into Galilee after His resurrection and, like a faithful Shepherd, would gather them together again like erring, frightened little sheep. That was a marvelous proclamation for the disciples; therefore, they all promise each other that they would firmly stand beside their Lord—especially Peter, who promised before them all to remain steadfast; even though all the others were to be offended, yet such would never be said of him. However, Christ announced to him that he would deny the Lord three times before the rooster crowed twice. Unlike the other disciples, Peter would not simply forsake Him; instead, he would also, in this single night, deny Him three times. For Peter that was a strange statement, and he felt that it was hitting home a little too closely. That's why he further stated: **Yes indeed, even if I have to die with You, I will never deny You.** But just as it was stated to him, so would it take place in the future.

First of all, here we have a true commentary about the entire passion history. Namely, everything which Christ experienced therein is to be examined as if God Himself is doing it, even as it is described by the prophet Zechariah in chapter 13—which Christ here introduces —that the Lord of Sabaoth says: **Sword, arise over My Shepherd and over the Man who is next to Me. Strike the very same Shepherd.** Accordingly, as we hear how Christ was bound, struck, wounded, and tortured, we are thus to view it as if God the Lord was standing there, beating, wounding, and binding Him, just as it is stated in Isa. 53: **We beheld Him as the One who was tormented and stricken by God and tortured. However, He was wounded for our misdeeds, was battered on account of our sin.** As Isaiah would say, God the Lord thus smote, tormented, and tortured His Son at the time of His passion, not because He was an enemy in His Person, but because He, as the true Shepherd, was giving Himself for His sheep, John 10. As He then took upon Himself our misdeeds (transgressions), God therefore seized upon Him, instead of the sheep and the entire human race, and punished Him on account of the sins that were laid upon Him. To that end, the apostle says in Acts 4: **Herod and Pontius Pilate—along with the Gentiles and the people of Israel—have done what the hand of God and His counsel had deliberated beforehand that it was to take place**; that is, Christ did not suffer something unforeseen. Rather, God knew about it from eternity and thus had decreed that Christ was to bring about the work of redemption through His suffering. Therefore, everything that proceeds from Christ's suffering, we are to view as if done by God's hand, as if it were the counsel of God.

  Yet one must not interpret this to mean that God the Lord implanted such murderous thoughts into the hearts of Judas, Herod, Pilate, and the rulers of the people or compelled them to act thus in order to accomplish His decree, for that would be contrary to Scripture, which testifies that God is not the cause of sin nor forces anyone to sin. Instead, one must understand this hand and this counsel of God within the context of Christ's suffering; namely, that God the Lord allowed the enemies of Christ enough leeway so that they were able to bring to completion the murderous plot against Him, which the Devil had inspired within them and which had been nurtured within them by their own hatred and envy. And God the Lord permitted the Devil and his tools [to accomplish] this, not because He had pleasure and delight in their evil deeds, but because He knew how to direct this suffering of Christ to a blessed end; namely, for the redemption of the human race. This is what the disciples mean to suggest when they say: **Herod and Pontius Pilate did what God's hand and His counsel had previously thought about**—not that they were forced to do it, but rather that it would take place. That we hear how God the Lord would thus smite Christ the Shepherd for our misdeeds (crimes) gives us glorious comfort. Because God punished Christ and smote Him on account of our sin, He indeed will no longer punish and smite us on account of our sin, if we regret them through true (genuine) repentance, and lay them on Him in true faith. Since God the Lord has laid the punishment of our sins upon Christ, we will now have peace, Isa. 53.

Accordingly, we learn here how dangerous it is to presume and to rely on one's own strength. In particular, Peter thought that his case was so certain and well-grounded that he could never fall. He should, rather, have petitioned God never to withdraw His hand from him and not let him sink. But he relied on his own strength. Thus, he fell away.

[These words] have been written for our warning, so that we learn to renounce all our strengths and solely cling to God's kindness. God the Lord is a constantly working power and strength. Anyone who simply clings to Him becomes one in Spirit with Him, 1 Cor. 6. His power is efficacious in such a person. God preserves him so strong and steadfast that no one is able to rip him out of God's hand, John 10. On the contrary, human beings are as nothing, Psa. 39; they weigh less than nothing, so great is He. Whoever in the slightest way ascribes anything to his own power, and turns away from God the Lord as from the constantly working power, such a one will fall away and will not be sustained. Thus, as David states in Psa. 39: **All men are as nothing, even though they live so confidently.** To this he adds: **So then Lord, in whom shall I trust? I place my hope in You.** It is as if David wanted to say: Since I am nothing and have no comfort within myself, I therefore hope in You alone. My hope is based solely on You. You will uphold (sustain) me. Since the Fall, the reliance on one's own power is perpetually born within us and is embedded in the deepest foundations of the heart. Thus it is necessary that we indeed pay zealously assiduous attention to pulling up this bitter root so that it does not sprout forth with the fruit of self-assurance and presumption. For when a person relies on his own strength and power, with the full intention of remaining steadfast by his own might, it soon follows that one becomes secure [cocky] and does not remember how highly important is the prayer through which our salvation is commended into the hand of God—from which also is obtained divine power for steadfastness.

As a result it is most wise that one daily holds before one's heart both of these passages: 2 Cor. 4, **We have our treasure in earthly** (perishable) **containers** [to show] **that the mighty power is from God and not from us**; [and] 1 Pet. 1, **By God's power you are preserved (sustained) unto the salvation which has been prepared.** If we truly ponder that the extraordinary power is God's and not from us, [and] also that through His might we are preserved for salvation, then all reliance on our own power and strength will quickly fall away. On the contrary, it will follow that a person will, with eager prayer, call upon God the Lord for strength of steadfastness and will commend the entire work of being saved into His almighty hand. God grant this to us through Christ. Amen.

O Lord Jesus Christ, You Arch-Shepherd of our souls, You who were smitten on account of our sin, give us grace that we, as obedient little sheep, put our heart-felt trust in this [foregoing fact] and steadfastly cling to You with true faith and nevermore forsake You. Amen.

The Second Sermon

The inward suffering and passionate prayer of Christ in the garden on the Mount of Olives.

Then Jesus came to a yard which was called Gethsemane, in which there was a garden. Jesus and His disciples entered it. However, Judas, who betrayed Him, also knew of the place, for Jesus often gathered there with His disciples. Then Jesus said to them: Seat yourselves here, until I go over there and pray. And He took with Him Peter and James and John, the two sons of Zebedee; and He began to sorrow and to speak and said to them: My soul is sorrowful [distressed] until death. Stay here and watch with Me; pray that you do not fall into temptation. And He removed Himself a stone's throw away from them and kneeled down, fell on His face onto the ground, and prayed that—if it were possible—the hour would pass. And He said: Abba, My Father, everything is possible for You. Remove this chalice from Me. Yet, not what I want, rather what You want. And He came to His disciples and found them sleeping. And He said to Peter: Simon, are you sleeping? Aren't you willing to watch with Me one hour? Awake and pray, so that you do not fall into temptation. The spirit is willing, but the flesh is weak. However, He went away for a second time, prayed and said: My Father, if it is not possible that this chalice leave Me, I drink it then so that Your will be done. And He came and found them sleeping again, and their eyes were full of sleep, and they did not know what to answer Him. And He left them again and went away and prayed the same words for the third time, and said: Father, if You so will, then take this chalice from Me;

yet, not My will, rather Your will be done. However, an angel from heaven appeared to Him and strengthened Him; and it happened that He wrestled with death and prayed even more intensely. But His sweat became like drops of blood which fell to the ground. And He arose from prayer and came to His disciples and said to them: Alas! Are you still wanting to sleep and rest? Why do you sleep? It is enough. Behold, the hour has come, and the Son of Man will be delivered up into the hands of sinners. Stand up, let us go. See, he who betrays Me is near. However, pray that you do not fall into temptation.

In Genesis 49 the patriarch Jacob prophesies about Shiloh, or Messiah, that He would wash His garment in wine and His mantel in the blood of grapes. By the garment of the Messiah is understood His noble manhood, His assumed flesh in which He had clothed Himself, covered as with a mantel—beautifully garbed in a long priestly robe as He allows Himself to be seen in Rev. 1. This, His robe, the Messiah will wash in the blood of grapes or in red wine, says Jacob; that is, His flesh will be sprinkled with red blood and will be washed. Afterwards it will provide sweet wine (that is, mighty comfort) to the believers. Later, as recorded in Acts 7, they will also be able to wash their clothes in His blood and make them shiny bright; that is, through the blood of the Messiah, they will be able to cleanse themselves from their blood-red sins. And, they will overcome by means of the shining, beautiful garment of righteousness which avails before God. These prophecies of the patriarchs were fulfilled by Christ the Messiah on the Mount of Olives, as He in the anguish of His inner (spiritual) sufferings sweated bloody sweat, by which His flesh was saturated and washed. This same history we now want to contemplate and attend to in three sections:

First, how it came to this: that the dear Lord endured such a burdensome inner (spiritual) suffering.

Second, how He conducted Himself with prayer towards His Heavenly Father in this situation.

Third, what sort of conversations He held with His disciples on this account.

I. To begin with, the evangelist records the place where this spiritually burdensome suffering of the Lord began. As Christ with His disciples went over the brook of Kidron up to the Mount of Olives, He discussed with His companions His approaching suffering and their flight. In the midst of this discussion, they came to a yard where there was a garden called Gethsemane. Judas, the betrayer, was familiar with this place because Jesus was accustomed to assembling there with His disciples. At the foot of the Mount of Olives were many pleasant gardens and farmsteads which the citizens of Jerusalem had developed there, as well as oil presses which they had built there. Among those citizens there was a good, pious man, who previously had often lodged the Lord when He was exhausted from a day of preaching and would come to him toward evening after He had said His prayers on the Mount of Olives—there the Lord would lodge with His disciples. Thus it came about from this customary practice that Judas was acquainted with the place.

That Christ then began His spiritual sufferings at Gethsemane, that is, by an oil press, indicates that He had now begun to tread the wine press, as prophesied in Isa. 63, and thereby acquired for us the oil of divine grace and mercy.* Since also our first parents brought sin and death upon the human race in the garden of Paradise, Christ also wanted to begin His

---

* Gerhard rather freely mingles oil presses and wine presses to make his point. Although oil could be made from treading olives, it was not the standard method. Ed.

suffering in a garden, through which He would make payment for sin and restore the lost purity. In the garden was made the promise about the Seed of the woman which would crush the head of the serpent; therefore, Christ wanted to initiate His saving work in the garden. The enmity between the blessed Seed of the woman and the seed of the serpent was established in a garden. Thus Christ also wanted to initiate this strife with the Devil and all his might in a garden. As the north wind blew through this garden—that is, as the storm of divine wrath and inner anxiety fell upon Christ in this garden—there dripped the fragrance of His spices, Song of Solomon 4 [vv. 10–16]. Christ shed His blood, which is able to give us the proper strong spice and power for our soul's need.

After this, the evangelist records the persons in whose presence this suffering of Christ occurred. He had with Him His twelve [sic. eleven] disciples, to whom He said that they should henceforth sit down in the garden while He had better go on the mountain and pray. He selected three (namely, Peter, James, and John) from among them, however, whom He led a bit nearer to the place where He wanted to pray.

Before us, then, this teaching is held up: that Christ also makes His own to be partakers of His suffering and tribulation, even as He takes along His disciples with Him into the garden. Yet, such suffering by Christians indeed bears no comparison to the suffering of Christ, neither to its greatness nor to its effects (results). Just as Christ here enters alone into such anguish (anxiety) and subsequently also alone is taken captive, it is agreed that He alone treads out the winepress, Isa. 63, and that no one from among the nations is with Him.

This is well pre-figured in Exo. 19, where it is recorded that Moses led the elders of the people to the foot of the mountain and took his brother Aaron a bit farther; nevertheless, He went alone to the top of the mountain in the dark cloud and there spoke with God. Thus Christ here takes His disciples with Him into the garden, three of whom He takes a little farther onto the mountain. However, He alone goes to a particular place where He speaks with God and carries out the office of reconciliation.

One also sees here that God always leads one person nearer to a cross than another and forever lays more suffering upon one person than another. Eight disciples remain seated in the forefront of the garden and see the agony of Christ from a distance; however, the other three come somewhat closer to the place [of Christ's suffering]. So it still is that God the Lord unequally distributes the chalice of suffering. And, if God thus wants to lead you ever closer to a cross, and make you Christ-like, then go along willingly and do not question why it is that others remain up front [i.e., farther away], on whom God does not lay as much and yet at the same time are good Christians.

But why would Christ select and take with Him nearer to the place of suffering precisely these three: Peter, James, and John? First of all, they had volunteered themselves more than the others. Peter said: **Lord, if I have to die with You, yet will I not deny You.** James and John volunteered that they really did want to drink of Christ's cup and were willing to be baptized with the water of tribulation with which Christ was to be baptized, Mat. 20. In order that this reliance upon their own strengths might be extinguished, Christ drew them nearer to Himself. God frequently still operates this way. He lays many great sufferings on you so that you see how completely beyond your power it is to have patience in cross bearing if God does not give it and remain at our side in the midst of our need. For true Christians must come to the point that they completely sink themselves in God's power and confess their utter powerlessness, since God's power is nothing if not powerful in the weak ones, 2 Cor. 12. But whoever is stuck on himself, and does not in genuine sincerity sink himself in God's goodness and power, such a one will certainly withstand [endure] nothing.

Accordingly, Christ held these three more dear than the others, just as it is clearly recorded by John [chap. 20] that Christ held him more dear than the others. Thus one can also perceive that Christ gave these three special names, Mark 3. To Simon He gave the name of Peter; James and John he called "Bnehargem,"* sons of thunder. Thus we are reminded that a heavy cross is an indication of exceptional divine love—just as a father deals much more sharply with a pious child than with an undutiful servant. David was a man after God's heart. Even so David stated: **You allow me to experience much and great anguish (anxiety)**, Psa. 71.

Furthermore, Christ took these three, rather than the others, into His suffering because they had viewed His transfiguration upon Mount Tabor, Mat. 17, and His raising of the daughter of Jairus in Mat. 9.† Even as they had viewed this glimpse of Christ's glory, He also wanted them to behold His outward degradation (humiliation). He wanted to teach that all heartfelt joy of the Spirit in this life is provided by God for this purpose: that one would later on be the better reconciled to suffering. And indeed, the more one grows in a mighty confession and spiritual perception of divine grace and power, the more suffering God takes care to generally lay on [a person]. For God takes pains to deal so graciously with His own that He allows a powerfully sweet taste of His goodness to precede whenever a bitter, strong drink [of anguish and sorrow] is to follow.

With this text one of the fathers also reminds us that if a Christian would endure great suffering for the sake of God's glory, then he has to have at his side the Faith-Strengthener—who is suggested by Peter, which means "rock"—so that he ground himself with firm faith upon Christ, the only Rock, 1 Cor.

---

* Obviously a misprint of the Greek word in v. 17: Βοανηργες. Ed.
† Although related in Matthew, only Mark 5 and Luke 8 specifically identify the three disciples who accompany Jesus to the house of Jairus. Ed.

10. Then also he must have the Sin-Conqueror—who is signified by James, for James means "a refuge"—so that he, through the Spirit's power, strives against sin. Finally, he must possess the Holy Spirit's grace—who is implied through John, for John means "kingdom of grace" or "kingdom of clemency"—so that he be equipped and comforted by the Holy Spirit.

Here, then, follows the description of the spiritual suffering which befell Christ at that time. At this point the evangelists are unable to find enough words with which to indicate the heaviness and greatness of His suffering. First of all, they say, Jesus had begun to be sorrowful. The joy of the Spirit started to disappear, and instead sadness came over Him. [2.] He began to shiver, αδημονειν—[a word] which actually refers to one's being confronted with an unavoidable danger and falling into shivering and fright. 3. He began to waver. He was anxious and fearful beyond measure; the same word is used by physicians when they speak of one who is lying in terminal illness. 4. Thus Christ Himself witnesses to this, His anguish: **My soul**, He says, **is grievously afflicted unto death.** Sadness wants to overwhelm Me on the spot. For the evangelists use a word here which does not mean generic, common sadness. Instead, [it refers] to a person's being overcome with such a degree of sadness, being so plagued and terrorized, that he does not know "what is in or out"; the heart is oppressed and heavy laden, understanding is numbed, the hands fall at one's side, [and] the feet will no longer carry one. 5. In anguish, He fell on His face to the ground. His strength deserted Him to the degree that He could no longer stand. 6. Soon He turned around and ran to the apostles and sought comfort from them, but then soon had to go forth again and walk still closer to the same place, by all rights like a person too anxious to stay in one place. 7. He pleaded that the Father might lift this chalice from Him. That must have been an awesome and bitter draught which He at that time had to drink, and great anguish that He felt, that the Son of God Himself desired that it be turned away [from Him]. 8. Then came an angel, who strengthened Him. That must have been a deep humiliation and a heavy burden that the Son of God required angelic comfort and strength. 9. It came to the point that He wrestled with death. It was, to Him, nothing other than that death had taken Him in its clutches so that He had to engage in battle against it. 10. His sweat was like drops of blood which fell to the ground. All His bodily powers were completely sapped from Him, such that also the arteries were unable to contain His blood. Instead, it gently ran down His body. 11. And so that one does not claim that this occurred only according to an external appearance, and not in genuine reality (as also some of the ancients speak about this), the prophet Isaiah adds the solid affirmation in chapter 53: **Indeed, He carried our sickness.**

What thus pressed upon Christ at that time that He became so anxious? It was the burden of God's wrath. For since the sin of the entire human race was laid upon Him, thus also the wrath of God, which is the usual consequence for sin, truly pressed down upon Him. Thus He says in Isa. 63: **I tread (tramp out) the grapes alone**; that is, as explained in Rev. 19, the wine in the winepress of the grim wrath of Almighty God. For just as a tender, little cluster of grapes, when it is tossed into the winepress, is crushed so that it produces red juice, so also the Son of God, the noble wine-vine of John 15, lies under the winepress of divine wrath and is crushed so that blood-red sweat drips from Him. **I am a worm**, He says in Psa. 22, as if He meant to say: It is as if I am a poor little worm who has to be squashed by the grim wrath of God. For God struck Him at that time, [as prophesied in] Zec. 13, and thus tormented Him, because all our sin was heaped upon Him, Isa. 53. In the language of Jesus, [i.e., Hebrew] there is an expression that means: The sins of mankind flowed over Him like a huge, rushing (roaring) flood. He Himself speaks of it in Psalm 42: **Your floods rush forth so that a depth surges here and a depth rages there.**

All Your waves and swells flood over Me. It was not as if just a tiny beaker of tribulation had to be drunk, but rather a huge flood of water, as He again refers to it in Psa. 69: **The waters flow over Me all the way to My soul. I am sinking into a deep slime (mud) where there is no bottom. I am in deep water and the flood wants to drown Me.**

We cannot comprehend this anguish of Christ, for it is with us just as it was with the apostles, who slept and slumbered through it all. Even so, we must speak of it, for this is the greatest suffering of Christ; namely, His inner (spiritual) agony and the hidden burden of the heart. Therefore, just as He began His suffering with such inner (spiritual) suffering, as we are here told, so He also concluded it with [spiritual suffering], as it is reported that He cried out on the cross: **My God, My God, why have You forsaken Me?**—to announce that in His suffering, this [inner anguish] is to be noted of first and foremost. One has various types from the saints in the Old Testament on practically every aspect of Christ's sufferings. But, regarding this inner (spiritual) agony and pain, one actually has no type. One would like to point to the fact that Jonah says that while in the belly of the "whale-fish" [*Wallfisch*] he cried out from the belly of hell, thinking that he was forsaken before the eyes of God, [and] that his soul despaired within him, Jonah 2. David, also, sometimes complained about the anguish in his heart; however, it is all to be regarded as nothing compared to the spiritual suffering of Christ; as insignificant as a tiny drop compared to a huge ocean. If, when other saintly martyrs were led to their death, they were joyful and confident, how is it that the Son of God here shivers and is in such agony before either Judas, or soldier, or any other outward enemies were present? The reason is this: at that time, He was burdened with the sin of all mankind and with the wrath of God and agony of hell; moreover, what death, Devil, hell and the gates of hell, because of sin, demanded by right and might of the human race, all this out of divine destiny they carried out against Christ. For as Christ loaded upon Himself all sin, God the Lord thus speaks to His Son in wrath and enters into judgment with Him, as is written in Joel 3: **The Day of the Lord is near in the valley of Jehosaphat, in the valley of judgment. Sun and moon will become dark, and the stars will lose their brightness, and the Lord will roar out of Zion and will let His voice be heard from Jerusalem so that the heavens and the earth will quake.**

The garden in which Christ endured these agonies is located in the valley of Jehosaphat, which became a valley of judgment for Christ, because in it God the Lord summoned Christ before His wrathful judgment for the simple reason that He had loaded on Himself the sin of mankind. In that place the sun, moon and stars kept back their light; that is, Christ found no comfort with His heavenly Father or with His disciples. In sum, He had no star to guide Him; instead, the thick cloud of sorrow encompassed Him, for at this time God the Lord roared out of Zion and let His voice be heard from Jerusalem. Jerusalem had been the city where God the Lord had His hearth and fire, as the Scriptures states in Isa.31 [v. 9]. There God had viewed His Son in wrath and let His voice issue forth in fury, as if to say: Are you the One who wants to bear all sin of mankind? As a result, shall I summon You before the judgment for everything people have committed against My Law? Do you want to pay for everything of which My honor was robbed by sin? Well then, I, as a righteous Judge, must allow My wrath and punishment to be pronounced over You; I must pour out My fury and ire over You; and I lay upon You such agony as would otherwise have pressed down on the entire world.

That now it is that Christ presses (forces) out these extremely agonizing words and gestures, namely the wrath of God, thereto came the power of the Devil and all his hellish gates. For the Devil, on account of sin, had taken captive the entire human race, which Christ wanted to win back from the Devil. Thus the

Devil opposed Him with the greatest might and pressed into the heart of Christ the sting of death which he had thoroughly honed and sharpened on the Law of God. Indeed, it came to the point that the agony of hell came over Him, which otherwise would have fallen upon all men on account of sin. Therefore, here there was no jest (pleasantry). Instead, in His wrath God truly viewed Christ as the greatest of all sinners—not on account of His Person, but because He had loaded upon Himself the sin of the world. God turned His countenance away from Christ, and even though He had already prayed that this chalice might be lifted, at that time He still received an answer of rejection, in that God said to Him: It can be no other way; You have to go on. And God set before Him an entire brook of wrath, permitting death, Devil, and hell to vent all their might against this Person, which they otherwise would have vented against the human race. Note well: that is why this agony and terror came to Christ, and that is why—as He descended from the Mount of Olives on Palm Sunday and proceeded to Jerusalem (John 12)—He reminded Himself of what He would endure soon thereafter, saying: **Now My soul is sad, and what shall I say**; that is, I am in such sorrow that I can say nothing.

    Now then, ponder what sin is, and what kind of anguish will result for those who do not seek forgiveness for sin in Christ and protection from the wrath of God. Here stands God's Son, who carries (upholds) everything by the power of His Word, Heb. 1, who is of the same essence with His heavenly Father. One might think that He will readily overcome and easily bear the burden of sins and divine wrath, and it will be for Him a light, little blade of straw. But look here, how this holy Soul agonizes; indeed, the more you reflect on Him, the better you will comprehend what a huge burden sin is. With the unrepentant, sin is regarded as an insignificant thing. Some intend to atone for it with their own deeds. However, this sad spectacle knocks down all these thoughts. For, if [sins] were such an insignificant matter, why was Christ Himself thus permitted to grieve [over them]? If they could be atoned for with one's own works, why was He allowed to be so fearful? One also sees here what the judgment of God and the anguish of hell are. Had God the Lord held the entire world accountable in His wrathful judgment, then all of mankind in one lump would not have been able to bear the burden of this divine wrath and judgment. Therefore, the damned, who did not seek and receive forgiveness of their sins through Christ, will constantly and unceasingly be in such agony; and, their ongoing existence will be nothing other than a continuous anguish and despairing. Truly, this Person, who stands here before divine judgment, has strong legs because He is of one essence with His heavenly Father; at the same time, He falls down to the ground in dread. Also, He did not know to stay away from sadness, and the world becomes too cramped for Him. How, then, will it go for those who are not reconciled with God, and instead go forth in steadfast certainty [cocky confidence] and godlessness?

Here also this powerful comfort against sin is offered to the believers, that they might not doubt the satisfaction and payment for sin, because Christ anguished under the burden of sin and God the Lord on account of sin brought Christ before His judgment. Thus from this time forth, He will not enter into judgment with the believers who are in Christ, Psa. 143. Since Christ sweated bloody sweat under the burden of sins, thus will God the Lord remove this burden from the believers as they cling to Christ. And thereby we understand what it means when we petition in the Litany: **By Your struggle-unto-death and Your bloody sweat, help us dear Lord God.** Accordingly, when the cold agony and death sweat overtakes you, thus remind yourself of this bloody sweat of Christ with which He paid for our sin [and] took from death its power so that it could not hold us accountable to the second and eternal death. Instead, death now must be merely a door for us to enter into eternal life. If it also ever happens that God gives us a little drink from this chalice of inner (spiritual) suffering and agony of heart, we are to be patient and are to remember how insignificantly this is to be regarded compared to the great flood which overcame Christ. Sink all your pains in this agony of Christ. Thus they will easily vanish like a tiny particle of dust in the sunshine. And that is precisely the reason that God the Lord at times portrays Himself as if He has hidden His countenance, allowing us to experience a bit of heart-anguish so that we may see what Christ endured for us and thank Him for it.

II. Secondly, it now follows how, under the burden of His spiritual suffering, Christ conducted Himself with prayer towards His heavenly Father, regarding which the evangelists record that He tore Himself away from His disciples. As He went approximately a stone's throw away from them, He knelt down, fell with His face to the ground, and prayed to God that—if it were possible—the hour pass away. **Abba, My Father,** He says, **everything is possible for You; take this cup away from Me. Yet, not what I want, but rather what You want.** And He repeated for the second and third time such a passionate, anxious prayer, petitioning rescue from this burdensome situation. And yet, in true humility and proper obedience, [He] gave everything over to the will of the heavenly Father. **My Father,** He states, **if it is not possible that this cup depart from Me, I drink it then. Thus Your will be done.** And He prayed this prayer amidst tears and in a clear, raised voice, Heb. 5 [v. 7], so that the apostles heard, about which it was subsequently recorded.

By recording here that Christ tore Himself away from His disciples, the evangelists thereby remind us, first of all, of the great love of Christ. His heart was, as it were, attached to the disciples. Thus [the text says] He ripped Himself away from them with pain. Christ still has such a heartfelt love towards all of His true disciples; His heart is, so to speak, attached to them.

Accordingly, they herewith remind us of Christ's great anguish and dread; namely, how He forcefully tore Himself away from the apostles. He could not stay with them. Instead, He had to go forth again to the place of His heavy, spiritual suffering. Also pertinent here is that He, because of anguish, fell upon His holy face, fell prostrate before His heavenly Father, and thus begged with yearning that this cup might yet be taken from Him. And although He prayed with such heartfelt emotion and lamentable wretchedness, yet He received no answer. Instead, God the Lord kept His silence, thereby indicating that it could be no other way. If the human race was to be helped, then all this had to overtake Him.

That Christ humbled Himself this way in prayer is not only an indication of His anguish of heart; rather, it is also prescribed as an example for us, that we, when we pray, should ponder well with Whom we are speaking, so that we properly humble ourselves before the high, divine Majesty. Christ is the true Son of God, holy and pure. We are poor, frail sinners. We are dust and ashes, Gen. 18. As Christ thus humbled Himself in prayer before His heavenly Father, what is proper for us? Of this, St. Paul writes to the Ephesians (chap. 3), **that he bends his knee to the Father of our Lord Jesus Christ.** Understand that he refers not merely to the knee of the body, but also of the heart, for God scrutinizes the heart. Furthermore, how our prayer is to be formulated is also portrayed to us in this prayer of the Lord: He calls God His Father, even though God sets before Him such a huge cup to drink. Thus, if God pours from the cross-chalice onto us, we must not allow our trust to fall (decline) on that account. Instead, in the midst of the cross, we are to regard Him as our Father. **Everything is possible for You**, says the Lord Christ. Thus must our prayer ground itself upon God's omnipotence, for God's fatherly heart and His omnipotence are the two supporting pillars upon which our prayer grounds (supports) itself. **Take away this cup from Me**, Christ said. Thus it is not improper that one petition God to avert or alleviate a cross. However, it must immediately follow thereupon and occur at the same time that one commits everything to the fatherly will of God. Just as Christ here says: **Yet not My will, rather Your will take place.** Even though Christ, as true Man, indeed felt human emotions and asked for the averting of this chalice, He nevertheless immediately forthwith put His will under the will of God [the Father]. We must do this much more, for many times we do not know for what we should pray, Rom. 8. However, as our dear Father, God's will is always the best.

III. In the third place, the evangelists record how the disciples conducted themselves toward their Lord and Master in such agony and also what Christ said to them. **Stay here**, the beloved Lord says to them, **and watch (be on guard) with Me; pray, so that you do not fall into temptation.** He requested them to stay awake with Him so that He might have from them a word of comfort in His agony; also, they were to pray so that they would not be overcome by temptation. Thereupon, Christ goes away and anxiously prays to His Father. When He comes back, He finds they were all asleep for sadness. Thus, they did not know what they should answer Him. Consequently, Christ says to them once more: **Oh, watch and pray, so that you do not fall into temptation. The Spirit is willing, but the flesh is weak.** And, since Peter, in particular, had volunteered himself so prominently, the Lord says to him: **Simon, are you asleep? Aren't you willing to watch with Me one hour?** If you are willing to go into death with Me, can't you hold off sleeping for even one hour for My sake? However, Christ's admonition has little effect on [Peter], for when He returns from His prayer the second and third times, He once again finds them as the other time—sleeping, sleeping until the betrayer arrives. Therefore the Lord says to them with ardent words: **Oh, do you then want to sleep and rest? Why do you sleep? It is enough. See, the**

hour has come, and the Son of Man will be betrayed into the hands of sinners. **Stand up, let us go. See, the one who betrays Me is nearby;** but pray, so that you do not fall into temptation.

 1. Just as the disciples are sleepy in the context of the great and burdensome suffering of Christ, so it also happens to us that our hearts are too cold and sleepy properly to ponder the suffering of Christ. If that were not the case, if our hearts were not totally asleep, then great remorse over sin would be awakened within us, for how could it be otherwise? If we do not take to heart that so much agony and suffering befell Christ on account of sin not His own, then we would most certainly tremble on account of our own manifold sins and be fearful of God's wrath. However, we often go along in the sleep of self-confidence and thus do not sincerely contemplate this matter. Also, if our hearts were not so cold and sleepy, then great love for Christ would be ignited in us. For if we truly take to heart what a great love Christ showed towards us—that for the sake of our redemption He allowed Himself to endure so much suffering—we would most certainly love Him with heartfelt passion, which does indeed occur. But here also we often pass along in the sleep of negligence and thus do not sincerely contemplate this fact.

 2. What Christ says here to His disciples: **Watch and pray, so that you do not fall into temptation**, we should regard as being spoken to us, as He personally teaches it to us from this text in Mark 13: **See to it**, He says, **watch and pray, for you never know when it is time. However, what I say to you, I say to everyone: Watch [be on guard].** For these are the two means by which we can guard against temptation; namely, watching and praying. Here the incitement of the flesh, the delusions of the Devil, and the deceptions of the world always make their presence known. Against these we can only prepare (mobilize) ourselves with watchfulness and prayer. By watchfulness is meant the opening of the eyes of one's heart, so that we pay proper attention to what the Devil has in mind as he attacks us from the right and the left, so that we do not fall into the sleep of self-assurance (cocky confidence) and thereby are overcome by the Devil. However, since our watchfulness, our caution, is at times inferior and inadequate, it must also be accompanied by prayer, by which we commend ourselves into the God's almighty hand, from which the Devil can never snatch us away. Through prayer we also become recipients of divine power to withstand temptation. Would to God that we would be as diligent in watchfulness and prayer as Christ faithfully here admonishes us to be! There would certainly be no lack in the midst of trials and temptations. Thus, watchfulness and prayer are highly necessary in order that we are not overpowered by trials and temptations.

3. We should also well consider that Christ here says: **The Spirit is willing, but the flesh is weak.** Consequently, when we already feel the beneficial movement of the Holy Spirit in our hearts, we should not become overconfident [cocky] or proud on that account, for we still carry with us the weakness of the flesh. And that is what St. Paul is talking about when he says in 2 Cor. 4: **We carry our treasure in earthly vessels.** A huge treasure is indeed entrusted to us; namely, that Christ resides in our hearts through faith, Eph. 3. Yet our flesh is such a fragile, earthly vessel, so that if we want to follow the lusts of our flesh, it can easily happen that we will lose this treasure. Here, then, appertains the strife between the Spirit and the flesh in [those who are] born again, whereof St. Paul speaks in Gal. 5. This conflict endures for a person's entire lifetime. And indeed, all certainty, all pride, all self-reliance in one's own power should rightly fall away from us as we hear that in this dangerous strife, which involves the crown of eternal life, the spirit indeed is willing but the flesh is weak. Therefore, the best counsel is, to petition and bid the strong Lord of Sabaoth with zealous prayer that He would be powerful in our weakness with His might, 2 Cor. 12, so that we be preserved by such power for the salvation set aside and held in trust for us, 1 Pet. 1. To that end, God help us through Christ. Amen.

O Lord Jesus Christ, who on account of my sin sweated bloody sweat, stand by me when the cold sweat of death breaks out on me. You who were crushed under the burden of divine wrath for my sake, rescue me from the impending wrath. Help me so that I may watch and pray so that the temptations may not overpower me. Amen.

The Third Sermon

Christ is taken captive in the garden through the betrayer Judas.

As the Lord Jesus was still speaking with His disciples, behold, Judas—one of the twelve—inasmuch as he now had allied himself with the troops and servants of the high priest and Pharisees and with the elders and scribes, went before the troops who came there with torches and lamps, with swords and with lances. The betrayer, however, had given them a sign and said: The one I will kiss, He's the one. Grab Him and by all means lead Him [away]. As Jesus then knew everything that was to happen to Him, He went out and said to them: Whom are you looking for? They answered Him: Jesus from Nazareth. Jesus said to them: I am He. But Judas, who was betraying Him, also stood next to Him. As then Jesus said to them: I'm the one, they all stepped back and fell to the ground. Then He asked them once more: Whom are you looking for? And they said: Jesus of Nazareth. Jesus answered: I have told you that I am He. If you then are looking for Me, let these go—so that the Word was fulfilled which says: I have lost none of those whom You have given to Me. And Judas came closer to Jesus in order to kiss Him. And immediately He stepped up to Him and said: The greeting of God to You, Rabbi, and he kissed Him. Jesus however said to him: My friend, why have you come? Judas, do you betray the Son of Man with a kiss? Then they stepped near and laid their hands on Jesus and grabbed Him.

In Song of Solomon 1, the Christian Church says: **Don't look [stare at me] that I am so black, for the sun has burned me so. My mother's children are angry with me.** With these words the Christian Church confesses that in her outward appearance she is so black; that is, so despised and unsightly, inasmuch as she has been scorched by the sun of tribulation and temptation, referring also to the people by whom she is most often frightened. My mother's children are angry with me, she [the Church] says. By [children] she is referring to the false brethren, those who proudly promote themselves as children of the Church, and yet persecute the true, genuine Church under the cloak (appearance) of piety. Because Christ, as the Head of the Church, wanted to endure (submit to) that which would happen to His members, the true Christians, and, as a faithful Physician, wanted to be the first to drink from the same chalice which He was going to proffer to His Church—now note this—He thus also wanted to endure this in His suffering, namely, that He would be persecuted and condemned to death by those who laid claim to the name and title of being the Church—such as the Pharisees, the high priests, and the clerics of Jerusalem—and indeed also that His own disciple Judas, who studied in Christ's school and received all kinds of blessing from Him, would actually betray Him, even as this [betrayal] had also been proclaimed beforehand, for example, in Psa. 41: **Also My friend, whom I trusted, who ate My bread, trampled Me under his feet.** Psa. 69: **I became a stranger to My brothers and unknown to My mother's children.** Psa.55: **If My enemy wanted to disgrace Me, I was willing to endure it; and if one who hated beat on Me, I would conceal Myself from him. You, however, are My companion, My guardian and My relative. We were friendly with each other and walked with a crowd in the House of God.**

In the text above, we wish to examine two aspects of how Judas arranged to effect such a betrayal of [Jesus]:

First of all, concerning the plot of Judas and what kind of accomplices he used for this deed.

Second, how Christ went out to meet him and what was spoken before Christ was taken captive.

I. While at this time Christ endured a great portion of His suffering in His soul—that is, the burden of God's wrath so crushed Him that He profusely poured out bloody sweat, from which the garments on His body became red like a treader of grapes as He trod out the grapes of divine wrath, Isa. 63—please note that His bodily suffering also continued. For in as much as His holy suffering was to be medicine for us against sin and eternal death, He wanted to suffer both in body and soul. Then, as He was still speaking with His disciples, wanting to rouse them from their natural sleep as well as from their spiritual sleep of overconfidence, there came Judas, the betrayer, one of the twelve disciples of Christ.

This indeed was a terrible turn of events: that one of the disciples of Christ becomes the betrayer of Christ. Judas was no ordinary Christian; rather, he was in his fourth year of studies in Christ's school. He had heard many outstanding sermons from Christ, and he had witnessed many divine miracles accomplished by Christ. Indeed, he himself had proclaimed Christ's teaching and had confirmed it with miracles, as we can conclude from Matthew 10. Even so, he is brought to the point where he betrays His Lord and Master and leads Him to the *Blutbank*.* Terrible it is that Solomon—to whom God the Lord appeared and gave such a wise and understanding heart that the likes of him never preceded nor came after him, 1 Kings 3—reached the point in his old age that his heart bowed down to foreign gods.

---

* Lit. "bench, table, or bed of blood." Gerhard is possibly referring to the bloody bed of the Brook of Kidron (see above), to the sacrificial altar, or to both. Ed.

However, it is even more terrible that Judas, who for such a long time learned divine wisdom from the Son of God Himself, at last so completely turned himself away and in ultimate despair fell into eternal damnation. [The experience of Judas] should indeed wipe the sleep of [false] security from our eyes; namely, that we somehow can never succumb to the delusion that it is impossible to lose the grace of God and the promise of life even though we do whatever we please. Not so! We obviously know that the Devil was kicked out of God's kingdom and Adam out of Paradise; how then can there not be security [cocky over-confidence] in this world?

Accordingly, we should at all times in true fear humble ourselves before God and ponder well what St. Paul says in Philippians 2: **With fear and trembling, see to it that you are saved.** We should also earnestly petition God that He would take our salvation out of our hands and take it into His own hands, just has He has promised in Isa. 49: **I have engraved [drawn] you on My hands.** Our salvation and [eternal] happiness could easily be ripped out of our hands; thus, we should not look to the strength of our own faith. However, God's hands are almighty. If we commend our salvation into His faithful hands, no one will be able to rip us out of His hands, as Christ very comfortingly states in John 10: **No one will be able to rip My sheep out of My hand. The Father who has given them to Me is greater than everything, and none can rip them out of My Father's hand.** God has emphatically given to us sure promises of eternal life. Therefore, our faith can confidently rely upon them. However, with this faith there must be a childlike fear (awe) within us, for we still carry with and in us our sinful flesh. Or, as St. Paul expresses it in 2 Cor. 4, we have this treasure in earthly vessels. As we steadfastly rely upon the goodness (grace) of God through true faith, we, with genuine fear (respect) are also completely to denounce our own powers. For the invincible Power by which we are sustained through faith unto salvation,

1 Pet. 1, is God's, and it is not from us, 2 Cor. 4. Thus it is that the true Christians in the Scriptures are described as follows: they waited upon God's goodness [grace] and at the same time also feared [had a healthy respect for] God. Christ's betrayer (His own disciple, Judas) was at one time one of these.

Secondly then, there arises the question: How did this poor, wretched man come to such a gruesome disaster? In John 13 it is recorded that the Devil implanted [the idea of betrayal] into his heart. But how did the Devil bring him to such a deed? The evangelists record that it happened because of greed. For he held the money-purse and carried what pious people gave Jesus. At times, through the prompting of the Devil, he stole some of this money, until through such greed he finally was brought to the point where he let himself be motivated to betray His Lord and Master for thirty little pieces of silver. Here we see how completely true it is what St. Paul records in 1 Tim. 6: **Greed is a root of everything that is evil.** The reason? Greed turns the human heart from God to temporal things. However, when the heart no longer clings to God the Lord with love and trust, nothing other than all kinds of sin will result. When the Devil fills the heart of man with greed, he may thereafter easily lead him wherever he wants to. "There is no trace of righteousness in a heart in which greed has set up its residence. Intoxicated with this poison, unfaithful Judas greedily longed for profit with the rope in place*" (Leo, 9. Passion-Sermon). When greed truly possesses a person's heart, that person no longer is afraid of God or men. He spares neither parents or sisters. He has faith in no friend. He has no pangs of conscience if because of [greed] he turns them into widows and orphans.

Thirdly, in what manner did Judas carry out the bloody assault of his betrayal? Through cunning and raw power. With cunning, because he pointed out Jesus with a kiss, which was

---

* A reference to Judas hanging himself? Tr.

a sign of special friendship. With power, because he took with him the troop of the Roman governor and the servants of the high priest, the Pharisees, the elders, and the scribes. They came there with torches and lamps, so that Christ might not escape from them in the darkness, [and] also with swords and lances, so that they might instill fear in the disciples of Christ and be able to out-man them in case they somehow attempted to defend [Jesus] with weapons.

    Here we should ponder how idolatry and false doctrine are commonly advanced through external sword and power and persecution of true confessors. The high priests, scribes, and Pharisees had long striven against Christ on account of [His] doctrine. Because, however, they saw that up to now they had not accomplished very much, they took their "arguments from the executioner's workshop," as Hieronymus states in his Apology to Ruffinus. So it goes still to this day: "The church of Cain is bloodthirsty." If black-colored ink doesn't help, they then grab for the red and dispute with those who oppose idolatry to the extent that they feel it [i. e., pain of bloodshed and death]. This occurs because the Devil is both a liar and a murderer, John 8. That's why he also defends his lies with murder and various kinds of tyrannies. Therefore, the great spiritual Babylon, the church of the Antichrist in the seventeenth chapter of the Revelation of John, is also pictured and portrayed as a woman who drinks of the blood of the saints; on the other hand, the true Christians are likened to slaughtered sheep, Psa. 44. And, in Song of Solomon 2 the Church is compared to a rose among the thorns. She is a beautiful rose before God's eyes, but she must endure being scratched by the thorns of persecution in this world. And, just as the heavenly Bridegroom is white and red, Song of Solomon 5—white because of His complete purity, and red because of His bitter suffering—so also must His spiritual bride become His likeness and image and apply herself in pure, unblemished service (worship) of God. Moreover, she will have to endure persecution patiently and, at times, also the shedding of blood. Thus she will also become white and red in the eyes of God, and will thus become an acceptable bride.

Accordingly, in Judas and in his companions we also see the nature and disposition of the enemies of the Church. For we see here, at the same time, the great foolishness and absurd madness of Judas. He knew that Christ with His divine power often miraculously escaped from the hands of His enemies. Even so, he hit upon the foolish thought that if only he had a troop of soldiers with him, [Jesus] would surely fall into his hands. Similar foolishness exists in the minds of those who persecute the Church. They know from experience that they cannot by force dampen the power of truth. Nor can the Church be uprooted through persecution. The blood of those who are killed for the sake of the truth is a fruitful seed from which later on comes forth an even greater and richer harvest of true Christians. Just as human blood, if one spills it on the trees, makes them fruitful, so also the blood of [martyred] Christians is a fertilizer for the spiritual acreage of the Church.* Thus, in Song of Solomon 2, persecution is called a time of cutting off [of pruning]. If one prunes the grapes in the blooming season of spring, their growth is greatly increased. So also, if with the sharp pruning knife (scythe) of death someone actually cuts away some members from the Church, it still does not diminish the Church; instead, it increases. The persecutors of the Church know all this; yet, at the same time they are so reckless and irresponsible that they do not desist in their undertaking. So also we note that Judas was afraid; else why did he take with him a troop of soldiers? Why all the swords and staves? Weren't [the disciples and Jesus]

---

* There may be no scientific evidence for the fertilizing effect of blood on trees; but this statement is to be taken for its illustrative purposes, just as the Lutheran confessors used scientifically mistaken medieval views for illustrative purposes in the *Book of Concord*. Tr.

a poor, unarmed band? But [these precautions] were brought about by Judas' evil conscience, which feared where there was nothing to be feared. So it still is with the enemies of the Church; even though they have in hand swords and staves, i.e., external power, yet their heart is never still [at peace] and is constantly filled with fear, for they carry their accuser in their hearts. This is also shown by the fact that they carry out their undertaking, not in the clear light of day, but rather in the darkness of night: **Whoever does evil, such a one hates the Light**, John 3. Their hearts were darkened and widely separated from the true light of divine knowledge. Therefore, they also love the outward darkness, which they use to their advantage.

Finally, we see from Judas and his gang that the enemies of the Church employ hypocritical deception. Judas kisses Christ, and yet leads with him swords and staves. Thus it still happens. The enemies of the Church exude honey-sweet words from embittered hearts, Psa. 55: **Their mouth is smoother than butter, and yet they have war on their mind. Their words are more soothing than olive oil and yet are naked swords.** This they learn from their father, the Devil, who, while seeking to destroy mankind, nevertheless deceives by means of a loving, outward appearance.

II. Jesus knew what would happen to Him, says the text. And why should He not know? Everything in His suffering quite obviously occurred through the thoughtful counsel and foreknowledge of God, Acts 2. In this counsel of God, Jesus was present as the Second Person of the Godhead. Accordingly, He goes forth to meet them and places Himself before them. **For whom are you searching?** He says. [We] **are looking for Jesus of Nazareth**, they answer. **I am He**, Jesus says to them. And therewith they saw that no might nor power was too strong for Him if He had a mind to resist. In His state of external and deepest humiliation, He permitted them a glimpse of His strength and power, in that, upon a single Word of the Lord, the entire troop wavered backwards and fell to the ground.

What sort of power will the voice of the Lord have when He will come to judge, since He did this [wonder] while allowing Himself to be judged? What kind of might will He have when He will come to rule, since He had so much might when He came to die? This falling back of the godless is much different from when true Christians—as well as Christ—fall upon their face in prayer, as the Scriptures testify. [The falling of the godless] happened out of fright and it is thereby announced that the godless will have to depart from God and be cast aside by Him. But that believers fall on their face before God occurs because of true humility.

However, here note the blindness of these godless ones. For as they behold the judgment of God and the power of this Lord, they still don't desist from their undertaking. For as Christ once more asks them whom they are seeking, they answer as before. Thereupon, Christ gives Himself over into their hands, while at the same time first winning safe conduct for His disciples. With this action, He fulfilled what He testified to His heavenly Father in John 18: **I have lost none of those whom You have given to Me.** If at that moment the disciples would have been apprehended, Augustine says in *sec. 112 of John*, their salvation would have been in a precarious state. Also, Christ first wanted to employ the service of the apostles for the spreading of the Gospel before they were to suffer.

Finally, as Judas gave the sign to his cohorts, in that he kissed Christ, Christ tried once more to see if He might not bring Judas to the knowledge of his grievous fall into sin. **My friend,** He says, **why have you come. Do you betray the Son of Man with a kiss?**—just so that no one until the end of time might happen to think that it was on the instigation and initiative of God that Judas had conceived these thoughts and accomplished this deed. For even though Judas' deed furthered the counsel of God for the redemption of the human race, yet such an end result was not intended for Judas [by God]; rather Judas sought satisfaction for his own greed. Much less did God implant such thoughts into the heart of Judas. Rather, God the Lord directed this horrible sin of Judas to a blessed end, in keeping with His unfathomable wisdom.

Here, then, we should ponder [several matters]:

1. Christ suffered willingly, especially since He presented Himself to those who sought Him. The fact that we know Christ suffered this way willingly and from a burning love for our salvation makes His suffering truly lovely and pleasing to us. The external suffering of Christ was never so great and burdensome; His inner (spiritual) love had to be more ready to suffer when it undertook the pressing need of our salvation. That is what made the holy sacrifice truly acceptable for the heavenly Father. For in the same way that all sacrifices in the Old Testament—which were to be pleasing to God—had to be ignited with the fire which fell from heaven, so also this holy Sacrifice—which Christ offered up before God the Lord by His suffering—is consumed by the heavenly fire of passionate love. And, to this end, He permitted His side to be opened [with a soldier's spear]; namely, so that we might behold His rich-in-love heart. Thus is now richly fulfilled what He states in Psa. 40: **Look, I come**—not by force, but of My own volition. **In the Book it is written about Me: My God, I eagerly do what You desire.** Consequently, also everything in His crucifixion is done with the intent that we may see His love. He bows His head out of love in order to view us in a kindly manner. He stretches out His arms in love in order to embrace us. His side is opened (pierced) so that thereby the fire of heartfelt love may gush out over us. He speaks of this in Song of Solomon 4: **My sister, beloved bride**, i.e., you believing soul, whom God the Lord has betrothed to Me by faith, and so have become My spiritual bride, **you have captured or wounded My heart.** Because Christ wounded His heart out of

love, He has thus endured such wounds and streams [of blood] from His body. That is indeed a marvelous power of love—that God's Son journeyed down from heaven to earth, was tied to a pillar, lifted up on the cross, locked up in the grave, and led into hell. If, then, our hearts are not once again drawn to Christ by such passionate love, they must most certainly be much heavier than any iron or lead. Should not this kind of fire warm up our hearts—and yes, also ignite them—so that they once again burn with love towards Christ, since it is quite natural that one would love the Person by whom he is loved?

2. By the fact that Christ alone is apprehended and endures the suffering by Himself, whereas His disciples go free, the fruit of His suffering is most winsomely portrayed; namely, the punishment is laid solely upon Christ so that we thereby may have peace, Isa. 53. He alone must endure such manifold suffering. Thereby, all His true disciples, that is, all believers, are brought to assurance (confident certainty) and freedom, as He says in Isa. 63: **I tread the grapes by Myself, and none of the people are beside Me.** If some of the disciples had also suffered on this occasion, someone might by chance fall into the delusion that Christ had not actually borne the burden of divine wrath all by Himself, and had thus not completely provided the payment for the sins of the world. However, since the disciples got off 'scot-free', and since Christ alone sweated bloody sweat from His body and alone endured the suffering, thus it is adequately demonstrated that He also had completed the work of redemption by Himself.

3. If Christ here speaks in such a friendly way with Judas, who of course was His betrayer and the Devil's bondman (slave), how much more patiently and graciously will He deal with those who, perhaps because of weakness, rashly precipitate a fall [into sin], as Psalm 37 states: **If he falls, he will not be thrown away, for the Lord supports him with His hand.** Just as a mother, when she sees that her dear child is about to fall, spreads out her hands so that it does not come to harm, so also does the Lord when His dear children—the true Christians—somehow stumble into sin. He supports (upholds) them so that they do not suddenly sink into hell. Instead, He sets them straight once again, and speaks in a friendly manner to the heart. God grant this to us also through Christ. Amen.

O Lord Jesus Christ, You who willingly gave Yourself up into the hands of Your enemies in order to atone for my disobedience, help, so that I give myself to You with my whole heart to live, suffer, and die according to Your will. Amen.

The Fourth Sermon

Since Christ won't allow Himself to be defended with the sword, He is, on that account, forsaken by His disciples.

However, when those who were with Him saw what was about to happen, they said to Him: Lord, shall we strike back with our swords? Then Simon Peter, who had a sword, pulled it out and struck at the high priest's servant and took off his right ear. And the servant's name was Malchus.

Jesus, however, answered and said: Let them continue what they are doing. And He spoke to Peter: Stick your sword into the sheath; for whoever takes the sword, such a one shall perish by means of the sword. Or do you think that I could not petition My Father to send Me more than twelve legions of angels? Should I not drink the chalice which the Father has given Me? But how would the Scriptures be fulfilled? This is how it must happen. And He touched his ear and healed him. In that hour Christ spoke to the high priests and rulers of the temple, and the elders, and to the troops which had come for Him: You have gone out with swords and staves like for a murderer to seize Me. Did I not sit daily with you and teach in the temple, and you laid no hand on Me? But this is your hour and the power of darkness, so that the Scripture may be fulfilled. However, all this took place so that the writings of the prophets were fulfilled. Then all the disciples forsook Him and fled. And there was one youth who followed after Him. He was clothed with a linen cloth over his bare skin. And the young men grabbed him. However, he let loose of the linen cloth and fled from them naked.

In Luke 9 it is recorded that as the Lord Christ was ready to undertake His final journey to Jerusalem in order to suffer and to die, He sent ahead messengers to a little village of the Samaritans so that they might reserve lodging for Him. But the Samaritans at that time did not want to receive Him or grant Him lodging. This moved the apostles James and John to such anger that they said: **Lord, if You want, we will, like Elijah, ask fire to fall down from heaven and consume them. However, Jesus turned to them and warned them and said: Don't you know which Spirit's children you are? The Son of Man did not come to destroy the souls of men, rather, to preserve them.** From this we may conclude that the apostles, out of anger and ill-timed passion, wanted to take harsh revenge against their Lord's enemies for this insult to Him. However, the gentle Lord had to restrain them. Not only could He not support them, but they henceforth had to exercise forbearance from such untimely zeal. For we hear in the lesson just read that likewise in the garden, as the Lord was being taken captive therein, [the disciples] wanted to strike back with spears and swords, which the Lord would not allow them to do. Instead, He restrained them for the best [reason], at which they were so confounded that they dropped their hands and feet and fled completely away. So they missed on both counts: one time they are too courageous, the next time they are too despairing.

At this time we want to deal with this point: namely, that the apostles initially wanted to defend the Lord with the sword, but later on forsook Him and fled.

I. When the disciples of the Lord saw what was about to happen (that is, as the godless gang attacked Jesus and intended to take Him captive), they thought about how they had volunteered to stand firmly by their Lord and give up everything for His sake. Thus, they asked the Lord, as was their habit, and said: **Lord,**

should we strike back with the sword? They had seen that at one single word from the Lord the entire troop fell back and to the ground. That made them so courageous that they, small in number, were willing to take on this large armed troop. Peter reminded himself of how he had promised steadfast allegiance in the presence of all the others, not waiting for Jesus' answer, but rather thinking that since Christ had previously said that in view of the imminent battle one might indeed now sell His cloak and purchase a sword for himself, there was not much about which to dispute here; and so he did not let the matter delay him for long. Consequently, he quickly pulled [his sword] from its sheath; and, as he became aware that one of the chief servants of the high priest stepped forward from the rest, wanting to be the first to lay a hand on Christ, Peter attacked him. He intended to split his head open, but the stroke did not happen [that way]; rather, he chopped off [the servant's] right ear.

We have here an example of an untimely zeal. The Lord Christ had faithfully admonished his disciples that they were to watch and pray so as not to fall into temptation. But to that [appeal] they were cold (indifferent) and sleepy. Yet now they are so courageous that amidst these troops [they] wanted to strike out with the sword. That's how it still goes; for what God has commanded us, we have indeed an entirely poor (inadequate) zeal. However, we are always ready and willing for that which pertains to an untimely (inappropriate) zeal. God has commanded us to gird our souls with patience, Luke 21, and promises us that by being still and hoping we shall be strong, Isa. 30. But we often forget this and obey instead a vindictive spirit and untimely zeal. Here Peter intended to defend His Lord with sword and power. But when it came to the point that he should confess Him, then he was much too faint-hearted. Here his hand was quick and ready for the sword, but later his tongue and confession were, so to speak, bound [i.e., disabled]. Indeed, Peter did not lack for an example to begin his defense. He knew that to

Abraham's renown it was later written in Gen. 14 that he, with a motley group, engaged the army of four kings and rescued Lot from their hands. Peter knew that it was accounted to Phinehas for righteousness—and that through a covenant he was given an eternal priesthood—that he, in wrath and in zealous devotion to God, impaled harlot and rogue, Num. 25, Psa. 106 [v. 30]. Thus Peter thought it was not only permissible, but that it would also redound to his fame if he fought to the death for his Lord and Master with the sword. However, in these examples there was one great dissimilarity which Peter did not take into account, and thus [he] acted against his apostolic calling. In this calling he and the other apostles were commanded, Mat. 19, that they were not to use staff, much less a sword, for weapons. Therefore, it is best that we do not look at the example of others, but instead each time look to the rule of our own calling and rather be prepared to suffer unjustly than to defend ourselves—in keeping with Christ's command in Mat. 5: **I say to you, that you should not strive against the evil. Instead, if someone slaps you on your right cheek, offer him the other cheek also.**

II. Secondly, as the Lord heard that the apostles with words, and Peter with action, demonstrated that they wanted to defend Him with the sword, He spoke to Peter: **Stick your sword into the sheath**, [as much as to say] I don't want to be defended in such a manner. Lay the sword aside. In its place take patience to hand, **for he who takes the sword will perish by sword.** He who is not girded on his side and given in hand a sword from God should never practice private wrath with a sword. Instead, leave the decision to the ruling authority, to whom God has given the sword and which does not bear it in vain, Rom. 13. The same will well defend his righteous cause. If that does not happen, then he should rather suffer than take his own revenge. For anyone who takes up the sword out of his own vengeance will perish by the sword—in keeping with the ancient law of God, Gen. 9: **Whoever spills man's blood, his blood shall once again be spilled by man.** Thus Christ did not intervene with the authority of secular rulers, nor did He forbid their use of the sword, for the [power of the] sword was given to government by God Himself. Instead, He forbade Peter, as an apostle and private person [citizen], to take up the sword for the sake of his own revenge and would so much as to say: Peter, it does not lie within your realm to fight with the external sword; rather, to you has been given a different sword, namely the Word of God, which is living and powerful and sharper than any two-edged sword. And [this sword] pierces through until it divides soul and spirit, also marrow and bone, Heb. 4. It is also called the Sword of the Spirit in Eph. 6. This sword slices off man's sin, and sustains him with life at the same time. With this sword you [Peter], as an apostle, shall fight as well as you can. That is also how the apostle [Paul] expresses it later in 2 Cor. 10: **the weapons of our knighthood are not of the flesh.** This is one reason why Christ forbade Peter the sword. Then [Jesus] says: **Do you think that I could not petition My Father to send Me twelve legions of angels?** In place of you twelve apostles I could doubtless provide another kind of assistance. I would petition My Father for more than twelve legion of angels. They would number in the thousands and could far more readily defend Me than you unarmed apostles. For just as one angel struck down eighty-five thousand men of the Assyrian horde, what indeed would many thousand angels be able to do? Just as angels once served Jesus, Mat. 4, so also they serve the members of Christ; and, when the need requires it, God often sends many angels to a Christian—as can be seen from the account in 2 Kings 6, where an entire mountain full of fiery horses and chariots surround Elisha.

In the third place, Christ says: **Shall I not drink the chalice which My Father has given Me?**—as much as to say: I have already prayed with heart-felt sincerity to My heavenly Father to divert this chalice from Me. However, since I see that it can be no other way, I would patiently and willingly submit to it. Now, in as much as Christ calls His suffering a chalice once again, He would have it understood that this measure of His suffering was foreordained within the counsel of the Holy Trinity—just as a person in setting a table usually sets each individual's chalice before him in advance. And even though it was indeed a bitter drink for Christ, nevertheless it was a salutary drink for us—even as many a medicine is bitter and yet useful for good health. By the same token, we should also regard all of our suffering as such a chalice, that God's counsel from eternity foreordained for each of us individually his portion of a cross [to bear]. And, as David says in Psalm 116: Though it indeed be a bitter drink, it yet will be a salutary chalice.

Finally, Christ says: **But how would the Scriptures be fulfilled? It must happen this way.** In the Scriptures, My sufferings have previously been proclaimed with prophecies and pictures. These must now be fulfilled, for it is impossible for the Scriptures to be broken, John 10. We should regard our crosses in precisely the same way; that is, the Scriptures must also be fulfilled through our suffering. For not only is the suffering of Christ proclaimed in the Old Testament, but also in the New Testament it is prophesied that the disciples of Christ must enter the Kingdom of God through much tribulation, Acts 14, [and] that they must become more like the image of Christ, Rom. 8. That is the other [aspect] of Christ's forbidding Peter to use the sword and the reasons He cited for the prohibition.

III. Thirdly, the evangelists then record that Christ healed the wounded servant again and re-attached his ear. This the Lord did to allow a glimpse of His divine omnipotence in the state of His deepest humiliation and to indicate (announce) that He is the One who, with the Father and the Holy Spirit, created mankind in the beginning, giving him body and soul, eyes and ears.

Furthermore, Christ herewith intended to avert the vile slander which might have arisen about Him and His disciples if one could have truthfully stated that they had defended themselves with strokes of the sword. It could have provided a great semblance [of credibility] to the enemies of Christ for their false accusations of insurrection if they could have set before Governor Pilate the wounded head of this servant, Malchus. To prevent this, Christ healed his ear again, and, in so doing, teaches us that we should avoid not only evil, but also all appearances of evil, 1 The. 5, and, indeed, never to give cause for our reputation to be maligned.

Thirdly, Christ wanted to teach by deed what He previously had taught with words in Mat. 5; namely, that we also are to do good to those who hate us and betray us. Is this not the greatest gentleness: that Christ here not only forbids the apostles' own wrath but, beyond that, also does good to His enemies by whom He was captured? Therefore, He may say truthfully in Mat. 11: **Learn from Me, for I am gentle (meek).** How far we are still from this gentleness of Christ—we, who often times pay back evil with evil, yea, who also offend our neighbor without cause.

Finally, Christ herewith intended to point out a mystery. For this servant of the high priest symbolizes the nation of the Jews, along with their high priests and teachers. Their right ear has been cut off; they hear everything from the left and wrongly. That which was held before them in the Old Testament signifies to them an earthly, worldly messiah. But ultimately the Lord Christ will have mercy on them and give them the right ear so that they correctly comprehend the mystery from the Old Testament about the Messiah, as it is proclaimed in Rom. 11: **Israel has experienced partial blindness and deafness until the fullness of the Gentiles has been established, and then all of Israel will be saved.** This is the third [point] in this text; namely, how Christ again healed the ear of the wounded servant.

IV. Fourthly, [the text deals with] how the Lord Christ hereupon addressed His enemies by whom He had been taken captive and took them to task about their evil intentions. For even in the hour in which the Lord healed the ear, He began to say to the high priests, the chief personnel of the temple, and to the elders who had come on account of Him: **You went out to capture Me like a murderer, with swords and staves**, etc. By noting that Christ spoke this in the very hour in which He had healed the ear, the evangelists would have us remember that Christ showed His miraculous kindness to His enemies because He wanted to hold before them (inasmuch as they indeed had not previously been moved to desist from their intentions by the terrible miracle which knocked them to the ground) that they should allow themselves finally to be so moved by this loving miracle of the healed ear. At the same time, He reprimanded them for coming out to Him with swords and staves as if He were a murderer, as much as to say: What's the meaning of this business? Did I not daily sit with you and teach in the temple, and you never laid a hand on Me? But this hour belongs to you and to the power of darkness. If you had any proper case against Me, you would have seized Me openly, but it is written: **He who does evil hates the Light**, John 3. Nevertheless, I know—Christ would say—[these things] will not happen to Me unexpectedly; rather, [they have] all been previously announced in the Scriptures.

Even that Christ was taken captive in the darkness of night His enemies had indeed thus employed to their advantage, for they knew that the people were attached to Him. However, it is indicated in Psalm 23 that He would journey through the dark valley of death on our behalf and, in Eph. 6, that the prince of this world, who rules in darkness, would rise up against Him—indeed, that the might of hellish darkness would for a time assault Him. However, Christ, even here in this darkness, lifts His eyes to the Light of divine Providence, and He comforts Himself in this same darkness which fell over Him with the fact that the Light of divine Providence would nevertheless not be darkened. Instead, God the Lord would again bring Him into the Light. We should also do and know the same, [that is,] nothing can happen to us without God's gracious will. Instead, all has first been confirmed by God and proclaimed to us in His Word.

 V. Fifthly, the evangelists record that when the disciples saw that the Lord no longer wished to defend Himself, but rather gave Himself into captivity, they all fled from Him. Thus was fulfilled what the Lord had announced to them in John 16: **Look, the hour will come that you will be scattered, each one to his own [place], and will leave Me all alone. But, I am not alone, for the Father is with Me.** One of the young men is especially remembered, obviously one of those who belonged to Christ and had his sleeping place on the Mount of Olives. He was awakened by the turmoil, tossed only a shirt over himself, and followed Christ from a distance, wanting to see how things would come out. As he found himself in midst of the godless troops, they grabbed at him. But he left his shirt behind and fled from there naked—just as he had seen the other apostles do.

 In this disciple we have an example of the bad habits ingrained within our flesh. As the Lord Jesus beat back the entire troop with a single word, [the disciples] became so courageous that they, in their insignificant number, engaged the large, armed brigade. But as the Lord Christ again restrained the streams of His divine power and allowed Himself to be seized and taken captive, they all fled from Him out of great fear. Thus, when we feel the slightest breath [i.e., suggestion] that God has taken our side, we are able fully to trust in God and be courageous. However, when it appears as if He has forsaken us, as if He is sleeping, and does not want us to defend ourselves but rather suffer, then our courage slips away so that we fall away from God. Therefore, during our lifetime we have more than enough to learn from the text in Isaiah 30: **By being still and hoping you will become strong.** Our flesh and blood is unable to learn or practice this. If God the Lord hides His countenance, Psalm 13, trust will sink (founder). However, we should rely more on the promises of God than upon our outward feelings. Thus we will be able to hope for help with good rest and quietness and ultimately experience the act of being helped.

Here we also see how one person will always forsake more and lose more for the sake of Christ than another person. The apostles flee altogether and take their clothes with them. However, the young man must [do them] one better. He also has to leave behind the loin cloth with which he was dressed. So it still goes. Many a person also suffers for the sake of Christ, but he still preserves his body, which is, as it were, the cloak of the soul. On the other hand, many a person must lose his body and life for Christ. Thus it always is: One must lose and give up more for the sake of Christ than another. Such inequality emanates from the all-wise counsel of God. Therefore, we should not be led astray; rather, [we should] accept with patience that which God lays upon us, be it a great or an insignificant cross. We should not look at others [to see] whether they have to suffer as much as we do. Instead, think about what the Lord Christ gave to Peter for an answer in John 21 when he became concerned about this inequality—that he should lose his life, while John goes away free. **What about this one**, he says, what am I guilty of that I should suffer more? **Indeed**, says the Lord, **if I want him to remain, what is that to you? You follow Me.** We should allow this to be spoken [to apply] to all of us: We should follow Christ as He leads us—through thorns and hedgerows [brambles]—moreover, leaving it up to Him how He would lead and guide others.

Finally, if we would properly follow the example of this young man, we should begin this way. When the Devil and his horde want to take us captive and tie us up with the cords of sin, we also should forsake cloak and all—all that is nearest and dearest to us. Our body and life are nothing more than a garment with which the soul is clad in this world [life]. Temporal goods are nothing more than a miserable covering for the body. If in times of temptation it indeed can be no other way, then so be it: leave body and life, goods and blood, behind. We would follow the Lord Christ bare and naked. We have a beautiful type of this in Joseph, Gen. 39, as Potiphar's wife tried to seduce and force him into illicit intercourse. He left his cloak in her hands and fled. If the godless world, the Devil's whore, tries to entice us into spiritual whoredom—that is, into idolatry, false doctrine, and shameful sin—we should leave behind our cloak (that is, goods and blood) rather than to consent to its temptation. God, give us such a heart through Christ. Amen.

O Lord Jesus Christ, You who at the time of Your suffering were forsaken by all Your disciples, let this redound for comfort and help to me, a poor sinner, who has so frequently fled from You until now. Unite my heart with Yours so that from henceforth I nevermore forsake You. Amen.

The Second Act

Comprising the history of the matters which have to do with Jesus before the ecclesiastical council in the house of the high priest Caiaphas.

The First Sermon

Christ was bound, was led first before Annas and next before the high priest Caiaphas; He was examined regarding His disciples and about His teaching and was struck in the face.

But the troops and the chief ruler and the servants of the Jews took Jesus and bound him. They first led Him before Annas, the father-in-law of Caiaphas, who was the high priest for that year. It was Caiaphas, however, who had advised the Jews that it would be good for one Man to be killed for the people. And they led Him to the high priest Caiaphas, that is to the prince of the priests, where all the high priests and Scripture-learned (scribes) and the elders had assembled themselves. Then the high priest asked Jesus about His disciples and about His teaching. Jesus answered him: I have freely and openly spoken before the world. I continually taught in the schools and in the temple where all Jews had assembled, and I have spoken nothing in secret. Why do you ask Me? Ask those who heard Me about what I said to them. Look, they know what I said to them. But as He said this, one of the servants who stood nearby struck

Him on the cheek and said, Are you going to answer the high priest like that? Jesus answered: If I have spoken evil, then prove that it is evil. But if I have spoken correctly, why do you hit Me? Annas had Him sent bound to the high priest Caiaphas.

We read in Judges 15 that the strong hero, Samson, willingly allowed himself to be bound by the three thousand men of the tribe of Judah, who were besieged by the Philistines and who would not free him until Samson delivered these their enemies into their hands. It is also there recorded that when the Philistines exulted with loud shouts over their enemy, the Spirit of the Lord happened upon Samson so that both cords on His arms became like threads which have been singed by fire, so that the bands on His hands melted. Thereupon, he took a jawbone of a mule and with it struck down his enemies in a heap. He also picked up the gate of the city in which he had been confined and took it with him up on a high mountain.

In this passage Samson is a type of our Lord Christ, the true Nazarene, Mat. 2, and the strong Lion from the stem of Judah, Acts 5. He, too, willingly allowed Himself to be bound by the Jews and turned over to the heathen judge. Yes, indeed, he allowed the cords of death to fall upon Him. However, He also finally ripped apart all these bands. He was once again not only personally liberated from all external and internal cords of death; rather, He also conquered all of His and our enemies. He stormed (assaulted) hell and returned from that slaughter as a victorious Conqueror.

At this time we, by divine grace, wish to speak of these bonds of Christ, namely, how He was led bound to the high priests by the godless gang which Judas had joined, and also of the substance of this first session before the council of the high priest, as presented in the account just read to us.

I. As Christ at this time was standing alone in the garden [of Gethsemane] and had been forsaken by all His disciples, the chief officer, along with His body of troops (soldiers) and servants of the high priest, stepped up and took the Lord Christ captive. And since they were fearful that He might overcome them, they tied Him up hard and tight so they might securely retain Him. Thereupon they led the captured and bound Christ down from the Mount of Olives, through the dark valley of Jehosaphat, over the brook of Kidron, on into town. It is easy to observe that along the way the scoundrels mocked Him as a poor captive and deplorably dragged Him like an evil-doer, until they had brought Him to the sheep door, so called because the sheep intended to be used for sacrifice were herded before this same door (gate). And, if one wanted to sacrifice a sheep from this herd, it was then led through this door up to the temple. And even though they were hurrying with their captive to the high priest Caiaphas, yet because an old, highly-revered senior—namely Annas, who had given his daughter [in marriage] to Caiaphas—lived near the gate, they wanted to show this courtesy to Annas, the high priest's father-in-law, thus they led the Lord Christ into His home. It might also have provided a bit of a delay [i.e., to buy some time] that the entire council might assemble in the quarters of the high priest Caiaphas.

We must, however, once again view these bonds of Christ in accordance with the explanation of Zec. 13; namely, that God the Father Himself fettered Christ with these cords. For what happened here was all done by God's counsel and God's hand, Acts 4. One takes care to bind and bring to judgment public transgressors. Because Christ had loaded upon Himself all the world's sin, He Himself stood before God's judgment as the greatest of sinners—certainly not as if He in His own person had committed a single sin, but rather because He took upon Himself the sin of others. Thus, God let Him be tied up and bound according to the types of Isaac, Gen. 22, and Samson,

Judges 15. The Devil had originally tempted (seduced) our first parents and thus ensnared them with sin. And so, from that time on the cords of sin came over all of us so that we are by nature slaves of sin, John 8, and sold into sin, Romans 7, [and] so that we are no more able to travel upon God's path and according to His commandments than a bound person is able to walk. For sins are genuine shackles of the soul, as it is written in Psa. 9: **The godless person is ensnared by the works of his hands,** and Pro. 5: **The iniquity of the godless person will make him liable, and he will be held captive by the cords of his sin.** Since the Devil at one time also had placed upon us the bonds of sin, the entire human race was thus in the cords of the Devil, as it is written in 2 Tim. 2, **that the obstinate rebellious ones are in the Devil's cords, by which they are held captive to his will.** From these bonds of sin ensue the cords of death and the bonds of hell, Psa. 116: **The cords of death had wrapped themselves around me, the anguish of hell flowed over me.**

Yes, indeed, we all were imprisoned in a pit in which there was no water, Zec. 9. For through sin the power of the Devil had overcome us, binding us with chains to eternal death and hell, even as the Devil himself, on account of his transgressions, was bound with the chains of darkness and cast into hell, 2 Pet. 2. So that we might acknowledge that according to our nature we are in all things tied up with these dangerous cords of the Devil, God ordained that the Devil bind the tongues of many, Mark 7, and to bind the feet, ears, and other members of many so that they were unable to use them. God ordained [these wonders] so that one might see from them how, on account of sin, the Devil actually held such power over all of us and that he not only bound our bodily members in this way, but rather also that we—bound hand and foot—might be hurled out into eternal darkness, Mat. 22. That this does not take place—and that we are saved from these dangerous cords of Devil, death, and hell—we have only Christ to thank. He willingly allowed Himself to be thus bound for our sake so that we might be rescued from the cords of sin. Therefore, it is written of Him in Zec. 9: **That He through the covenant of His blood released the captives from the pit in which there was no water.** And He Himself says in Hos. 13: **The sin of Ephraim is bound together, and his sin is retained; however, I will redeem them from hell and rescue them from death.** According to our nature we all are lying in the deep pit, out of which we are unable to climb by our own power. Also, in this pit there is no water of comfort nor any refreshment.

However, Christ releases us from this pit through the blood of His covenant. He is thus so firmly bound that His blood springs forth from the nails so that we might be helped. Our sins are bound as in a little bundle before the eye of God so that for His sake we might be eternally bound [united] to Him. But if we are hereby to be rescued so that our souls might be tied in the little bundle of the living ones with the Lord our God, 1 Sam. 25,* then Christ first had to let Himself be bound and win for us that great grace, so that through the proclamation of the Gospel would be announced to the captives their release and to the bound the loosening of their shackles, Isa. 61. This He Himself teaches us when he says in Luke 24: **Did not Christ have to suffer this and enter into His glory,—and cause to be preached in His Name repentance and forgiveness of sins among all nations.** In essence He says: Christ had to suffer this way, and in His suffering allow Himself to be bound, so that through His Word He could proclaim the untying [loosing] of sins. For since Christ was thus bound, He has thereby won for the Christian Church the "loosening key," so that by its power poor repentant sinners may be freed from their bonds of sin. For that reason we should now confess this with thanksgiving and say with David, Psa. 116: **You have torn loose my fetters; to You**

---

* Very likely a reference to Abigail's action of bundling up things and making her plea before King David, Tr.

will I offer thanks. We also should be on guard that the Devil does not again wrap the cords of sin around our neck, so that it does not happen to us as is written in Isa. 5: **That one couples himself with loose cords to do wrong, and with wagon ropes to commit sin.** For that would result in our being overtaken by the cords of corruption. Rather, we should ponder that Christ was bound so that we might be released from the shackles of sin to walk unhindered on God's path, so that we may be bound to Christ with firm faith, and also so that we may be diligently on guard against the ropes of the Devil.

 These bonds of Christ should also be a comfort to all those who would be fettered on account of their confession of the divine truth, that, with St. Paul, they may [be confident] that because they believe in the bound and crucified Christ, and confess Him, bonds and cross are an honor for them. **Remember my bonds**, says St. Paul, Col. 4. Even more so should we be reminded of the bonds of Christ, who was put into chains in accordance with the type of Joseph in Gen. 40 and the example of the prophet Ezekiel, Eze. 4, who were also bound. He has therewith sanctified and glorified all bonds which might be laid upon us on account of the Name of Christ and the truth, so that one need never be ashamed of them. Rather, with St. Ignatius, we regard them as precious pearls.

 2. Also, it should not be overlooked that Christ was led into Jerusalem through the sheep gate, through which one at other times led the lambs brought as offerings. For He was the little Lamb of God, who wanted to let Himself be sacrificed for the sins of the entire world. All the other atoning sacrifices of the New [*sic*—no doubt a misprint for Old] Testament had pointed to this Sacrifice; and, by this leading and dragging of Christ was fulfilled that which Isa. 53 had previously proclaimed: that He would be led like a Lamb to the place of slaughter and not open His mouth. As Abraham was about to sacrifice his son, Isaac, as a burnt offering to God the Lord, he was restrained

by an angel. He looked behind him and noticed, hanging in a thicket of thorns, a ram, which he sacrificed as a burnt offering in place of Isaac, his son, Gen. 22. Christ our Lord is the true little Lamb and atoning Buck (Ram), upon whom God cast all our sins and who allowed Himself to be captured, seized and bound so that He might present Himself there as a sacrifice and offer Himself for our sin in His body upon the tree, 1 Pet. 2. This He did so that believers, as true children of Abraham, might be preserved for [eternal] life. Abel sacrificed to God from the first-fruits of his herd in Gen. 4, and God considered it a [valid] sacrifice because it emanated from faith, Heb. 11; that is, He was reminded thereby of this little Lamb of God which would be offered up to His heavenly Father as a sweet fragrance. In Exo. 12 God the Lord commanded that [the Jews] must first let their bound Passover lamb lie before their eyes before they slaughtered it. Thus Christ, our Passover Lamb, to whom the former pointed, here also allowed Himself to be seized and bound before He willingly gave up His life on the timber-trunk of the cross. Because in Christ all these and other types of the Old Testament were fulfilled, Christ was willing to let Himself, as the true little Lamb, be led to the sacrifice through the sheep gate.

II. What all occurred in the residence of [the high priest] Annas the evangelists do not record, except that they allowed Christ to be bound on the basis of unproven and outrageous matters [i.e., false testimony]. Neither did Annas permit himself to be displeased with what the executioner's thugs did with Christ. As, then, the high priests and rulers of the spiritual consistory at Jerusalem had meanwhile assembled themselves at the house of Caiaphas, the current presiding high priest, they also led the captured and bound Christ there in order to discuss among themselves how to bring charges against [Him] before the secular, Gentile rulers, who at that time had criminal jurisdiction. In their deliberation they found it best if they would present their accusation in this manner: to portray Christ as a heretic and a rebellious insurgent who had advanced a new teaching which was contrary to the Law and to the worship service as it had been hitherto conducted and by which the people were incited to be so bold as to engage in rebellion. That's what the evangelists mean when the say the high priest asked Christ in the first session about His disciples and about His teaching. All this was thought through with extraordinary cunning (deceit). For since God the Lord Himself commanded in Deu. 13 that one should without mercy slay a false prophet, and also since the Romans punished insurrectionists especially severely, they intended that this accusation would most certainly make the secular authorities consider it carefully. For that very reason this accusation was also a huge sham, in that even though Christ never taught contrary to God's Word and the truth, He nevertheless at times, in teaching and worship, demolished errors and cast out falsifications. And many times He had a huge crowd of people with Him.

As for the accusation of sedition (rebellion), Christ gave no answer; for they themselves knew that Christ had never rebelled against secular authority and that He never endeavored to have the people cling to Him in order to cause a rebellion, but rather only to instruct them. To the accusation of heresy He responded by appealing to his audience: **I have freely and openly spoken to the world. At all times I have taught in the school and in the temple where all the Jews assembled together, and never have I spoken secretly. Why then do you ask Me? Ask those who have listened to what I have said to them. See, they know what I have said.** In effect He says: If you are concerned about My doctrine, then for that very reason you ought not to have dealt thus with Me, because at all times—without fear (reserve)—I have conducted [My teaching] openly and consistently. To some degree I have also answered the charge of sedition. Because I taught openly, my teaching gives witness that I never encouraged rebellion. For those who do those kinds of things shy away from the light and assemble themselves in a secret place.

However, as Christ said this, the servant gave Him a slap across the cheek. Some of the [Church] fathers claim that it was Malchus, whose ear Christ had healed shortly before. He wanted to ingratiate himself, while at the same time casting off the suspicion that he was inclined to be kindly disposed towards Christ for doing this kind deed for him. For that reason, he struck Him in the face and said: **Should You be answering the high priest like that?** Shouldn't You be thinking about in whose presence You are standing and be more careful about what You are saying? Christ responded decisively: **If I have spoken evil, then prove that it is evil; but if I have spoken truthfully, why do you strike Me?** Christ intended thereby to demonstrate His innocence, that these things happened to Him without His being guilty or deserving them.

1. Christ was here led back and forth from one place to another—out of the garden through the dark valley, then to Annas' residence, next, from Annas to Caiaphas, and later, as the story records, from Caiaphas to Pilate. From there [He was taken] to Herod, once more back to Pilate, and finally to the place of the cross. Moreover, He was also everywhere mocked and despised and was given a slap on the cheek in open court. All these things He endured on our behalf. We had incurred indebtedness so that we should have been eternally cast out of Paradise. However, Christ willingly allowed Himself to be led out of the garden, through the valley of Jehosaphat, where they used to throw all the outlaws. With this He opened the door of Paradise to us and has taken the curse from us. We had rebelled against God and tried to rob Him of His glory so that we would be like God. However, Christ here let Himself be accused as a heretic and a rebel in order to benefit us. We should have been accused before divine judgment on account of our sins. But Christ allowed Himself to be led before the spiritual court and to be accused before it, so that we might be pronounced free before God's judgment and henceforth can pray Psa. 143: **Lord, do not enter into judgment with Your servant.** On account of our transgressions, eternal shame and disgrace should have fallen upon us. However, Christ here permits Himself to be put to shame in public court by a slap on the cheek so that we might be rescued from eternal disgrace. For the Scripture and examples testify that a slap on the cheek is something shameful and disgraceful, Job 16: **They have disgracefully slapped me on my cheek. They have taken out their anger with each other on me.** The same disgrace Christ has taken from us and [taken] upon Himself.

In Deu. 25 God the Lord ordained that whenever someone is identified before the court as being godless and having done wrong, the judge should direct him to fall down and let him be publicly beaten before the court, and thus shame him. Here Christ stands before the court as the greatest of evil-doers—not that He in His own Person ever in the least did anything wrong, but rather because the sin of the entire world was laid upon Him. Thus was He given a slap on the cheek in open court by the servant of the priests; and such the lords of the court allowed him to do as he pleased. However, we are to view it as if God's hand had done it, Acts 4. God strikes Him so shamefully because [Christ] took upon Himself our shame with which we had disgraced God. The dear Lord Himself speaks of this in Psa. 69: **I have to pay for that which I did not steal (plunder). For your sake I bear disgrace. My countenance is full of shame. Don't let those who wait for You be shamed on My account, Lord Sabaoth; don't let those who search for the God of Israel be made to blush with shame because of Me.** Behold, hence it is that those who wait on the Lord and put their trust in Christ will not be shamed, since Christ was thus put to shame by a slap on the cheek before a court for their sake. Hence it is also that the believers can with true confidence pray in Psalm 25: **Don't let me be shamed, for I trust in You.** We must [of course] be ashamed of ourselves, Dan. 9; also, we dare not lift our eyes towards heaven, Luke 18. However, Christ here allows Himself to be put to shame, so that we may step before God with joy and confidence, Heb. 5; may lift up our heads on Judgment Day, Luke 21; and be made worthy to stand before the Son of Man. Since this worthy, precious Stone, the Lord Christ, was cast aside by the builders of the ecclesiastical establishment [*den Bauleuten des geistlichen Kirchenbaus*], [that is] was put to shame in the council of the high priests and scribes, so He now has become for us a precious Corner- and Foundation-stone for our salvation, Psa. 118, so that upon [this Stone] we as living stones can be built up as a spiritual house and into a holy priesthood, to offer God spiritual sacrifices which are acceptable to Him through Christ, 1 Pet. 2. In sum, Christ permitted Himself to be led up to Jerusalem in order there to offer Himself up to God as a sweet fragrance. The reason He gladly and willingly let Himself be presented before the high priest was that God had commanded that everything that was to be sacrificed had to first be shown to, and approved by, the high priest, Lev. 17.

2. By responding not only to the false accusations of sedition, but also to the unjust hitting by Malchus, Christ thereby first of all establishes His innocence. For just as with His silence He demonstrated His patience (forbearance), so also with His response He demonstrates His innocence. He therewith furnishes an explanation as to how we should interpret Mat. 5, where He states: **You should not fight against evil; rather, if someone slaps you on your right cheek, then offer him the other cheek, too.** One should not interpret this to mean that Christians are culpable [and deserve] to suffer at the hands of everyone and are never permitted to employ the protection of civil authority—as the apostate Julian had thus explicated [this text] in former times. For here we hear that Christ defended Himself against the injustice of this servant. **If I have spoken**

the truth, He says, **why do you hit Me?** In essence He says: You high priests sit there in God's place and hold court. You should not allow an innocent person before the court to be thus unjustly struck. It is the same way that St. Paul speaks to the high priest Ananias in Acts 23: **You sit and judge me according to the Law and allow me to be beaten contrary to the Law.** In keeping with this example, a Christian may indeed defend his innocence before civil authority against false accusations and force. But how then are Christ's words fulfilled: **You are not to strive against evil. Instead, if someone strikes you on the right cheek, then offer him the other cheek, too?** It is to be understood in regard to the disposition of the heart. Christ requires true patience from His own. They are not to be vengeful (vindictive). Rather, when they suffer evil and are beaten, their heart is to have the attitude that they gladly are willing to suffer more evil if God were so to ordain it. Accordingly, this is to be understood that Christ wants to forbid self revenge, or that no one is to be his own judge and avenger. Instead one should call out [appeal] to the civil authority for help. If he meets with no help, he is much rather to suffer wrong than to avenge himself. God, give us this kind of heart through Christ. Amen.

> **O Lord Jesus Christ, You who were bound on account of my sin, free me from the bonds of sin and eternal death. You who were disgracefully slapped in the face, protect me from the eternal disgrace and from the blows of the Devil. Give me a patient heart to suffer all wrongs with patience. Amen.**

The Second Sermon

Concerning the fall and reclamation of Peter.

Simon Peter followed Jesus from afar with another disciple up to the palace of the high priest. [The other disciple] was acquainted with the high priest and went in with Jesus into the high priest's palace. However, Peter remained standing outside the door. Then the other disciple who knew the high priest went outside and spoke to the doorkeeper and led Peter inside. But the servants and domestics were standing there, having made a charcoal fire below in the middle of the palace [courtyard], for it was cold and they warmed themselves. Peter, however, stood beside them and warmed himself so that he might see what it all meant. But the high priest's maid, the doorkeeper, saw Peter in the light warming himself. Considering him carefully, she said: And you also were with this Jesus from Nazareth; aren't you one of this Man's disciples? But he denied before all of them and said: Woman, I'm not the one. I don't know Him; neither do I know what you are talking about.

Simon Peter, however, stood and warmed himself. And a short time after the first denial, while he was going to the front court, the rooster crowed. And one of the other maids saw him and again said to those standing nearby: This one also was with Jesus from Nazareth. Then she said to him: Aren't you one of His disciples? And another said: You too are one of His. And he denied again, and added an oath to it: Man, I am not, and I don't even know the Man.

And after a short while, within the same hour, another person corroborated the others that were standing there, and said: Truly, you are also a Galilean, for your speech betrays you.

Then one of the high priest's servants, a friend of the man whose ear Peter had chopped off, said: Didn't I see you with Him in the garden? Then Peter began to curse and swear: I don't know the Man about whom you are speaking.

And while he was still speaking, the rooster crowed a second time. And the Lord turned around and looked at Peter. Then Peter remembered Jesus' words which He had spoken to him: Before the rooster crows two times, you will deny Me three times. And [Peter] went out and cried bitterly.

In Jer. 17 it is reported that the human heart is an obstinate and cowardly thing. Thus are we informed not only that some human hearts are actually too obstinate and too arrogant, while others actually are too timid and too cowardly, but rather [also] that in the course of time a person's heart is at times too defiant, at times too timid. This [condition] emanates from the deep internal and outward corruption of our nature through the fall into sin. Thus the prophet also adds: **Who can understand it?**, as if to say: The human heart is rotten to the core, so that a person himself never knows what kind of evil lies hidden in the heart until it finally breaks out into outward deeds. Just as a seed hidden in a field is not recognized until it sprouts forth and bears fruit, so also there lies in the deep foundation of the human heart an evil seed, which has been sown there by the Devil. What an evil and rotten seed it actually is one does not see and believe until it ultimately makes itself known through various weeds of sin and offenses.

We have an example of this [sinful condition] in the beloved Peter, whose heart also was [both] defiant and timid. While there was still no danger present, and as the Lord previously proclaimed to him how he would be offended by Him in the same way as the other disciples, [Peter] was audacious and defiant enough. **Even if they all are offended by You, he says to the Lord, I will certainly not be offended.** Indeed, he commits himself to the point that even if he had to die with the Lord, he still would not deny Him. However, when the time came for the rendezvous, and it was now time to show such steadfastness with deeds, behold, the heart of Peter then became so timid and despondent that not only did he forsake the Lord along with the rest of the disciples, but he went so far as to curse and to swear that he did not know Christ and that he never had anything to do with Him. The reason that the evangelists record this in such detail is that from [the example of] Peter's fall into sin we may acknowledge the weakness of our corrupt-to-the-core nature, and from his reclamation may acknowledge God's immeasurable compassion and mercy.

At this time we intend to deal with these matters:

I. As Christ was led from the residence of the high priest Annas to the palace of Caiaphas, Peter followed at distance. This [action] was a already a prelude [precursor] to his abandoning of Christ. However, Peter's intention was to see what else they were going to do with Christ. Along the way he encountered a disciple of the Lord. Nearly everyone maintains that this disciple was John, because it was his practice that whenever he had to record something about himself, he withheld his name. However, because it would [reflect negatively on] John, the apostle and evangelist, after studying for so long in Christ's school, still to maintain such a good relationship with the high priest and his servants, St. Augustine maintained that this was some other secret disciple of the Lord. There were many at that time who indeed believed in Christ; but they did not openly confess it, so that they would not be placed under the ban by the Pharisees, John 12. Against this backdrop, Peter expressed himself [said what he did] so that he, for all that, might readily see what the outcome would be for His Lord and Master. This disciple, then, since he was known in the house of the high priest, negotiated with the woman guarding the door whether she would allow this man—unknown to her that he was a disciple of the captured and bound Jesus—to enter. He simply was eager to see what was going to happen to Him. Thus, there would be no danger in it.

Therefore, Peter went into the house of the high priest; and since various servants (such as the soldiers of the chief ruler, the servants of the council, and the servants of the high priest) assembled there together, Peter thought no one would readily recognize him among them. Since, however, it was nighttime and was cool, the servants had made a fire of wood and charcoal, to which Peter drew close and warmed himself. The inner fire of love for Christ began to extinguish itself. Now as various conversations about Christ were heard among the servants, the door-keeper stepped close and looked specifically at Peter. She said to him (not with evil intent, but out of pure compassion): Aren't you also one of this Man's disciples? When Peter would not respond, she became impatient and began to speak more loudly to him. Then Peter thought: This will never do. If I say nothing, then the whole matter is exposed. Therefore, he began to make excuses: Woman, I'm not the one. I don't know Him. Also, I don't know what you are talking about. Note: It was not a soldier, or the high priest, or an imposing matron who here questioned Peter; rather, it was a maidservant. Nor did she ask out of malicious intent, but rather, as Theophilus and others maintain, out of sympathy. Nor does she call Christ a seducer; rather, [she asks] simply out of compassion for a man. Nonetheless, Peter falls away and denies that he knows Christ. As this happens to Peter, he still stays a while longer at the fire, fearing, however, that he might be set upon some more. Therefore, he goes out into the courtyard to see if he can escape. But while he is in the courtyard, the rooster crows. Had he stayed indoors, he would not have heard the crowing on account of all the great tumult. But God saw to it that he heard the signal which Christ had given him as a reminder, namely, the crowing of the rooster. Peter hears it well, but he disregards it and does not think about the words of Christ. And since he is unable conveniently to escape, he once again enters into the palace and steps up to the fire so that he not make himself look conspicuous.

Then another maid comes up beside him. She presses him hard and insists that he also had been with Jesus of Nazareth, no matter how much he denied it. At that every man focused his eyes on Peter, and those standing around began to inquire further. The one said: Are you then one of His disciples? The other said: Truly, you are one of them. Then Peter thought to himself: Now you have to get yourself out of this predicament, or it will go very badly for you. Therefore, he did not just let it lie with a plain denial; rather, he added an oath and swore that he did not know the Man. Over an hour later one of the servants who was standing around stepped up to him and insisted even more strongly: Truly, you are one of them, for you are a Galilean. Even though the Jews commonly understood each other in their speech, yet there was a difference among them in their language, just as there is among us with the high German and the Saxon language. Yet one more person comes forward, who was a friend of Malchus, whose ear Peter had chopped off in the garden. He says: How much can you deny? Didn't I see you in the garden with Him? This frightened Peter even more, and he thought to himself: Now this must be answered earnestly (sincerely); otherwise I am going to be turned over to the high priest. Thus, he began to curse and swear. He gave himself over to the Devil and disposed of his portion of God's kingdom, all over whether he knew this Man. Indeed, the words of the evangelists might well be understood as saying that Peter actually cursed Christ Himself and said: What do I have to do with this accursed Man?

1. Here we need to consider how entirely unfit (useless) are human strength and human free will for sustaining us in God's grace and for protecting us from sin. Above many others, Peter had special knowledge of Christ, as is to be understood from Mat. 16. Even so, when he looked to [depended on] the strength of his faith and his own power, he not only fell into the sin common to all the other apostles (that they fled from their Lord) but he also denied [Him], swearing an oath and cursing himself over it. Even some of the fathers [ancients], such as Hilary and Ambrose, actually wanted in some measure to excuse this terrible fall of Peter—as if Peter spoke this way because he wanted to remain in the palace of the high priest and be able to await the end result. And when he says: I don't know the Man, it so much as meant: I don't acknowledge Him as a simple man, because He is also God's Son. When he says: I am not His disciple, that in essence must mean: I fled from Him. When he says: I don't know what you are talking about, that in essence means: I know nothing about your deliberations. Origen makes allegories out of [the events] and states: The first maid symbolizes the Jews; the second maid represents the Gentiles; the servants, who caused the occasion of the third denial, symbolize the heretics. However, with the tears that followed, Peter sufficiently demonstrated that he did not want this fall of his to be excused. Christ expressly called it a denial. To this, then, Hieronymus correctly states: I would rather that Peter denied than that the Lord had deceived. If we want to excuse Peter, we are doing no other than castigating Christ for lying. If we rightly consider it, there is here a heaping up of many sins: **1.** We have here audacity. Peter proceeded into danger, for which he had no calling. He followed Christ into the high priest's house. **2.** Distrust—[Peter] did not trust that God would sustain him, even though Christ had obtained safe conduct for His disciples. **3.** Faint-heartedness—Peter let himself be frightened by the speech of a single maid while there yet was no danger. **4.** Lying—Peter did not keep the promise he had made to Christ, he also denied the truth. **5.** Denial—He did not want to admit that he was a disciple of Christ. **6.** Perjury—He called upon God to witness his lying. **7.** Cursing—He cursed himself, putting at risk his own salvation. **8.** Obstinacy (stiff-neckedness)—He was so obdurate [impenitent] that he did not take note of the fact that the rooster crowed. **9.** Great offence (scandal)—Until now, several of the rulers among the Jews had believed in Christ, even though secretly, John 12. They had heard a portion [of Peter's denial] and thought: His foremost disciple [denies Him]; why should we then continue further to rely on Him?

It appears from the seventh chapter of John that certain of the high priest's servants had previously thought much of Christ. Without doubt they must have been greatly offended by this fall of Peter. Thus it is apparent that it was indeed a horrible sin on Peter's part and that, accordingly, we should understand from it that we indeed can never be sustained in the grace of God through our own power, and that we can accomplish nothing at all in divine matters by our own strength.

2. But no one dare think: This is a great, burdensome sin which Peter committed, [but] it is not my care; I shall shield myself from such. That's why we should take note of how far the denial extends and what it means to deny Christ. It is not only the Jews, Gentiles and Turks who deny Christ when they claim there is no true God; nor is it not only the heretics who deny Christ when they deny His Person and His office. Rather, as Augustine concludes from this text in *sec. 113 of John*: "Peter denied Christ as he denied being His disciple. Thus Christ is denied not only by the person who says [that] Jesus is not the Christ, but also by that person, who, while he is a Christian, denies being one." Also, those deny the Lord Christ who either from fear or for other reasons do not want to confess that they are His disciples. Professing that one is a disciple of Christ occurs at the time that he openly and freely confesses the teachings of Christ, as He says in John 8: **If you remain in My Word, then you are My true disciples.** On the contrary, therefore, those also deny Christ who don't want their faith to be made known or who don't abide in Christ's doctrine. Accordingly, it also means that one professes to be a disciple of Christ if one patiently and willingly takes up the cross which God sends to him, even as the Lord Christ says in Luke, chapter 9: **If anyone wants to follow after Me,** that is, wants to be My disciple, **let him daily take his cross upon himself.** Thus, those also deny Christ who don't want to suffer on account of Christ and for the sake of His Name or who don't want to carry their cross with patience. Therefore, the Lord Christ once more says in Luke, the fourteenth chapter: **Whoever does not carry His cross, such a one cannot be My disciple.** Finally, this also means that one professes to be a disciple of Christ if he treads in Christ's footsteps and follows the life of Christ with love, humility, gentleness and with His virtues. That's why Christ says in John, chapter 13: **Love one another, as I have loved you; thereby everyone will recognize that you are My disciples.** In John 15 He says: **You are My friends, as you do what I have bidden you to do.** In Mat. 12: **Whoever does the will of My Father in Heaven, that person is My brother, sister and mother.** Therefore, whoever would not enter into the life of Christ [i.e., tread in His footsteps], and instead continues in sin against one's conscience, such a person also denies Him, even though he praises Christ with a full [big] mouth. As the Lord Christ testifies in Mat. 7: On that Day [the Last Judgment] He will say to the evil doers, I don't know you—thereby sufficiently [clearly] announcing that they denied Him in this world. For He will deny those on that Day who deny Him in this world, Mat. 10. Paul writes about the same matter in Tit. 1: **They say they know God, but they deny it with their deeds.** God judges according to deed and truth, not according to appearances and mere words. Thus, the Lord Christ is denied before God by godless living. **Christ is**

the Way, the Truth and the Life, John 14. Whoever does not place his faith in Christ's words, such a person denies Christ, for Christ's word is truth, John 17. Whoever does not want to walk in the life of Christ, such a one also denies Christ, for Christ's life is the true way upon which we should walk before God. But whoever thus denies Christ's truth and the way of Christ's life, such a person will also not find [eternal] life.

3. We should also contemplate how Peter came to such a fall, in order that we avoid the same. He was entirely too daring (presumptuous)—meaning that it all depended upon a good heart and good intentions. When he noticed others who were not like him in this matter, he held them in disdain. Thus he experienced how very little we are capable of if God does not sustain us. Therefore we should indeed not rely on the strength of our own faith, or on our good intentions. God's power does it, and it alone must do everything. Indeed we should always keep in our heart the admonition which Christ gave to Peter and the other disciples: **Watch and pray, so that you do not fall into temptation.** Peter also got himself into danger and trouble by mingling with the godless servants of the priests and warming himself by their fire. So it still is. Many a person also wants to warm himself at the fire of worldly glory, temporal riches, and great power; but over these [temptations] he falls into denying Christ's teachings and, on that account, falls into the eternal fire of hell. Many a person associates with wicked, godless people. He can easily also thereby come to the point that he denies the sufferings of Christ; that is, that he also steps onto the way of sinners, Psa. 1.

Finally, Peter is offended at the cross of Christ. When he saw in the garden that at a single word from the Lord the entire troop fell back, it heartened him and made him courageous. He alone advanced into the crowd, and he thought that his Lord and Master would well protect him. Shortly after, when he sees that Christ is being taken captive, he, together with the other disciples, flees from the Lord. However, since he had love for Christ in his heart, he could not renounce Him completely. Instead, he followed after him from a distance. As he saw anew, however, that the Lord was not going to free Himself—as had often happened before—through miraculous strength and divine power, but rather saw that not only did the chief rulers treat Him disgracefully (abusively) and mock Him as a poor miserable man, but also that the servants despised Him and that one among them struck him in the face, Peter's heart began to sink until he fell completely away from Christ. So it happens still. Many are offended at the cross of the Christian Church, that God conducts His rule in the Church in such great outward weakness—and not with thunder and lightning so that the enemies of the Church are immediately smashed to pieces. However, we should here take to heart the admonition and the comfort of Christ, Mat. 11: **Blessed is the one who is not offended by Me.**

4. We also see here how Peter falls into one sin after another. Once he falls into the Devil's sieve, he receives a thorough shaking; and he would ultimately have fallen away completely had not Christ once more reclaimed him. Sin is such a rapidly growing weed; "Sin is fruitful [prolific]; it never quits at its starting point," says Gregory. If a person once begins to err, he becomes ever more distant from the right path. So then, anyone who once steps onto the pathway of sin stumbles ever further into error. If one betakes himself out of the sunlight into a dark situation, then he stumbles (thrusts himself) into it more and more. So then, if a person once turns away from the true divine Light, he then falls ever farther from one work of darkness [into another]; that is, from one sin into another. Therefore, David states, Psa. 9: **The godless person will be tied up in the work of his hands.** In essence, he intends to say: Just as a wild animal, when it comes into a net, wraps (tangles) itself up more and more in it, so it also goes with a person who gives himself over to the ropes of the Devil: he becomes ever more tangled up with those

ropes. Thus it says in Pro. 5: **The misdeeds of the godless will make him liable, and he will be held captive by the ropes of his sin.** This, then, should be a serious warning to us, that we indeed never allow a single sin against our conscience. Rather, we should remember that the Devil always rushes mankind from one sin into many others if one lets him.

5. That Christ here was denied by His own disciples, such He also suffered for our sake. With our sins we had incurred such a debt that we, on that Day, would have had to be denied by Christ before God and all the angels, because we have denied God with so many and varied sins. However, Christ has stepped into our place. And as He stood before the court in highest betrayal and mockery, he allowed Himself to be denied by His own disciples, who were ashamed of Him and His Word, so that we would not have to be put to shame on account of our sin for all eternity.

II. As Peter thus fell from one sin into the next, and the rooster crowed for the second time—which was disregarded by Peter in the same way as he did the first [time], so that he did not recall what the Lord had earlier predicted: **Before the rooster crows two times, you will deny Me three times.** Behold, the Lord turned around and looked at Peter. Now the high priest's palace was built in such a way that a portion was elevated. At this location the high priest had questioned Jesus. Down below in the house [living quarters] were the servants, who stood and sat around a fire. Peter was standing with them, so that the Lord could indeed see him well. All the roosters might well have screamed themselves to death before Peter would have come to the knowledge of his sin. However, such a look of the Lord Christ is so powerful that Peter's heart was thereby enlightened and reclaimed, for he remembered the Word of the Lord: **Before the rooster crows two times, you will deny Me three times.** Moreover, he also remembered what he had heard from the Lord, Mat. 10: **whoever denied Him, him He would in turn deny before His heavenly Father**; that is, He would not be [that person's] Advocate before His heavenly Father. Neither would he recognize him as His disciple. Peter then remembered that this Word of the Lord also applied to him, and that he had committed a serious fall into sin. The confessing of such sin produced an inward pain of the heart, which burst forth in outward tears. For Peter went out of the palace of Caiaphas and wept bitterly. Nevertheless, he did not at all fall into despairing doubt. Rather, he also remembered the words which the Lord had spoken often—that He had come into this world to call poor sinners to repentance, and also that He had especially promised Peter that He would pray for him, that his faith would not cease. Peter comforted himself with this. Then he departed from the godless mob, and later on he again confessed [Christ] three times, John 21, just as he had denied Him three times.

Here then we have:

1. a reflection of divine mercy. Peter continued to sin and did not think back. However, Christ, although He stood bound before the court, mocked by the high priests and struck by the servants, forgot as it were His own misfortune and remembered poor Peter, as the Devil, so to speak, rattled him around in his sieve. It sickened Him not a little that His own disciples had denied Him; still, He forgot all that and looked with friendly, gracious eyes at Peter. He did not turn His fatherly heart away from Peter. Instead, in His great suffering He thought to Himself: O, poor Peter, how he is fallen into such deep slime of sin. I have to bring him out of it again. Take note: God the Lord still must do that with us today if we are to come to repentance. He Himself has to view us with the eyes of compassionate mercy and convert our hearts to Him, if we are to be made His own, as it is written in Jer. 31: **Lord, you reclaim me, and I shall be converted.** Thus, then, St. Augustine correctly states in *Enchiridion* 82: "God's mercy is required when we repent. It is also necessary if we are to desire repentance." When we are stuck in sin, God indeed gives us lots of rooster-crowings; that is, many signs and reminders that He would beckon us to repentance. While there are many kinds of chastisements, the preaching of the Law, and all sorts of good deeds (*or*, blessings) ... yet to all these must come the gracious look and the mercy of God, by which our hearts are converted, if we are to repent.

And by His action, the Lord Christ here demonstrates that His office was not only to win for us our redemption by His precious merits and bring about heavenly blessings for us. Rather, beyond that, this also pertains to it: that He Himself must work mightily in our hearts so that His suffering and death not be lost on us, but be imputed to us through genuine repentance. On our own we cannot make ourselves fit to become partakers of these precious merits—no more than Peter here could do it.

"Those whom Christ looks upon, weep over their sins." Thus the great mercy of God becomes even more apparent from the fact that after this grievous fall into sin it once again received Peter back into grace. How could Peter have done it any more rudely? He was an apostle and a disciple of Christ; at the same time, he so rudely sinned against, not just an ordinary man, but against Christ Himself. He not only denied Him, but cursed about it and execrated himself [imprecated evil upon himself] about whether he knew Christ. "Thus this sin is immense in the act, whether one looks at the person of the sinner or at the Lord against whom this sin was committed, or looks at the way and manner in which the sin was perpetrated." Even so, he is taken back into grace. This example should then deeply imprint itself into the heart of each individual, especially in a person who has stumbled (fallen) into a particularly serious sin, so that no one despair of God's mercy. Rather, what St. Paul says of himself, 1 Tim. 1, **that Christ had demonstrated all** [of His] **patience with him as an example to those who would believe unto eternal life**, [applies] precisely also to Peter. For with these examples of

Peter and Paul—the two foremost apostles and proclaimers of the Gospel—God intended to demonstrate clearly that which is expounded to us in the Gospel, [i.e.,] how great is His mercy.

    2. Here we also have a mirror of what constitutes genuine repentance. If poor sinners, along with Peter, wish to obtain this grace of God, then with Peter they must also genuinely repent. [Such repentance] is here very beautifully portrayed for us, namely, that to it pertain [contrition and faith]. **1.** Contrition—As Peter reflects on what he has done, heart-felt contrition and sorrow ensue, which he demonstrates with his bitter tears. So also must we, with a broken and crushed heart, come before God if He by His mercy is to free us from our sins. **2.** Faith—Not only is Peter heartily sorry for his grievous fall, but he also remembers the comforting promise that Christ would pray for him that his faith not cease. Accordingly, he apprehended within his heart the comforting fact that God wanted to accept him into grace for Christ's sake. Thus must we also hold before us God's promise and Christ's merit, and conclude therefrom that God wants again to pick us up and take us back. If, then, this contrition and such faith are rightly created in our hearts, therefrom will follow improvement of our lives, just as Peter here removed himself from evil associations. These are the elements of genuine repentance. Nevertheless, we also see here in the example of Peter that all things in our lives take place in the midst of great weakness. Peter rightly should have publicly stepped forward and before the high priest and each and every one publicly confessed Christ, so that the offense that had been given would have again been averted (removed). But, there was also weakness running through his repentance. So it still is with us. Our repentance also takes place in weakness. Underneath it there is always imperfection. God will turn such weakness into good for us, if only our repentance is heartfelt and we do not approach with impenitence. God grant all of us grace to repent. Amen.

O Lord Jesus Christ, look upon me, a poor sinner, with Your eyes of mercy, the same eyes of mercy with which You looked upon Peter in the assembly-room, upon Mary Magdalene at the banquet, and upon the malefactor on the cross. Grant to me also, O You, almighty God, that with Peter I bemoan my sin from the heart, with Mary Magdalene sincerely love You, and with the malefactor on the cross may live eternally with You in Your kingdom. Amen.

The Third Sermon

Christ is accused by false witnesses and is condemned to death by the high priests as a blasphemer.

The high priests, however, and the elders and the entire council sought false witness against Jesus in order to put Him to death, and they found none. And no matter how many false witnesses stepped forward, they yet found none whose testimony agreed with that of another. At last two false witnesses stood up and came forward and gave false testimony against Him, and said: We have heard that He has said: I can and will destroy the Temple of God, which is made with hands, and in three days build another one, which is not made by hands. And yet their testimonies did not agree. And the high priest stood up among them and questioned Jesus, saying: Have You no response for these who testify against You? But Jesus remained silent and gave no answer. Then the high priest questioned Him and said to Him: Are You Christ the Son of the Most Highly Praised One? I charge You by the living God that You tell us whether You are the Christ, the Son of God. Jesus said to him: You said it; I am. Yet I say to you, from now on it will happen that you will see the Son of Man sitting at the right hand of Power and coming in the clouds of heaven. Then the high priest tore apart his clothes and said: He has blasphemed God; why do we need any further testimony? See, now you have heard His blasphemy; what do you think? Then they all condemned Him and said: He is guilty of death. The men who held Jesus captive mocked Him, spit in His face, and hit Him with their fists. Some of them—particularly the servants—covered Him up [blindfolded Him] and hit Him in the face and said to Him: Prophesy to us, Christ; who is it that hit You? And they spoke many other abusive/slanderous things against Him. Then in the morning all the high priests, the scribes, and the elders of the people assembled together and deliberated about Jesus so that the entire council might promote His death. And they led Him up before their council and asked: Are You Christ? Tell us. But He said to them: If I tell you, you still don't believe it. If I question you, you don't answer Me. Yet you still won't release Me. Therefore, from now on Son of Man will sit at the right Hand of God's Power. Then they all said: Are You then God's Son? He said to them: You said it, for I am He. Again they said: Why do we need further testimony? We ourselves have heard it from His own mouth.

In Jer. 20 it is recorded that the high priest Pashur, who had been appointed the overseer in the House of the Lord, allowed the prophet Jeremiah to be struck and thrown into captivity until the morning. Previously in chapter 18 it is noted how this Pashur, along with other of his colleagues in the priesthood, had plotted against Jeremiah and laid the groundwork for keeping the orderly succession from him; about that [matter] their decision (sentence) was certain and infallible. **Come**, they said, **let us advise (counsel) against Jeremiah, for priests can not err with the Law, and the wise cannot fail with their counsel, and the prophets cannot teach wrong. Come here, let us kill him with the tongue, and give no credence to any of his sayings.** What the prophet Jeremiah experienced at that time was precisely what was later encountered by the great Prophet Christ—to whom all the other prophets and their teachings pointed. For the evangelists record that the high priests, the scribes, the Pharisees, and the elders (that is, the entire ecclesiastical council) had assembled themselves in opposition to Christ. They set up false witnesses against Him and thus took upon themselves to kill the Lord with the tongue. Nor did they want to give any credence to His sayings, even as the beloved Lord then said to them: **If I tell it to you, you still won't believe it.** Indeed, they allowed Him to be spit on and hit in the face before their court—thinking that they were performing the highest service to God, since they were directed to examine matters of religion and faith, and since they could not err in their conclusion and sentence.

At this time then we want consider and attend to [the following]:

I. The matters which were taken up with Christ in the middle of the night before the ecclesiastical council.

II. How He was once again placed before them in the morning and had to make His final statement.

I. In the first hearing, the high priest had asked Christ about His disciples and about His teachings. And as Christ appealed to His listeners in his answer, it resulted in His being struck in the face—which was indeed an unfair process. Therefore, Christ then also insisted that they should convince Him that He had spoken or done anything wrong. This [request] went to the hearts of the ecclesiastical rulers, that they were to reflect upon testimony as God the Lord had instituted it in Deu. 19. They were, however, no longer seeking clarity and truth, but rather false witness. They were searching not for what was right, but rather merely for an appearance of right. Accordingly, they produced [as witnesses] the kind of people about whom Christ laments, Psa. 41, **They come to see** [but] **do not mean it from the heart. Rather, they search for someone whom they might slander,** [then] **go out and tell tales.** They had at times listened to the Lord superficially and paid attention for their own advantage so that they could thereby jeopardize Him (expose Him to danger), just as—sad to say—there still are hearers who do not listen for their own instruction, but rather to defame the preacher. Even though many false witnesses then stepped forward, yet their testimonies did not agree with one another. Falsehood and lying cannot be entirely disguised; rather, they are exposed if one scrutinizes them closely.

Finally two false witnesses got up, stepped forward, and spoke: We heard that at the beginning of His sermon on the Passover He said: I can and will demolish the temple of God, which is made with hands, and in three days build another one, which is not made with hands. This was a willful perverting of Christ's words, especially since Christ did not say: I can and will destroy the temple of God. Rather, these are the words recorded in John 2: **Tear down this temple, and on the third day I will raise it up.** He was referring not to the outward [visible] temple in Jerusalem, but rather to the Temple of His body, which He would again bring forth from the grave on the third day. Let everyone guard himself against such a malicious perversion, for a false witness is an abomination to God, Pro. 6. If we happen to experience such a thing at the hands of others, we should remind ourselves of Christ's example. Such perverting and slander does indeed hurt painfully, as it is written in Pro. 18: **The words of the slanderer are blows and pierce through the heart.** Yet also in this one should possess his soul in patience, as Christ did here. For as the high priest stood up and asked whether or not He would respond to those who had testified against Him, Jesus kept His silence. For public lies are not worthy of an answer, and willful slanders must be borne with patience. This, then, was the second interrogation which had been employed against Christ.

However, when the high priest saw that this approach was getting him nowhere, he took a different tack, and said to Him: **Are You Christ, the Son of the living God?** And since Christ had previously kept silent, he charged Him by the living God to tell him whether He was Christ, the Son of God. In His preaching Christ had so often taught that He was God's Son and the promised Messiah. He had also permitted His disciples to confess Him as such. Thus, the high priest thought: If we just can get Him to admit this, then as a result of such an admission (which they regarded as blaspheming God) we will have a proper accusation to bring against Him. Thus he charged Him by the living God, that is, he made Him swear, and admonished Him that He should tell the truth if God in heaven was dear to Him. Since an oath is not a joking matter—and in the case where there is something to be stated before the authorities under oath, nothing should be concealed—so Christ would no longer keep silent. Instead He said: **You said it, I am the One**; that is, what you say, I admit (confess). I am indeed the Son of the living God and the promised Messiah. Christ indeed well knew in what great danger it placed Him if He would publicly declare this before this court. However, He would not for that reason withhold His confession. He did it as an example for us, that we are not only with the heart to believe unto righteousness, but also with the mouth to make confession unto salvation, Rom. 10. Where true faith is in the heart, it also breaks forth into the confession of the mouth, Psa. 116. And where there is light in the heart, it also shines forth before everyone, 2 Cor. 4.

Because we possess this same Spirit of faith, it subsequently is written: **I believe, therefore I speak.** Thus because we also believe, therefore we also speak. Here St. Paul teaches that all who truly believe also freely confess publicly. But anyone who would fear danger in this should consider that the Word of Christ in Mat. 10 is to be feared even more: **Whoever denies Me before men, him I will also deny before My heavenly Father.** That was thus the clear confession of Christ, [i.e.,] that He was the true Son of God; but since He knew that they would be offended at His despised (abject) outward appearance, He adds: **Yet I say to you, from now on you will see the Son of Man sitting at the right hand of Power and coming in the clouds of**

heaven. Herewith He points them to chapter 7 of Daniel and to Psalm 110, so that they might learn that the Messiah would not be a worldly [king], but an eternal King, exalted to the right hand of God. Outwardly, however, he would be regarded as a son of man, that is, as an ordinary, unsightly (plain) man. The high priest regarded this as a blaspheming of God. Therefore, he tore his clothes and said: **He has blasphemed God; what need do we have for any more witnesses? See, now you have heard His blasphemy of God. What do you think?** It was indeed also the usual custom in the Old Testament that one would tear his clothes because of impatience, wrath, fright, and mourning—as one sees with Jacob in Gen. 37, with Moses in Num. 14, with David in 2 Sam. 1, with Jephtha in Jdg. 11, with Hezekiah in Isa. 37, and with Paul and Barnabas in Acts 4, all of whom tore their clothes as they unexpectedly were overtaken by fright and grief (affliction, worry). For all that, it is revealed here in a veiled manner that the order (succession) of the high priestly office should now come to an end, and that the only true High Priest of the New Testament was now at hand. For God had forbidden the high priest to tear his garment, Lev. 10. Nevertheless, Caiaphas here does it, to announce thereby that this was indeed a much too great and horrible blaspheming of God. But God destined it thus: That at the same time is herewith announced that the high priestly office should be ripped up in the same way also that temple curtain was later to be ripped apart at the death of Christ. The true Essence was beginning [at hand]; therefore, shadows and types had to pass away.

The high priest hereupon conducted a hearing concerning what they thought of the proceeding. But they all condemned Him and said: **He deserves to die.** And so the Lord Christ was publicly declared to be a blasphemer of God by the entire assembled council, and they concluded that He deserved to die. However, since the first three hearings against Christ became somewhat protracted, and it was already midnight, the ecclesiastical authorities wanted first to get some rest before they sent the captive Christ to be given over to Pilate in order to petition him to carry out their sentence. Consequently, they parted company and turned Christ over to the servants to guard Him until morning. Regarding what this godless rabble engaged in with the Lord Christ from midnight until morning, the evangelists have this to say: **The men, however, who guarded Jesus mocked Him and spit in His face and struck Him with their fists. Then certain ones covered** [blindfolded] **Him and slapped His face and said: Prophesy to us Christ! Who was that who hit You? And they said many other slanderous things against Him.** Christ was not unknown to these servants prior to this time. They had heard Him preach and seen His miracles. Indeed, what's more, as they were sent out by their rulers to seize Christ, they returned from their unaccomplished task, saying: **There never was a man who speaks the way this Man does**, John 7 [v. 46]. On that occasion they had received the power of Christ's words into their hearts. But now, since they saw how Christ had been captured and bound, condemned by all the ecclesiastical council and forsaken by men, they not only separated themselves from Christ, but they also helped to spit on, mock, and beat Him. This is indeed a terrible example of falling away [apostasy], and all these servants follow it. As the sixth chapter of Hebrews states [regarding those who believe and fall away]: They had once been enlightened by and had tasted of the heavenly gift and had been made participants of the Holy Spirit and had tasted the benevolent Word of God and the power of the world to come. Later, when they fall away, they themselves crucify the Son of God anew and hold Him in derision. These then are the ones who, against the witness of their own heart, willfully deny the perceived divine truth. God preserve all of us from this! They also cover Christ's face [blindfold Him] and mock Him, thinking that God does not see their evil, and devote themselves to hypocritical sanctimoniousness. Also, they mock

God's messengers, despise His Word, and mock His prophets, as is charged against the Jews in 2 Chr. 36.

This, then, is what happened to Christ prior to midnight in the assembly of the ecclesiastical council, and how the servants dealt with Him until the morning. However, we must once again examine and contemplate this portion [of Christ's passion] according to the explanation of Peter in Acts 4 as to what [part] God's counsel and hand play here.

1. Christ is here falsely accused; and that which was proclaimed in Psa. 27 is fulfilled in Him: **False witnesses stand up against Me, and they treat Me unjustly without any fear.** And Psa. 35: **Sacrilegious (blasphemous) witnesses step forward who accuse Me of that of which I am not guilty.** Why then did Christ experience such? All of us together are accused before God's judgment on account of our sin, and indeed rightly and justly so. God's unchangeable Law accuses us, which is a witness against us, Deu. 31; thus Moses accuses us with his heavy tongue, John 5. For the voice of the Law decrees that all are under sin, Gal. 3; our own conscience accuses us, which is the handwriting against us, Col. 2, so that our own heart condemns us, 1 John 3, and our own thoughts accuse each other, Rom. 2. The Devil accuses us and clamors for us, as it is written in Rev. 12, that the hellish Dragon accuses us before God day and night. He walks among the children of God and demands that God stretch out His hand over us and assail us, Job 1. The holy angels accuse us, for they are the fellow servants, Rev. 22, who are saddened by this and bring it before them and our heavenly Lord when we do not properly conduct ourselves towards our neighbor, Mat. 18. All creation accuses us, which we have abused through sin. As St. Paul writes in Rom. 8: Creation waits with anxious hoping, longing, and fear to become free from servitude to this perishable existence. And in James 5 it is recorded of the godless rich who have misused their riches and clothes and their gold and silver, that their gold and silver will rust away [corrode],

and their rust will be a witness against them. Behold, these all are our accusers: God's Law, which we have transgressed; our conscience, which is captive to sin; the Devil, who accuses us, as he with his cunning tries surreptitiously to procure us; the angels, who on account of our sins shrink from us; creation, as we with our abuse spoil it. All these have become our accusers before God's judgment. We can never be counted free (acquitted) from these legitimate and just accusations except for Christ's sake. He allowed Himself to be falsely accused and condemned in public court so that we from now on can joyfully say, Rom. 8: **Who dare charge with blame the elect of God? God is the One who makes righteous. Who dare condemn? Christ is the One who died so that there is no longer any condemnation for those who are in Christ Jesus.**

2. Christ is here accused of wanting to tear down the temple of God in Jerusalem. Why did that happen? God the Lord created the first man so that he should be a temple and residence for the Holy Trinity. However, since he turned himself away from God, through his sin he became a dwelling of the Devil—even as Christ says of the evil spirits in Luke 11, that they reside in brutal, malicious criminals. For this misery to be averted and for the great grace to be achieved for us, so that God the Lord might once again set up residence within our hearts, John 14, Christ here allows Himself to be accused as a destroyer of the temple in Jerusalem, in which God the Lord dwelt among the cherubim and in which he had His fire and flock. He also permitted the Temple of His body—in which the fullness of the Godhead resides bodily, Col. 2—to be torn down (demolished) by death, so that we thereby could be reconstructed into a spiritual building and temple [and] so that it can now be said of those who believe in Christ: **Don't you know that you are God's temple and that the Spirit of God resides within you?**, 1 Cor. 3. And again in 2 Cor. 6: **You are the temple of the living God, even as God says: I**

will live within them and walk with them; and I will be their God, and they will be My people.

3. Christ here remains silent as He is falsely accused. Why did that happen? When our first parents were summoned before God after their fall into sin, they should rightly have been ashamed and should have confessed their sins. But they tried to make excuses. Adam laid the blame on Eve, whom God had ordained as a helpmeet. Eve laid blame on the serpent, whom God had created along with all the other creatures. Thus, when one really thinks about it, the blame was ultimately placed on God, who had created both Eve and the snake. And we, too, are of a mind gladly to conceal and excuse our own sins, even though every mouth is muted by the accusation of the Law, and the whole world is guilty before God, Rom. 3. And it is with us as recorded in Job 9: A man cannot stand justified before God; [and] if he has the desire to quarrel with God, he is not able to answer for a single one out of a thousand of our sins. Since we all are lacking in the reputation we should have before God, we would all have to be speechless before God's judgment, just like the man of whom Christ speaks in His parable in Mat. 22: He was speechless because he did not have on a wedding garment. So that this may not happen to us, Christ here remains silent, as if He knew of nothing with which to take exception in His vindication [i.e., as if He could not answer His accusers in His own defense]; and He remains dumb like a patient little lamb before its shearer, Isa. 9.

4. Christ is here condemned by a unanimous decision of the ecclesiastical court for confessing that He is the Son of God. Our first parents wanted to be like God. If this wrong was to be atoned for, if we were once again made to share in the true divine nature, 2 Pet. 1, and if we were again to be given the power to become the children of God, John 1, then, for that reason, the true only-begotten Son of God had to allow Himself here to be publicly condemned for confessing to be God's Son.

So also the Lord publicly confesses that He thus suffers as the Christ, that is, as the truly anointed King and High Priest, and that He takes His kingdom upon His shoulder, Isa. 9. And, as the true High Priest, He intended to offer Himself up to God as a sweet fragrance. For that reason—since Christ is God's Son [and] our King and eternal High Priest—His suffering and death has such a power that it serves as payment for our sin. Thus, to that end God disposes [so directs things] that in the midst of His passion Christ publicly confesses to be God's Son and our only King. Then one indeed pays [proper] respect to the kind of Person who suffers here, for within stands [the One] of greatest and highest rank.

5. Christ is condemned by the ecclesiastical council as a blasphemer of God. Our first parents began the greatest blasphemy of God, in that they wanted to take [usurp] His glory and later nevertheless tried to make excuses. We all, with our sins, do nothing different, as we try to take from God His glory, omniscience, righteousness, and truth ... as if He does not see our sins, or as if He will not punish them, or as if His threats are not sincere. Now if there was going to be payment for this, then Christ had to allow Himself to be accused and condemned as a blasphemer of God; yet He always spoke the truth and never took anything evil into His heart or mouth.

6. Christ is here mocked. For our sins we had all deserved that the Devil would be able to mock us into all eternity, since we had lost the glory which we were to have before God, Rom. 3. As the first parents turned away from God, they were justly mocked, so that God the Lord said in Gen. 3: **Look, Adam has become like one of us, and he knows what is good and what is evil.** If we, then, were to be delivered from such misery so that we would not have to permit ourselves to be mocked eternally by the Devil, then Christ had to step into our place and allow Himself be mocked by the military thugs. We must regard this as if it was done by the hand of God, which takes the shame

(disgrace) from us and lays it upon Christ.

7. Christ allowed Himself to be spit upon and to be hit in the face, which customarily befell those who were to be put to public shame. Thus, if one did not want to make love to [marry] His deceased brother's wife, then his sister-in-law stepped up to him and spit in his face, Deu. 25, Ruth 4. So also Job complains, ch. 30, that even the least of them was not reluctant to spit before his face. Christ allowed this to happen to Him, thus fulfilling what He Himself says in Isa. 50: **I turned My back to those who flogged me, and My cheeks to those who plucked them** [i.e., pulled out My beard]; **I did not hide My face from shame and spit.** Isa. 53: **We saw Him, but there was no form which would have pleased us. He was the most despised/scorned and unworthy**, even though He usually is the most beautiful One of all the children of men, Psa. 45. This He allowed Himself to undergo for our sake, so that we would not have to put to shame before God's face, Psa. 69. **The shame of those who shame You falls upon Me**, the dear Lord laments. "As He allowed Himself to be spit upon, He washed the face of our soul; as He allowed His face to be blindfolded, He took away the blindfold from our hearts"—Hieronymus.

8. Christ was regarded by these thugs as a fool and adventurer, for they covered His face, hit Him, and said: **Prophesy to us, Christ, who is it that hit You?** This also He endured for our sake. We had lost God's image, and thus also the wisdom in which we were initially created, so that from then on a covering [blindfold] was pulled over our hearts, and our understanding was darkened so that we did not know God. Then Christ stepped into our place. And, even though He indeed is the Wisdom of God, 1 Cor. 1, in whom all the treasures of wisdom and knowledge are hidden, Col. 2, yet He still allowed Himself to be regarded as a fool and [permitted] a covering to be pulled over His face, so that He could once more win for us the true divine Wisdom, which imparts a shining brightness to our heart. Through it the illuminating light of the knowledge of the brightness [glory] of God arose in the face of Christ, 2 Cor. 4 [v.6], so that in us, as a result, all of the Lord's glory is reflected by our uncovered faces, and we become transfigured into the same image from one glory to another [from glory to glory], as from the Spirit of the Lord, 2 Cor. 3 [v.18]. Yes, indeed, He has redeemed us to the highest blessedness (salvation) by it, so that someday we shall see God as He is, 1 John 3, face to face, 1 Cor. 13.

II. Even though the hearings and dealings against Christ before the ecclesiastical council lasted until midnight, yet the ecclesiastical authorities soon gathered together again in the early morning. No sleep was so dear to them that it would make them neglect their undertaking. So it still is with Christ's members. [Their] persecutors do not shrink from any effort or labor, and they often times are more effective in doing evil than Christians are in doing good. However, it was their intention and objective to hear Christ's own confession from Him one more time, and once again falsely charge Him of a capital offense before Pilate. Accordingly, the high priest summoned all his colleagues—the scribes, the elders of the people, and the entire council; that is, the large respectable crowd of members of the large consistory of Jerusalem—and asked the Lord: **If You are the Christ, then say it to us.** But, since Christ indeed knew very well that they were not asking out of love for the truth, but rather in order to accuse Him, He answered this way: **If I tell you, you won't believe it.** I have previously testified with words and deeds that I am He, and you still would not believe Me. **But if I question you, you won't answer, and you still won't release Me.** Even if I wanted to instruct you with further questions and inquiries, you still are not serious [sincere] because you have already determined to get rid of Me. Thus, I will patiently endure this and raise My heart to the glory that will follow. **For from now on the Son of Man will sit at the right hand of God's power.** Through this My suffering, I will enter into My glory. Here, then, Christ teaches that a person should look beyond the cross to the ensuing certain joy and glory which the unfailing truth of God promises to all those who carry their cross after Christ [i.e., who in their cross-bearing follow Christ]. Thereupon, as He once more publicly confessed to be God's Son, Christ was condemned as a blasphemer of God. **Why do we need any further witness**, they said. The accusation of Christ is our intercession; Christ's condemnation is our acquittal. Amen.

O Lord Jesus Christ, You who for the sake of my sin were falsely accused, rescue me from the accusation of the Law and of my conscience; You who remained silent in the face of false accusations, help me so that I do not have to be silent before God's judgment; You who in an innocent manner were shamed and spit on, rescue me from the eternal disgrace and shame; let Your innocent, suffering condemnation be my eternal acquittal. Amen.

The Third Act

Which encompasses the history of the affairs that have to do with Christ before Governor Pilate in the judgment hall.

The First Sermon

Christ is led before Governor Pilate, which, when observed by the betrayer Judas, causes him to fall into despair.

The entire troop arose and bound Jesus, led Him from Caiaphas in the house of judgment, and delivered Him up to the governor Pilate. And it was still early. As Judas, who had betrayed Him, saw that He had been condemned to death, he was repentant, and he brought back the thirty pieces of silver to the high priests and elders, and said: I have done evil in that I have betrayed innocent blood. They replied: How does that concern us? You see to it. And he threw the silver pieces into the temple, left there, and hanged himself; and his belly burst apart, and his entrails poured out. However, the high priests took the silver pieces and said: It is not appropriate that we place these into the divine coffer, for it is blood-money. So they deliberated and with the silver pieces—that reward of unrighteousness (injustice)—purchased a potter's acreage for the burial of pilgrims. And it thus became known by all those who lived in Jerusalem that this field is called in their language—to this very day—Hakeldama, that is, a field of blood. Here was fulfilled what was said by the prophet

Jeremiah: They took thirty pieces of silver which was paid for the one being bought, whom they purchased from the children of Israel, and exchanged these pieces for a potter's field, as the Lord had commanded me.

In Psalm 22, when, by the instigation and inspiration of the Holy Spirit, David wanted to record a glorious prophecy concerning the suffering of Christ, he gives the Psalm a title which indicates he intends to speak of a hind (doe), which was hunted early [in the morning]. Since the whole Psalm is only about Christ, one thus should and can understand that this title deals with none other than Christ. He is compared to a hind because in the same way that a deer lures snakes out of the holes in the rocks with the breath of his nose, then steps on them and devours them (and as a result an exquisite thirst arises within him, Psa. 43), so also Christ, as the promised Seed of the woman, trampled the head of the hellish serpent, Gen. 3, devoured death in victory, 1 Cor. 15, after which the Lord Christ also cried out from the cross: **I'm thirsty.** However, David does not liken the Lord Christ to a stag who shows off and defends himself with his antlers. Instead he compares Him to a doe; for Christ, in His state of humiliation—and, above all, at the time of His suffering—did not show off His divine power, which He kept inwardly hidden and did not use. Otherwise He indeed could easily and without any effort have protected Himself against His foes, as He adequately demonstrated in the Garden, when the entire troop fell back at His single word. Finally, David does not compare Christ to an ordinary hind. Instead he calls Him a "hind of the rosy dawn," which according to the Hebrew manner of speaking is actually to be understood to mean a beautiful doe, just as in Isa. 14 the king of Babylon is called a "son of the rosy dawn," a beautiful, chosen king. However, we can reasonably stay with Luther's interpretation, [i.e.], a hind which is hunted in the early morning. How this is actually fulfilled in the work of Christ, we hear about in the first portion of this account; namely, that the high priests, the scribes, Pharisees, and the entire council gathered in the early morning and had delivered Him over to the Gentile judge, Pontius Pilate—regardless of the fact that they had spent a good part of the previous night with Christ and had cut short their sleep. All this produced horrible jealousy and hatred against Christ, so that they—just like the unleashed, foolish dogs mentioned in Psa. 22, cited above, who chase hinds in the early morning—drive Him from one judge to another. In the second part of the text just read is described the despair of Judas—how he hurled the thirty little pieces of silver into the Temple, openly confessed Christ's innocence, and, since he received little comfort from the high priests, hanged himself. Also [related here] is how the high priests, not wanting to place this blood money into the coffers of God, instead bought with it a plot of land in which to bury the pilgrims. We intend briefly to consider both of these matters; God grant that we may do so fruitfully.

[I.] 1. As Christ was innocently condemned to death by the scribes, high priests, elders, and the entire council for the second time that morning, they tied Him up anew and were united in their resolve to lead Him before the Roman governor so that he might confirm their sentence and hold Him for execution. For the Roman eagle had grasped the Jewish nation in its claws, and the Jews no longer had the final or criminal jurisdiction; rather, if someone was to be sentenced to death, it had to take place through the Roman governor of the land. Thus, from the house of the high priest Caiaphas, the lords of the consistory—which included seventy [representatives] from all the tribes of Israel, as well as also the scribes as the judges, the Pharisees as the representatives and defenders of the rights of a community,* and the elders of the people (the respectable gray heads)—set out early in the morning and proceeded in a

---

* Gerhard uses the Latin, Syndici.

long train to the judgment hall, where they had requested Pilate to appear. (For this was not Pilate's residence; rather it was a public judgment hall.) They thus allowed Christ to be brought here [in the condition] into which He had been so deplorably placed overnight by the spit and blows of the servants, so that He might be held in the most extreme contempt by the people. Up to now the people had regarded Christ with respect and esteem. The further intention of these lords of the consistory was to file together through the narrow streets in an imposing procession to the judgment hall. This was quite extraordinary, for they usually let their servants bring the evil-doer before the governor with a declaration of what he had done wrong.* That Christ now here was delivered up to a Gentile judge is not to be regarded as occurring solely because of the hatred of the Jews. Rather, the evangelists themselves provide us with a commentary: It occurred as a fulfillment of the prophecies about Christ, that He would be delivered up to the heathen [Gentiles]. And Peter states even more clearly in Acts 2 that this took place according to the deliberate counsel and foreknowledge of God. Had Pilate granted the Jews the authority to judge Christ according to their own law and to their own peril, they would gladly have accepted and would have dealt with Christ as they did with Stephen, Acts 7, whom they allowed to be stoned in a fury even before a sentence was forthcoming from the Roman governor. However, in this case they were afraid of the people, who up until now had been attached to Jesus. Thus they wanted to force it on the governor's bosom that he should take [this matter] upon himself. The people would not so readily revolt against it (they thought), because Pilate had recently displayed a horrible severity against certain Galileans, whose blood he had mixed with their

---

* A note on Gerhard's sentences: The above consisted of a single 23-line sentence of interconnected thought in the original German, making it a "grand champion" of sorts, superseding the 17-line sentence in his *Treatise on Baptism*. Tr.

sacrifices, Luke 13. Moreover, they had conceived such hatred against Christ, which could not have been appeased had Christ been punished with only a mild (less painful) death.* Instead, since it was customary for the Romans to allow certain evil-doers to be crucified—which was a horrible, pitiful death—behold, they endeavored to see to it that Christ would have such a death inflicted upon Him. That was the godless intention of the Jews. However, God had so disposed that His Son would be sentenced to death not only by the Jews, but also by the Gentiles, so that herewith would be shown that Jews and Gentiles, that is, all mankind, were guilty of this death, and that all mankind with its sins helped cause the murder of the only beloved Son of the Lord God. Moreover, [this took place] so that the fruits of this death would come to both Jews and Gentiles if they trusted in it in true faith. Thus, Augustine says, *Epist. 171*: "The suffering of Christ is the ransom payment for the whole world." In the Holy Scriptures, particularly in Rom. 2, all mankind is divided into two groups: either Jews or Gentiles. Accordingly, since it was not only the Jewish high priests, scribes, and elders who condemned Christ to death, but also that Pilate accepted such a charge and willingly complied with their judgment, it is thus to be concluded that all mankind are guilty of Christ's death, be they Jew or Gentile.

2. We also note here the incivility of the human heart; namely, how the high priests, scribes, and elders of the people were so swiftly and indefatigably driven to maliciousness. For they had spent nearly half the previous night with their dealings against Christ. Nevertheless, at the dawning of the new day, they did not allow their burning hatred against Christ to rest; on the other hand, the disciples of Christ slept and slumbered. So it still goes: when worldly pleasure and luxury are present,

---

* Gerhard may be referring to the more humane Roman method of beheading. Ed.

no sleep enters into the eye. However, if one is supposed to hear God's word—or with King David, proclaim praises to God at midnight—then the heart and the eye always want to become sleepy. All this originates from the great corruption from our hearts via the inherited (original) sin by which we are inclined towards the worldly; for all the thoughts and aspirations of the human heart are evil and worldly from one's youth, Gen. 6 and 8. If there is an opportunity to hurt the neighbor, cheat him, and to overcharge him, there is always plenty of clever ingenuity, intelligence, and burning greed to accomplish it. However, if it is appropriate to advise the neighbor, seek the best for him, or to practice other kinds of godliness, then our intellect is darkened, and the will to do it is sluggish and lazy. The heart has an aversion towards doing it. We should confess this great incivility (rudeness) of our corrupt nature; and we should petition that God would subdue such incivility through His Holy Spirit and, on the contrary, ignite within us a fiery zeal for every good work by means of this [His] heavenly fire, because for that purpose Christ has given Himself, [i.e.,] to rescue us from all unrighteousness and to cleanse for Himself a people for His own possession that would be eager to do good works, Tit. 2.

II. As Judas the betrayer saw that the Lord Christ had been condemned to death, he was sorry about it. Judas had never had the slightest thought that it would come to this with the Lord Christ. Rather, he thought that Christ, as had happened several times before, would tear Himself loose again. For all that, he still would have come away with thirty pieces of silver, and later on he would again easily find grace and reconciliation with Christ. However, when he saw that Christ made no effort to free Himself, but instead was condemned to death by the entire council of the ecclesiastical authorities, and was furthermore led before Pilate so that their bloody sentence would be carried out, he was sorry about it. His conscience awoke within him, whereas previously he would not permit himself to be aroused from the sleep of sin by any of Christ's admonitions. He then became so frightened that he hurled the thirty pieces of silver—the wages of betrayal—into the temple; and he confessed openly and publicly before the high priests and scribes (who were conducting the worship service in the temple) and before all the people in attendance that he had done wrong, that he had betrayed innocent blood. He thus gave clear testimony of the Lord Christ's innocence. However, for his anguished conscience, he received a sorry bit of comfort from the high priests; for they said to him: **What is that to us? You see to it,** [as if to say,] if you have done something against your conscience, you will have to make amends for that. As he was dismissed with such a sorry comfort, his conscience was overcome with anguish, so that he went out and hanged himself; and, as it is recorded in Acts 1, his middle burst in two, and all his intestines spilled out.

With such a horrible downfall for Judas, the high priests should have reflected on and desisted from their murderous intent against the innocent Christ. But they knocked that thought out of their eyes and hearts, not realizing that they were stuck in the same sin as Judas. Moreover, in the true style of hypocrites, they concerned themselves with the insignificant: they did not want to place such money into the coffers of God. Instead they purchased a plot of land from a potter, in which the foreigners [travelers] who might come up to Jerusalem and die there could be buried. This occurred, however, because of God's special divine dispensation, that it might thus be fulfilled what the prophet Zechariah had earlier proclaimed, chapter 11, where the prophet speaks in the Person of Christ thus: **If it suits you, then bring forth what I am worth; if not, then defer payment. And they weighed out as much as I was worth, thirty pieces of silver: And the Lord said to me, throw it away, so that it will be given to the potter; alas, an insignificant sum that I was held to be worth by them. And I took the thirty pieces of silver and hurled** them into the House of the Lord, so that they would be given to the potter.

1. Just as we have in the account of Peter's conversion an example of divine mercy towards the repentant, so also we have in Judas a horrible example of the wrath of God against the deliberately unrepentant sinner. We must take care not to misuse (take advantage of) Christ's suffering and death, which He endured for the sake of our sin, by impenitence and carnal security, to the extent that we would think that since Christ has paid for our sin, we are from now on freely allowed to sin. For [this payment] will have little consequence for us if we go forth wantonly sinning against conscience. And so I say, in order that we do not then think this way and so misuse Christ's suffering, behold, right in the middle of the Passion history this horrible example of Judas is held before us, so that we learn from it how those who deliberately proceed to sin against every warning and admonition cannot comfort themselves with the sufferings of Christ, nor hope to receive mercy. Instead, they can await nothing but terrible judgment and the fire of anger which will destroy the hateful [ones], Heb. 10.

For beloved, is this not a horrible example of divine wrath against a deliberate, impenitent sinner, that Judas—who was no ordinary Christian, but an apostle who for nearly four years had been instructed by Christ, had preached to other Christians, and confirmed his proclamation with miracles—I repeat, [is this not a horrible example of divine wrath] that he finally through his impenitence fell into despairing doubt, hanged himself, and thus became a child of eternal damnation? Accordingly, just as we may use the example of the apostle Peter for our comfort, so also this example of Judas should stand before our eyes as a warning. If the Devil wants to drag us into sin, we should remember the example of Judas; if out of weakness we have fallen into sin, we should behold the example of Peter. The example of Judas should protect us from over-confidence, the example of Peter from doubt. The example of Judas should dampen ["put a lid on"] our outward man, so that we do not follow our evil lust into sin. The example of Peter should console our inner man so that we do not in anxiety despair on account of sin.

2. We also have here a reflection of the Devil's cunning. As he planted into Judas' heart the idea that he should betray Christ, he made the sin so sweet and easy that Judas did not listen to the faithful admonition of Christ. He went out in blind delusion and did not allow himself to be warned. However, as he later acquiesced under the weight of sin, the Devil made it appear to be so huge and heavy that Judas did not see the Sun of divine mercy and the payment of Christ. For that reason the ancients said that the Devil has, so to speak, twin mirrors which he holds before a man. The first mirror is the minimizing mirror. With it he makes the sin quite small and insignificant. He holds this mirror up to a person when he wants to tempt a man into, and drive him towards, sin. The second mirror is the magnifying mirror. With it he makes the sin quite large and thick. He holds this mirror up to a person when he has toppled him into sin. With this trick the devil deceives very many people, so that they either commit sin against their conscience with great eagerness; or later despair in vexation over the sin. We should equip ourselves against this, so that we remind ourselves before we fall into sin what a weighty and dangerous thing sin is. If, however, we ever do fall into sin, we should remember that Christ's merit and the mercy of God are much greater than the former—yes, much greater than all of the world's sin combined. Sin is a work of the Devil and of the corrupt human nature; on the other hand, the mercy of God and Christ's merits are the work of God. For that reason, God's grace and Christ's merits are indeed greater than sin. If, in that regard, the Devil wants to convince us that our sins are greater than what can be forgiven us, we should remind ourselves that the Devil is herewith doing nothing other than to present his work as God's work, and thus wants to put himself before God the Lord. Therefore, we should never believe him nor follow him. It is also a major element in the Devil's cunning that he does not immediately try to draw a person into great, terrible sins. Rather, he begins with the most insignificant and then leads a person ever more deeply into sin. Thus, with Judas he did not immediately plant the thought that he should betray Christ, for with this approach he could not have so quickly brought Judas to this point. Instead, he first begins with the most insignificant [temptation], by planting a lust for wealth in the heart of Judas. Now those who want to become rich, fall into temptation and the cords of the Devil, 1 Tim. 6. Accordingly, he puts greed into his heart; now then, greed is the root of all evil. From this greed it followed farther that Judas would pinch off [steal] a little bit from the alms that were given to Jesus, and as he noticed that God did not strike him down with lightning and thunder, he became bolder and contemplated how he might steal even greater portions. As Christ admonished him to refrain from that, he presented himself as outwardly pious, allowed [Jesus] to wash his feet, and partook of the Holy Supper. Yet in his heart he remained a rogue and a skinflint. When the Devil had brought Judas to this point, he planted into his heart that he should betray Christ. And even though Christ faithfully warns Judas and expressly holds before him that it would have been better that he had never been born than that he should consent to this great sin, the Devil plugs up Judas' heart so that he ignores all this and does not take Christ's Word to heart. We should let this be a warning to us, so that we learn to recognize the Devil's cunning tactics, Eph. 6, resist the evil one in good time, take to heart the warnings which are presented to us in God's Word, and indeed never to close our hearts, Psa. 95, Heb. 3. Instead, we are to live in heartfelt fear of God, earnestly pray, and, if we indeed fall into sin, to rise up quickly again and cling to the promises of the Gospel. In the future we should zealously guard against sin and therewith be sustained unto eternal life.

3. Furthermore, we here have a mirror of an evil conscience. As Judas went forward in his sin, his evil conscience slept; indeed, it slept so soundly that Christ could not awake it with any kind of warning. However, by this time the sin was initiated, and the evil conscience awoke once again, causing such anguish for Judas that he did not know how to endure it. Instead he ran for a rope and thought he would thus put an end to his anguish. The words of God the Lord to Cain in Gen. 4 state it correctly: sin rests dormant at the door. But one should not let it have its way, even if sin lies quietly like a satisfied puppy and rests for a long time. His resting is not to be trusted, for the puppy rests at a door that is always opening and closing. This puppy will be easily awakened by the creaking of the door. And when it awakens, it will be sufficiently alarming. St. Paul also addresses this issue in Rom. 6. Sin may indeed rest for a long time, but through the voice of the Law it quickly comes alive. That's why we should never act against conscience, for when the conscience later awakens, it is likely subsequently to become too burdensome for us. A conscience is indeed a sensitive thing. It is easily injured, but afterwards difficult to heal. A person can easily disquiet this inner witness, but scarcely be able to soothe it again. One can inscribe many debts into the book of conscience, but afterwards they do not allow themselves to be easily erased. A person can easily saddle the conscience with a heavy burden so that it is pressed down and crushed and he thereby sinks into ruin. For this reason it is advisable that we practice a good knighthood [devoted service], maintaining faith and a good conscience, 1 Tim. 1.

4. We also here have mirrored for us the selfsame terror which will press down upon the unrepentant sinners and the damned into all eternity. In Judas's hanging himself and spilling (pouring) out his intestines is portrayed for us not merely temporal punishment—which usually overtakes the greedy in that either they themselves, or through their descendants, will have to empty out whatever they unjustly scratched together;* but rather, this [incident] especially foreshadows the great terror which will some day overtake and eternally crush the damned, so that the worm of their conscience will nag them forever, Isa. 66, so that they will seek death but not find it, Acts 9, so that their soul will wish to be hanged, Job 7. For if Judas could not bear the anguish of his evil conscience for a few hours, but was driven to a rope by it, what kind of terror will there actually be in the hearts of the damned when they discover that they will have to remain in such pain and anguish for all eternity? The contemplation of eternity will create in them a most severe sense of woe (heartache), because all hope for relief from such anguish, or even an amelioration of it, has been cut off from them. Behold, as a result a constant despair will well up in their hearts. God grant that we carefully consider this, so that we become enemies of the sin which, as it were, adds logs of fuel to this hellish fire and increases the burden of this anguish of heart.

Finally, the fact that an acreage for the burial of pilgrims was purchased with the blood-money for which Christ was sold, portrays for us the following mystery: We poor Gentiles are pilgrims and strangers before God the Lord, Psa. 39: **Strangers (foreigners) outside of the community of Israel, strangers to the covenant of the promise**, Eph. 2. All of us should have been hurled into the accursed valley, just as the Jews threw the bodies of foreigners into this one, had not Christ allowed Himself to be sold for our sake, and thereby purchased (earned) for us a little place and bed of rest [the grave] in the acreage of the heavenly Potter—for God the Lord compared Himself to a potter, Isa. 29: 45, Jer. 18, Rom. 9. In this Acre of God we, through Christ and for the sake of His merits, may rest in exquisite peace until

---

* In typical analogical fashion Gerhard makes the point. Ed.

Judgment Day, when our bones shall blossom forth to eternal life, Isa. 66, and we shall be gathered into the barns of the eternal cottages (dwellings) like pure seeds of wheat, Mat. 13. Abraham was a stranger in the land of Canaan, and he acquired nothing more than a plot for the burial of his descendants, Gen. 23. In the presence of God, we are all strangers (aliens) here on earth, Heb. 9.* Thus it should be our greatest desire that we receive a gentle resting place in God's acre and obtain eternal life. This comes to pass when we retire to rest and fall asleep in true faith in Christ, who for our sake let Himself be sold (betrayed) and killed. He wants to give that to all of us by grace. Amen.

O Lord Jesus Christ, You who were accused before the Gentile judge, Pilate, let also us poor Gentiles partake of Your suffering. Direct us with Your Holy Spirit so that the Devil not mislead us into despair, doubt and other gross sins. Instead, give us grace so that we will be sustained in true faith to the end; and finally, grant that we may be sown into God's acre as pure wheat seeds, to blossom forth anew unto eternal life. Amen.

---

* Seemingly a rare memory lapse—Gerhard must have been thinking of Heb. 11: 13, Tr.

The Second Sermon

How Christ was accused before Pilate and gave a good witness about His kingdom.

The Jews however did not go into the judgment hall, so that they would not become unclean [and] so that they might eat the Passover. Then Pilate went out to them and said: What charges do you bring against this man? They answered and said to him: If this Person were not an evil doer, we would not have delivered Him over to you. Then Pilate said to them: Then you take Him and judge Him by your law. Then the Jews said to him: We are not allowed to kill anyone. Thus was fulfilled the word of Jesus which He spoke indicating the kind of death which He would die. Then the high priests and elders began adamantly to accuse Him, and said: We found this One subverting the people and forbidding the payment of taxes to Caesar; and He said: I am Christ the King. Then Pilate went once more into the judgment hall and called for Jesus, and he questioned Him and said: Are You the King of the Jews? Jesus stood before Him and answered: Do you say this by yourself, or have others said this to you about Me? Pilate answered: Am I a Jew? Your people and the high priests have surrendered You to me, what have You done? Jesus answered: My kingdom is not of this world; if My kingdom were of this world, My servants would have vigorously battled that I not be delivered up to the Jews. But now My Kingdom is not from here. Then Pilate said to Him: So are You nevertheless still a King? Jesus answered: You said it. I am a King; I have been born and have come into the world for the purpose that I should testify to the truth. Anyone who is of the truth, hears My voice. Pilate said to Him: What is truth?

In the first book of Moses [Genesis], the 39th chapter, it is recorded that Potiphar's adulterous wife accused pious, innocent Joseph before her lord (husband), as if he had wanted to shame her and commit adultery with her, even though she herself was the one with the villainous heart and intended to bring about his downfall. In this story Joseph is a type of the Lord Christ. Christ Himself was accused before Pilate by the adulterous sort (breed), as they are called in Mat. 12—namely, the high priests and scribes—as if Christ had spread false doctrine (which the Scriptures label as spiritual adultery) among the people. All the while they had a hypocritical, godless heart, and, by their falsification of divine truth, were the most malicious harlots and adulterers in God's sight.

This false accusation by the spiritual authorities in Jerusalem, which they tried to prove against Christ in a shameless manner before Pilate, is described for us in the text just read. In it we are informed of:

I. How the spiritual authorities dared to demand of Pilate that he condemn Christ to death on the basis of their blatant accusation, without a hearing and without any knowledge of the matter.

II. As they were unable to obtain such [a verdict] from Pilate, [we are further informed] of how they accused Christ of being a misleading and inflammatory Teacher and also of how Christ responded to them.

I. When the ecclesiastical authorities came before the judgment hall, they did not wish to go in so that they would not become unclean and thus be prevented from celebrating the

Passover. In Num. 9 it was ordained by God that if one entered a home with a dead person inside, he was regarded as being unclean and had to cleanse himself by means of certain ceremonies. The Jews also applied this [principle] to their man-made regulations; namely, that anyone who entered a house in which an evildoer was to be sentenced to death, he too would become unclean. Pilate, even though he indeed could have refused to come out to them, nevertheless accepted their excuse. [Thereby] he gives an example to all rulers that they likewise should not always be concerned about their reputation [i.e., official dignity], but instead allow their leniency and friendliness to shine through. And, as he allowed his servants to take into custody the captive Christ from the high priests, he asks: What kind of charges do you bring against this Man? You bring a prisoner here and petition that He be sentenced to death. Now, it is in every way proper that you at the same time submit a sure, articulate charge against Him, so that one might know what the offense is, and might know whether and how He is to be punished.

That was a puzzling pronouncement for these ecclesiastical authorities. For they had made up their minds that if they jointly came to Pilate in such an imposing procession, he wouldn't raise many questions. Instead, with such an imposing group bringing in Christ, he would [they thought] quickly sentence Him to death. Therefore, they speak, as it were, with a single defiant voice: **If this One were not an evildoer, we would not have turned Him over to you.** Don't you know that we also have a conscience? In a unified council [by unanimous consent] we have sentenced Him to death. That's how it should remain. Pilate, however, would not pronounce the sentence merely on the basis of their accusation. For it was not the Roman way for a man to be given over to be put to death before the defendant, in the presence of his accusers, had been given opportunity to defend himself against their accusations. [Note the example] of Festus, another Roman governor, as recounted in Acts 25. And

Valerius Publicola had made a law that no case was judged without a trial. Pilate did not want to go against this Roman practice and law. Therefore, he says to the high priests and scribes: **So then, you take Him away and judge Him according to your Law.** In essence he is saying: This is very strange to me; you boast that you are a special, peculiar people of God and regard us Romans as being accursed and godless people. If you have such an unjust law from your God that one should and can sentence a person to death even before accusations and hearings take place, then you may do so according to such a law; but that is not the practice with us Romans. To that they responded: **We are not allowed to kill anyone.** You well know that such [permission] must be obtained from you. You know that according to the way of the Roman Caesar you must condemn an evil-doer to death. Such criminal jurisdiction has been taken away from us. The evangelist writes, **This happened so that the Word Christ [spoke] be fulfilled as to the kind of death He would die**, namely, John 3, that He would be lifted up (on a cross), and John 12, that He would be lifted up from the earth. [It is stated] even more clearly in Mat. 20 that He would be crucified by the Gentiles, for such mode of death was not the practice among the Jews, but rather only among the Romans.

1. That Christ here before the court is called an evil-doer was the greatest injustice against His Person. For Augustine says in his *Treatise 114 on John*: Ask those whom Christ rescued from the bonds of the Devil, those whom He made well from their illnesses, cleansed from leprosy, those whose ears, eyes and mouth He opened, those whom He awakened from the dead if Christ was an evil-doer. Since, however, Christ had taken upon Himself all the world's sin and transgression before the divine court of justice, behold, He is here resoundingly called an evil-doer before the seat of judgment; for He stood there not only before the world's judgment, but rather also before the Judgment of God. And, since God the Lord had laid all our sin upon Him, Isa. 53, behold, He is also publicly named as an evil-doer.

2. We also have here a true reflection of hypocrisy by the high priests and scribes. They knew very well that they should have entered into the judgment hall. However, the fact that they presented false witnesses against Christ, that they accused Christ before the tribunal, that from the horrible demise of Judas they truly realized that Christ was innocent, and the fact that they demanded of Pilate that he should promptly (without hearing the case) condemn Christ to death [shows that] they truly had no conscience about doing all these things. It is just as Christ reproached them in Mat. 23: **Filtering gnats and swallowing camels.** Here we have illustrated the way of the hypocrite: Without any fear, his conscience allows him to violate the mandates of man and the commands of God.

3. We observe also here how far evil can penetrate into those who are among the people of God when they follow the Devil and their lusts, that is, much farther than it ever does among the heathen, who are outside the Church and separate from the people of God. The high priests, scribes, Pharisees, and elders were the true people of God. Indeed, as the foremost among them, they should have been the very essence [of godliness]. Pilate was a Gentile; even so the wickedness of the high priests, scribes, etc., was so great that they demanded to allow that Christ be condemned to death without even a hearing of His case. Regarding that matter, they had a far different law from God, as Nicodemus testifies about all of them in John 7: **Does our law also judge a man even before he receives a hearing and confesses what he's doing?** More honesty and sincerity remain in Pilate's character from the light of nature [than in the scribes, Pharisees, et al.]. So it still is today; many among those who praise Christ are not ashamed to perform such acts as even the heathen abhor, just as Paul testifies of the Corinthians, 1 Cor. 5 [namely], that there was in vogue among them the kind of whoredom of which even the heathen were not known to speak. However, such false Christians will one day receive a severe sentence of judgment, as the Lord had proclaimed to them in Luke 12: **The servant who knew the will of his Lord and did not prepare himself, nor did His will, he will have to suffer many whip lashes.** Thus, it is better to be a heathen than to live like a heathen under the name of Christianity. On Judgment Day the intelligent (prudent) heathen who assiduously assumed an outwardly pious lifestyle, will all the more severely accuse such false Christians.

II. As the high priests and elders saw that they would not be able to persuade Pilate to condemn Christ to death merely on the basis of their demand, they brought forth their charges. They formulated their grievances in a manner intended to induce in Pilate an extreme hatred towards Christ. Their accusation consisted of three points: First, they accused Christ of being a heretic. We found this One subverting the people from the ancient religion. He caused them to stray from their true faith, as it properly reads in the original language, and He introduced a new heretical doctrine. That, however, was nothing [i.e., a baseless charge], for Christ always proved His teachings from Moses and the prophets. Next they said that He was a rebel (rabble rouser), that He forbade the paying of taxes to Caesar. But that too was [a baseless charge]. For He had first explained Himself for two days against the Pharisees and the servants of Herod that a man should give to Caesar what was the Caesar's. He Himself had also paid tribute at Capernaum. Thirdly, they said: He wants the people to cling to Him and detract from Caesar. He passes Himself off as a king.

Pilate let stand the first point of the accusation, for as a Gentile he cared very little about religion. He knew that the second accusation was false. Therefore he examined Christ privately about the third point and said to Him: **Are You the**

King of the Jews? He knew that the Jews daily hoped for the kind of king who would rescue them from the power of the Romans. That's why he was specifically commanded by the Roman Caesar to take diligent precaution that no one present himself as a king of the Jews, or be raised up by the people as a king, so that no uprising take place as a result. Therefore, he could not allow this point to be neglected. Rather, he thought that because of his office, it was his duty to learn the true reason for this charge. Therefore, he went into the judgment hall and asked Christ if He acknowledged being a king of the Jews. To this Christ answered: **Do you say this by yourself, or have others told you this about Me?** I ask you whether in the slightest you see anything about Me that would indicate I am such a King of whom the Roman Caesar would have anything to fear? However, if others have said this about Me—that I want to drive the Caesar out of the land—then you must not put too much stock in it. One can also take this statement to mean that Christ wanted to know what Pilate meant by this question. For there were two viewpoints on this matter: that of the Scriptures and the pious Jews, who hoped for a spiritual and heavenly King, and that of the Gentiles and scribes, who labeled a king as someone who had an earthly kingdom. Therefore, in order that I may give a correct answer, says Christ, I must know whether you are asking me as a Jew or as a Gentile. Pilate said: Am I a Jew? What do I care about the Jewish religion? Your own people, and indeed the foremost among them, the high priests, have accused You before me. They are continually talking about their future King, and now that You present Yourself as the One, they don't want to accept You. What must You have done?

Thereupon, the Lord Christ gives a glorious confession before Pilate regarding the kind of King He is and the nature of His Kingdom. **My kingdom is not of this world.** You need not fear that I intend to encroach upon the worldly kingdom of the Roman Caesar. I indeed am a King, but not a worldly king.

I have a kingdom, but it is a heavenly kingdom. **If My kingdom were of this world, My servants would fight on that account so that I would not be accused by the Jews. But now My kingdom is not from there.** And as Pilate concluded that since He had a kingdom, He also had to be a King, Christ answered: **I am a King; I have been born for that purpose.** In the fullness of time I was born of a virgin—as Augustine explains it—and I came into the world to testify to the truth. I am the kind of King whose office it is to preach (proclaim) the truth, to bring people to the true knowledge of God, and to show them the right way to salvation. Whoever is of the truth, whoever is born of God, hears My voice and follows after it. When Pilate heard that this was only about dispute of the Pharisees and scribes with Christ concerning the nature of correct teaching and divine truth, he said: **What is truth?** If there is nothing here that would detract from the Caesar, should one instigate such a fuss on account of truth?

  1. That Christ is here now falsely accused, such also He endures for our sake, as was explained and elucidated above. God had committed the Law to the high priests, scribes, and Pharisees, as is recorded in Mal. 2: **The lips of the priests should preserve the teaching (doctrine) so that one can seek the Law from their mouths.** However, here they falsely accuse Christ as if He had acted contrary to God's Law; in this way, Christ redeemed us from the accusations of the Law. That Christ was also accused before Pilate because [it was said] He had arrogated to Himself false honors, had wanted to be a king, and had forbidden the payment of tribute to Caesar, all this He suffered as payment for the sins of the first parents—which we also had inherited. They [our first parents] had arrogated unto themselves false honors; they wanted to be like God; and they did not want to render the tribute of obedience which they owed to God the Lord. To atone for this [sin], Christ here suffered these false accusations. Although He indeed could have easily defended Himself, He quietly remained dumb like a little lamb which is led to the slaughter (chopping block); and He did not open His mouth. Thus He rescued us, so that on Judgment Day we would not have to be struck dumb before the divine Judgment.

2. We should also ponder the confession of Christ before Pilate, which St. Paul extols for us in 1 Tim. 6, calling it a good confession, which it most certainly was. For it includes very much—actually everything that is relevant to Christ's kingdom. Initially, Christ states that His kingdom is not a worldly kingdom which stands in external splendor or is defended by outward force. Rather, His kingdom is within us, as we read in Luke 17. He reigns in our hearts through the Holy Spirit. Since it is not a kingdom of this world, it is, then, a kingdom of the cross, wherein the servants of this kingdom are not recognized. Instead, they lie hidden under the cross, and are secretly hidden from the spite of the Enemy, as David says in Psa. 31; that is, God rules and protects the kingdom of Christ in such a manner that reason cannot grasp how it is done. Because it also is not a worldly kingdom which from the outside has a stately appearance, it is thus despised by many. Later in the Passion [story] we will hear of how the soldiers gave a reed into the Lord Christ's hand, so that they might demonstrate that His was indeed a reed kingdom, that is, a weak kingdom, and that the kingdom of Christ appeared to be so weak that it might actually soon collapse. Further, since it is not a worldly, earthly kingdom, we too (who would be its members and subjects) should not first seek worldly goods, temporal benefits, and external fortune (happiness). Christ's kingdom is in the world, but not of this world. We should not seek after that which the world regards as a high priority. Instead, we should strive for heavenly blessings.

If Christ's Kingdom is not a worldly kingdom, if Christ is not a worldly King, what can we expect from Him? Christ here also testifies about that: **For this I was born, and came into the**

world so that I should testify to the truth. My kingdom, He intends to say, is a Kingdom of the Truth, for in it one can learn the truth, for God's Word is Truth, John 17. Whoever is not in this kingdom of Christ, he cannot come to a true knowledge of God. That's why Christ's teaching is often called the Word of Truth, Eph. 1, Col. 1, James 1. It is also a Kingdom of Truth, because in this Kingdom the true heavenly blessings (reconciliation with God, forgiveness of sins, the gift of righteousness, etc.) will be distributed to us, John 1. **Grace and truth come to us through Jesus Christ.** Earthly goods are not genuine, true blessings (Christ calls them unrighteous mammon in Luke 16) because they are subject to unrighteous use. As Luther explains the selfsame text: They are also to be called foreign (alien) goods because they will be taken from us, or even we from them. In this text, the Lord Himself contrasts these same temporal goods with the spiritual, eternal blessings. These spiritual blessings He calls our real and proper blessings, since they remain ours forever and shall never be taken from us. Behold, because now these true heavenly blessings are distributed to us in the Kingdom of Christ, the Lord Christ thus calls it a Kingdom of Truth. But how can one know who belongs to this Kingdom, and who may hope for such blessings? Christ also here teaches us this: **Whoever is of the Truth, such a one hears My voice.** Christ is the Truth, John 14. Accordingly, whoever hears Christ's voice, believes it, remains in Christ by faith, and also in whom Christ lives, such a one is of God, John 8. That is, [he is] born of God; such a one is of the Truth, that is, of Christ. Thus he belongs to the Kingdom of Christ. Such a one will also be taken from this Kingdom of Grace into the Kingdom of eternal Glory. God help us to that end through Christ. Amen.

O Lord Jesus Christ, You who in an innocent manner were accused as an evil-doer for the sake our sins, let Your holy suffering redound to the good of us poor evil-doers. You

King of Truth, make us partakers of Your Kingdom, guide us into all Truth, and transfer us from the gracious Kingdom of Truth into the Kingdom of eternal Glory. Amen.

The Third Sermon

How Christ was adjudged to be innocent before Pilate and was sent to Herod.

After Pilate had said that, he went out once more to the Jews and said to them: I find no guilt in Him. And when He was accused by the high priests and the elders, He gave no answer. But Pilate asked Him again, and said: Have You no answer? See how severely they accuse You; don't You hear anything? And He no longer answered him a word, so that the governor was very puzzled. However, [the accusers] persisted and said: Beginning in Galilee, He has stirred up the people by His teaching across the entire Jewish territory. When Pilate heard this, he asked whether He was from Galilee? Perceiving that He was under Herod's jurisdiction, he sent Him over to Herod—who happened to be in Jerusalem that very day. But when Herod saw Jesus, he was very happy; for he had eagerly wanted to see Him for the longest time, because he had heard many things about Him and hoped he would see a sign from Him. So he asked [Jesus] about many different things; but, He answered him nothing. The high priests and scribes, however, accused Him with great intensity. But Herod, along with his servants of the court, despised and mocked Him, laid on Him a white garment, and sent Him back again to Pilate. On that day Pilate and Herod became friends with each other, for previously they had been each other's enemy.

In Exo. 12 God the Lord commanded the Jewish people that when they wanted to slaughter their Passover lamb, they had to select and choose one that had no flaw or imperfection. What is signified by this Passover lamb is taught by St. Paul, 1 Cor. 5, where he writes: **Our Passover Lamb is Christ, who was offered up for us.** It is also recorded in Isa. 53 and 1 Pet. 2 concerning this very same little Lamb of God that there was no flaw or sinful imperfection in Him. He had committed no sin or wrong; also, there was no deceit in His mouth. **For we should have such a High Priest who was holy, innocent, and unspotted, set apart from sinners**, Heb. 7. Not only do the prophets and apostles testify of this innocence and purity of Christ; but in the Passion story others—indeed, including the most vicious enemies of Christ—have also publicly acknowledged this with their testimony. [Even] Judas, the betrayer, discovers that he has betrayed innocent blood.

The high priests and the ecclesiastical council at Jerusalem acknowledge Christ's innocence by the fact that they could not get results with their accusations in any other way than by planting false witnesses against Him. Pilate's wife admonished her lord [husband] that he should have nothing to do with this righteous One. The women of Jerusalem testify with tears that the Lord experienced injustice. The captain and others who were standing beneath the cross confess: **Truly, this was a godly Person and the Son of God.** Indeed, also creation testifies to Christ's innocence: the sun becomes dark, the earth quakes, the rocks are ripped apart. Two such testimonies about Christ's innocence are also presented to us in the text just read: how Pilate did so with words, [and] Herod with his actions—in that he had a white garment placed upon Christ and thereby indicated that he found nothing in Him worthy of death. Let us give our attention to this matter as we now consider it.

First, how Pilate testifies that he could find no guilt in Christ, but failed thereby to assuage the premeditated hatred of the Jews.

Secondly, how Christ was led before Herod and was mocked by him.

I. When Pilate heard that Christ acknowledged being a King of the Truth, and that a conflict had thus arisen between Him and the Pharisees as to which party taught and defended the truth, he scorned all this; and, in keeping with his worldly wisdom, he regarded it as so much foolishness that someone would take such a matter so seriously. **What is Truth?**, he said. Otherwise it is nothing over which to lose one's head. At this he leaves the judgment hall, goes outside to the Jews, and says to them: **I find no guilt in Him.** I have indeed confronted Him as to whether He intended to instigate a rebellion against Caesar. But, He made it clear that He was seeking no worldly kingdom or rule. As the high priests and elders perceived from this that Pilate did not wish to proceed further, nor consent to their sentence of condemning Christ to death, they all the more intensely began to accuse Him anew. Also, without a doubt they wanted to affirm their accusations with many lies. However, Christ remained silent because Pilate had already acknowledged His innocence. Pilate was puzzled by this and said to Christ: **Won't You answer? Look at how intensely they accuse You. Aren't You listening?** The high priests knew how to use this silence of the Lord Christ to their advantage. Thus, they proceeded with their accusation and especially to urge [insist] that He had stirred up the people by teaching up and down across the entire Jewish land, beginning in Galilee and going as far as Jerusalem.

Here we should take note of the clear testimony of Pilate which he gave concerning the innocence of Christ; namely, that as pertains to His Person nothing was found in Him which was worthy of death. For this is also one of the foremost facts to be noted about the suffering of Christ; namely, that He was absolutely innocent. Had Christ inherited the least sin or committed one Himself, then His suffering could not have redounded to our good. However, since He suffered everything in innocence, it could thus be sufficient for our reconciliation (atonement). Many martyrs and saints have suffered much, but none of them suffered anything for us. For even though they well may have been innocent before the judgment of men and experienced injustice, they nevertheless were not innocent before the judgment of God. For it is written that before God no man is innocent, Exo. 34. But Christ was able to suffer for us because He was innocent in all things—not just before men, but also before God's judgment. His conception is holy, His birth is holy, His life is holy throughout, and—since He is the righteous Servant of God—He thus was able to give His life as a guilt-offering, Isa. 53. Concerning this innocence of the Lord Christ, the Christian Church speaks of Him as its beloved Groom in Song of Solomon 5: **My Friend is white and red, chosen from among many thousands.** He is white because of His innocence. He is red on account of His deep red blood that sprinkles forth from Him. He is chosen from among many thousands, because none from among so many thousands of angels and men is capable of pouring out his blood for others. The patriarch Jacob also speaks of this in Gen. 49: **The eyes of the Lord Messiah are more red than wine, and His teeth more white than milk**; that is, even though He will in His suffering have red eyes because of crying and bloodshed, yet His teeth shall be whiter than milk, i.e., no deceit will be found in His mouth.

  2. By remaining silent before Pilate and no longer answering the false accusations of the Jews, Christ thereby fulfills the prophecy of Isa. 53: **As He was punished and afflicted, He did not open His mouth, like a lamb which is led to the slaughter block; and like a sheep that is dumb before its shearer, He did not open His mouth.** So also the prophecy of David in Psa. 38: **Those who are after my soul, hunt me down; and those who wish evil for me, talk about how they want to harm**

me, and go around with idle cunning. But I have to be like a deaf man and not hear, and like a mute person who does not open his mouth. And I must be like one who does not hear and who has no objection in his mouth. Herewith Christ also fulfilled the type of Isaac, Gen. 22, who with patient heart and mouth allowed himself to be bound by his father as a sacrificial victim. Christ, however, wanted thereby to pay once and for all for the wordy [i.e., empty] excuses of our [first] parents. When they fell into sin, they knew how to excuse themselves skillfully. Adam placed the blame on his wife, Eve. Eve, on the other hand, laid the blame on the snake, Gen. 3. They gladly would have liked to placed the blame on God Himself, who had created the woman and the snake. By keeping His silence, Christ wanted to pay for these hypocritical excuses [of our first parents]. He also herewith wanted to ransom (redeem) us from the accusations of the Law and our conscience. For when we are accused before God's throne of judgment by His Law, by our own conscience, and indeed by all of creation, our mouths are stopped up, Rom. 3, since we have no excuses to proffer, Rom. 1. For that reason, we must be silent like the servant who did not have a wedding garment, Mat. 22. So that we then might be rescued from these accusations, and so that on Judgment Day we won't have to be silent before God and all the angels, Christ remained silent, although He very easily could have defended Himself against these false accusations. "Above all else, when Christ did not answer, He was silent like a lamb; when however, He did answer, He taught like a Shepherd."

  With this silence, Christ also wants to teach us that one should patiently endure injustice and calumny (slander). We must often trust to God and time, and wait until our innocence is acknowledge at a later time. One clearly cannot stop up the mouth of every slanderer. If God, our own heart, and various pious people exonerate us, what more can a person ask for? The exoneration by God and our own heart comforts us much more than the slanders and false accusations of this entire world can ever frighten us. The Lord speaks of this in Isa. 30: **If you remain silent, then you will be helped; by remaining quiet and hoping you will be strengthened.** The tranquility of the heart is often sustained much sooner and better by silence than by rambling, long-winded defenses. For who can stop up all the slanders of the mouth? **I will bear the Lord's wrath, for I have sinned against Him** (says Micah in chapter 7), **until He prosecutes my case and justly deals with me. He will bring me into the light so that I have my pleasure in beholding His grace.** In essence he is saying: Even though I may not be exonerated by men, who so slander and malign me, I nevertheless am excused by God; thus, I will bear my case with patience and commit it to God in silence. In His own time He will bring to light my innocence and reveal it to everyone.

II. The Jews would not desist from their accusations. Instead they stubbornly insisted that Christ with His preaching had tried to stir up an rebellion, since He never stayed in one place. Rather, He wandered around, and the people became attracted to Him from one place to the next, especially in Galilee, where He was often found. And, as one well knew, the Galileans were continually disposed towards rebellion, Acts 5. When Pilate heard [the word] Galilee, he thought he would be given occasion for an honorable [face-saving] way to be free of this poor, captive man. He did not want to have to act against his conscience and condemn this innocent man to death, contrary to everything that was right and just; nor, however, did he wish to burden himself with the ill-will of the high priests and elders. Accordingly, when he perceived that Christ was a native of Galilee and thus under Herod's jurisdiction, he thought it would be for the best to send this captive to Herod, who at this time had gone up to Jerusalem for the Passover. He would know best whether there was any validity to the accusation that Christ instigated a rebellion in Galilee with His teaching. Thereupon, Christ was led from the judgment hall through the old city up into the new city to Herod's palace; the entire ecclesiastical council followed Him in a long train.

Now when Herod saw Jesus, he was elated, for he had wanted to see Him for the longest time. For he had heard many things about Him, and he hoped he would see some sign from [Jesus], regarding which he also asked the Lord various [questions]. Herod had the notion that Christ would perform some sort of fantastic miracle in order to please him and gain favor and be set free again. However, since Christ knew very well that Herod was asking out of curiosity and thoughtless frivolity, and not out of a desire for the truth, He answered him nothing—even though He previously had engaged the heathen governor of the land, Pilate, in conversation. For it is written, as Solomon says in Pro. 26: **Do not answer the fool according to his foolishness, so that you do not become like him.** As the high priests and scribes saw that Christ would not answer Herod, nor do a miracle to please him, they sought to accuse and denounce Him as a seditionist, notwithstanding that by all rights this accusation had been cast aside before Pilate as worthless and false. For hatred and jealousy know no shame. They are not satisfied with just one lie. Instead, they only seek the oppression of the neighbor, rightly or wrongly, with lies or with the truth.

When Herod heard that Christ had claimed before Pilate that He was a King, he despised and mocked Him, together with the servants of his court. Realizing that he was in no danger on account of this poor captive (as if He would drive Caesar from the land), Herod therefore placed a white garment on Him and sent Him back again to Pilate. It was customary with the Romans that if one was elected as mayor, a white garment was placed upon him. Since Christ had confessed to being a King, Herod made a mockery of Him, and also placed such a kingly garment on Him. By this he also wanted to show that this foolishness was more to be mocked than to be severely punished—that such a poor and forsaken-by-man Person could hardly pass as a King. Also, since in former times those who had been condemned to death had black clothes placed upon them, with this white garment Herod wished to give Pilate to understand that he found nothing in this captive which was worthy of death—just as Pilate later declared. Even though Herod could coax no word or miracle out of Christ, it so much pleased him that Pilate had given him the honor of sending Christ to him that he once again became friends with Pilate. For previously there had arisen a misunderstanding between them, in that Pilate had encroached upon his jurisdiction and had gruesomely beheaded several of his subjects in Galilee and had mixed their blood with the sacrifices, Luke 13. However, as he now saw that Pilate once more had sent him a captive from Galilee, he again became his friend and let his wrath sink away. So it still goes today; if something is going against Christ and His Church, then the most malicious enemies stand together.

    1. Here, then, is described for us a bit of corrupt worldly cunning. Pilate knew that the Lord Christ was innocent. At the same time, he did not want to release Jesus and burden himself with ill-will on account of such an action. Therefore, he sent Him to Herod so that he could begin to take on responsibility for the Lord Christ. Thus it still often happens. High-ranking people, especially of the [royal] courts, know that many people experience bad things, and they could well come to their rescue. However, they don't do it, perhaps so that they do not thereby fall into disfavor with others or inconvenience them. Before God, however, such behavior is inexcusable, no matter how fine an appearance of worldly wisdom (intelligence) it might have. For here a person is obligated to rescue the neighbor in his situation apart from appearance, disfavor, or enmity. Furthermore, high-ranking officials often know that poor Christians are ill-treated by persecutors. However, they do not embrace their interests, so that they do not on their account incur the disfavor of important people or cause other inconveniences. So it must be with the members [of Christ's Body], that they experience what befalls the Head, Christ. Consequently, when we see such things, it should not surprise us or cause us to wonder. One can indeed paint such actions with a nice color, as if it were sufficient that a person refrain from oppressing the neighbor, even though he does not save (deliver) him. However, [such behavior] does not stand the test. For before God it is one and the same whether a man allows the neighbor to be oppressed, even though he might have helped him, or he actively participates in oppressing the neighbor—just as the Lord God regards it as unrighteousness not only if one takes what is his neighbor's, but also if he does not assist him when he is clearly capable of doing so.

  2. Christ is here mocked as an adventurer and a Shrove Tuesday carnival king, and is derisively cloaked with a white garment. He suffered this for our sake! In like manner, He allowed Himself to be paraded around the city as a spectacle so that He might rescue us from the Devil's mockery. And even though it was Herod's intention to mock Christ with this white garment, it is nevertheless hereby signified in a hidden manner by the Lord God that Christ is our eternal King and High Priest. For not only did the high priests in the Old Testament, in keeping with God's ordinance, wear a white cloak under their priestly vestments, but it was also the custom of the Romans to adorn with a white garment those who were elected to the office of mayor (at that time a position of great honor and authority, like unto the mightiest of kingdoms today). Since, then, Christ was the true High Priest of the New Testament, God thus saw to it that the white high priestly garment was placed upon Him. In contrast, the putative high priest, Caiaphas, ripped his clothes. Because Christ is the true, eternal King of His believers, a royal white garment is placed upon Him. Herod actually intended it to mock Christ, but God let it happen this way to provide a sure, positive sign. Since Christ here also in His suffering put on a white garment, in which He was scorned and mocked, He thereby won for us [the privilege] some day also to stand before the throne of God clad in white garments and to say in eternity: **Glory and honor, and wisdom, and thanksgiving, and praise, and might, and power be to our God from everlasting to everlasting**, Rev. 7. For just as Christ as our only eternal King and High Priest has made us into kings and priests before His heavenly Father, Rev. 1, so also has He through this white garment won for us the white garment of innocence and salvation so that we, along with the twenty-four elders who have harps and golden vessels filled with incense, may say to Christ, the Lamb of God: **You were slain and have purchased us with Your blood; and, you have made us into kings and priests before God**, Rev. 5. When the angels appeared after His resurrection and also after His ascension, they let themselves be seen in long, white garments. Since, then, Christ by His suffering wanted to win for us the blessed fellowship of the angels, so that we along with them may be clad in white garments and stand eternally before the throne of God, behold, in the midst of the story of His suffering, He allowed Himself to be clothed with a white garment.

In the Old Testament, when a high priest wanted to enter into the holy place and perform his sacrifice for the sins of the all the people, he had to put on—at the command of God—clean, white garments. By the same token, God frequently reiterates that the priests should wash their garments. Accordingly, since Christ, as the true eternal High Priest, wanted to offer Himself up to His heavenly Father as a sweet fragrance for the sins of the entire world, He allowed Himself to first be dressed in a white garment, thereby winning for us the white cloak of righteousness. For all our righteousness is actually like a soiled (stained) rag, Isa. 64. However, what has been won for us through Christ is that we shall overcome through faith. We shall one day also walk with Christ in heaven dressed in white garments, Rev. 3.

3. We also here see what frequently takes place in [royal] courts: that Christ is once again in His members [i.e., physically] repeatedly mocked and despised. Initially Herod was glad to see Jesus, and he hoped to become renowned because of Him, if only Christ would perform many miracles to please and honor him. But since Christ regarded him unworthy of any answer because he was a godless scornful person, He was mocked by Herod and his palace servants. There are still many courts like that, and one finds very few courts which measure up to David's boast of his royal household in Psa. 101.* If one does not at all times act and speak in a way that pleases the great lords of the courts, the same thing happens to him as to Christ, who was mocked in Herod's courtyard. If one would do something contrary to the truth to please them, then it happens to him as happened to Peter, who denied Christ in Caiaphas's courtyard. If, against his conscience, one actually would oppress the godly, then it happens to him as happened to Judas, who concluded his life at the end of a rope. Therefore, let everyone take heed (beware) that he does not let himself to be taken in by the superficial sham of the favor of the court to undertake anything which would go against Christ, against the members of Christ['s body], against righteousness, or against his own conscience. **For the essence of this world will disappear**, Paul says in 1 Cor. 7. The favor of the court is very unreliable and falls away in the blink of an eye, but God's grace lasts forever. On the Day of Judgment, no man is going to answer for you, even though you have already done him many favors. Rather, each person will have to give an account for himself. Each person's conscience will either be his accuser or his excuser. Furthermore, in this life no favor of the court can give as much joy as the inner testimony of a good conscience. However, a bad conscience distresses far more than

---

* No doubt Gerhard is especially referring to v. 7: "No one who practices deceit will dwell in my house." Tr.

all human favor and outward benefits can delight. That's why it is not worth undertaking the least bit of wrong against conscience in order to please any human being. God help us that we always use the world in such a way that we never misuse it.

4. The fact that Christ is here placed before a third seat of judgment, that of Herod, and further that He thus was accused three different times—once before the ecclesiastical consistory, next before Pilate, and finally also before Herod—all this He also suffered for the sake of mankind. The first Adam was, on account of his sin, summoned and accused three different times before God's judgment. God the Lord called to him in Paradise: **Adam, where are you? Have you not eaten from the fruit of the very same tree of which I had previously told you, the day you eat of it, you will die the death** [surely die]? After this, as he was he was driven from Paradise to farm the fields, he had to hear: **Cursed be the land because of you; with grief and sorrow you will have to nourish yourself from it your whole life long. It will produce thorns and thistles for you; and you will have to eat the plants of the fields. In the sweat of your face you will eat your bread until you once more become the soil from which you were taken. For you are soil, and you will become soil.** This was the second sentence God pronounced against Adam. The third invitation to appear before God's judgment still remains; namely, in that on the Last Day Adam, along with all his descendants, will be placed before the judgment throne of Christ to hear the final sentence. Here take note: so that Adam and all his descendants who cling to Christ in true faith will not have to be ashamed before God's judgment here in this life or on Judgment Day, Christ allowed Himself to be accused and condemned before three different judgment thrones. He did all that for our benefit. May He grant that we acknowledge it with thankfulness. Amen.

O Lord Jesus Christ, You who were innocently accused and condemned, may Your innocence redound to my benefit as a poor sinner. You who endured every wrong with great patience, let Your patience be a comfort to me in my disobedience, and may it be held up as an example for me to follow. Let the white garment with which You were vested cover my blood-red sins, so that I may some day, clad in a white garment, eternally praise You before Your throne. Amen.

The Fourth Sermon

How Pilate recommended that Christ be scourged and was warned by his wife about shedding innocent blood; Barabbas is given preference over Christ.

Pilate called together the high priests and the leaders and the people, and he said to them: You have brought this Man to me as one who stirs up the people; and behold, I have held a hearing for Him in your presence. And, I find nothing of which this Man is guilty. Neither does Herod, for I have sent you to him, and behold, no one has brought up anything against Him that is worthy of death. Therefore, I will chastise Him and turn Him loose. However, on this festival it was customary that the governor had a prisoner of their choice released to the people. This time, however, he held a prisoner who stood out from the rest, namely, an evil-doer and murderer named Barabbas. He had been thrown into jail with the seditionists. In the rebellion which had occurred in the city, he had committed a murder. And the people came up and petitioned that he do the usual thing. And as they were gathered together, Pilate answered them: You have a custom that I release someone to you at the Passover. Whom do you want me to release, Barabbas or Jesus, the King of the Jews, the One called Christ? For he knew the high priests had delivered Him up because of jealousy. And as He sat on his throne of judgment, his wife sent someone to him with the message: Have nothing to do with this Righteous One, for today I have suffered much in a dream because of Him. However, the high priests and elders persuaded the people and instigated them to ask for Barabbas and do away with

Jesus. Then the governor answered and said to them: Which of these two do you want me to set free? Then the entire horde shouted out and said: Away with this One and free Barabbas to us. Then Pilate once more called out to them, and, wanting to let Jesus go free, he said: What then shall I do with Jesus, of whom it is said that He is the Christ? Once more they cried: Crucify Him! Crucify Him! He spoke to them yet a third time: What evil has He done? I find no cause for death in Him, therefore I will chastise Him and release Him. But they screamed out all the more and said: Crucify Him! And they laid into him with loud shouting and demanded that He be crucified. And their shouts and those of the high priests gained the upper hand.

In Psalm 118 David prophesies about the Lord Christ: **The Stone which the builders rejected has become the Cornerstone. The Lord made this happen, and it is a miracle to our eyes.** That this prophecy solely and alone points to Christ, He Himself teaches, Mat. 21, as does St. Peter, Acts 4. This very same Christ, our Savior, is called a Stone because He is the sole, solid Foundation of our salvation. He has been made by His heavenly Father to be the Cornerstone of the spiritual House of His Church. However, this Stone was rejected by the builders. By the builders are meant the Pharisees, scribes, and high priests of Jerusalem, who were living at the time when Christ traveled about in the days of His flesh [earthly life], as Peter explains, Acts 4. For these very scribes and high priests were ordained by God to be spiritual builders, so that they should raise up other people as living stones into a spiritual house, as Peter writes (1 Peter 2). They were to build themselves and others on the foundation of the apostles and prophets, of which Jesus Christ is the Cornerstone, Eph. 2. However, they actually constructed evil, because they rejected the Foundation and Cornerstone, the Lord Christ. They did not acknowledge Him as the Messiah, and they would not direct others to Him. Instead, they were offended by Him; they maligned Him and condemned Him to death. Furthermore, they tore down the proper foundation, as David states in Psa. 11. How all this happened, how the high priests and scribes rejected Christ, the Cornerstone of salvation and eternal bliss, how they instead gave preference to the gruesome murderer, Barabbas, the evangelists have recorded in the text just read. In it we heard:

I. **How Pilate twice undertook to free Christ from the hands of the Jews. He proposed to them that he would chastise Christ and then free Him. But since they were silent [did not respond to the offer], he placed Him next to the murderer Barabbas, allowing the Jews the freedom to request, in keeping with their custom on the preceding Passover, one of the two go free.**

II. **How Pilate's wife let her husband be warned to be cautious about what he undertook to do with this innocent Man, the Lord Christ.**

III. **How the high priests and elders asked for Barabbas, and also stirred up the people to the extent that they unanimously demanded that Pilate release Barabbas to them, [and,] on the other hand, that he condemn Christ to death on the cross.**

Under the guidance of divine grace, we intend briefly to deal with these matters.

I. Pilate had sent the Lord Christ to Herod, fully hoping that by this means he would be rid of Him. For he saw and well knew that Christ was innocent of everything. But as his plan failed, and Herod sent Christ back to him again, he thought of another way. Accordingly, he called the high priests and leaders and all the people together and said to them: **You have brought** this Man to me as if He was trying to subvert the people; and see, I gave Him a hearing before you. And in every matter I found no cause to accuse Him [of any crime]. Neither did Herod; for I sent you to him, and behold, no one brought anything against Him worthy of death. Therefore, I will chastise Him and let Him go free.** In essence he told them: You indeed accused this Man of being a heretic and rebel and have demanded that He be sentenced to death. However, you have not been able in the least bit to prove any of your charges against Him. Just as I have, so has Herod given a hearing to your charges; but, with a white garment, he also testified to the innocence of this Man and sent Him back to me. Since He then is entirely (undoubtedly) innocent, I will let Him go. Nevertheless, since I have up to now perceived your special hatred and animosity against Him, in order to please you I will have Him chastised or whipped. Indeed, you won't be able get anything more out of me than that. For it was the Roman practice when someone had done something wrong, yet not worthy of death, they just let him be whipped.

So Pilate then thought to himself: Even though Christ will be whipped despite being innocent, I will nevertheless spare His life, and still rescue Him from the hands of the high priests. While the high priests and leaders were silenced for a while by this proposal by Pilate, and as they were considering which points they wanted to pursue further in their charges against Christ, the people meanwhile assembled themselves and went up to Pilate and asked him if he would release to them one of the prisoners because the Passover was at hand. The Jews had introduced the custom that at the Passover a prisoner was released—or was requested to be released. They would thus be reminded of the great deeds of God, who had freed them as poor captive slaves from the house of servitude and led them out of Egypt. God the Lord had not commanded them to do this, but they had introduced this custom out of their personal devotion, even though it would have been better if they had been satisfied with the remembrance of the Passover lamb, which God had specifically instituted for them to remind them of their rescue from Egypt. They should have been content with this remembrance, and by it let the evildoers to their just desserts. When the people reminded Pilate of this old custom and petitioned for the release of a prisoner, Pilate thought that a most appropriate means had been placed in his hand to free Jesus without having to whip (scourge) Him first. As a result, he placed the two before them, namely Christ and Barabbas, in the certain hope—since Barabbas was a common public murderer and rebel—that the Jews would surely ask for the release of the Lord Christ and would not wish the high priest's bloody intention against Him.

In this section we must first contemplate the public testimony to His innocence, which the Lord Christ received from Pilate and which occurs several times [during the proceedings], so that we indeed take careful note and grasp with our hearts that Christ did not endure such suffering on account of His sins; for even the Gentile judge also acknowledged His innocence and publicly testified of it. Thus, then, as Christ suffers innocently, we need immediately to conclude from this that He suffered on account of our sins, even as Isa. 53 teaches us to draw such a conclusion: **We regarded Him as One who was tormented and beaten by God and tortured; but He was wounded for the sake of our transgressions and was battered on account of our sin; the punishment was laid on Him so that we might have peace.** There is no other person on earth who in all things suffers innocently, because after the Fall into sin, inherited (original) sin is perpetually ingrained in human nature. Therefore also can no person earn something for himself or for someone else by his suffering. No one can redeem his brother nor reconcile someone to God, **for it costs too much to redeem one's soul, so that** [payment of the debt] **must be eternally deferred**, Psa. 49.

But, among all mankind, Christ alone suffers in total innocence. It is not only through the unity of Person as true God and Man, but rather also according to His assumed human nature, that He is completely holy, pure, and innocent. He can suffer for our sin—and His suffering can redound to our good—because it is the suffering of a completely innocent Person and of the Son of God. Since Christ is the holy One from His mother's womb, Luke 11, the most Holy One, Dan. 9, He is able to sanctify Himself for us, John 17 [:19].

Furthermore, from the fact that Pilate would allow the Lord Christ to be scourged in order to please the Jews—even though he knew and acknowledged that Christ was innocent in all matters—we are to learn that Christ's members also frequently experience such [treatment]. In this they are also to become like Christ, their Lord and Head, Rom. 8. Also, mighty potentates oftentimes know very well that true confessors of Christ experience injustice from the betrayers of the Church. Even so, they do not assist [the Christians] but allow it to continue to take place, so that the true disciples of Christ are tormented and betrayed, and they don't have to get involved in opposing the [perpetrators of this injustice]. Instead, they can rest undisturbed. However, that tends ultimately to produce the same result as happened to Pilate. He wanted to maintain the good will of the Jews, and so he allowed the innocent Christ to be whipped. He was thereby in the end actually brought to the point of condemning Christ to death on the cross. The same result still occurs with all those indifferent people who know very well that the true confessors of Christ are being treated unjustly, and nevertheless do not take up their cause. Ultimately, they will actually become betrayers of the Church and wicked Christians.

II. When Pilate had placed the murderer Barabbas beside Christ and now awaited a statement from the Jewish people regarding which of the two they would ask him to release, Pilate's wife sent a message to him: **Have nothing to do**

with this righteous Person; today I have suffered much in a dream on account of Him. To be sure, some would interpret that this dream was given to Pilate's wife by the Devil so that the redemption of the human race—which was accomplished through Christ's death—would be hindered. However, as St. Paul says of the crucifixion of Christ in 1 Cor. 2 [:8]: If the rulers of this world had recognized the hidden wisdom of God, they never would have crucified the Lord of Glory. So also say we: If the Devil had known the counsel of God concerning our salvation and the redemption of the human race by means of Christ's death, he would not have driven the Jews so intensely to clamor that Christ should be crucified. Therefore we stick with [the explanation] that God the Lord gave this dream to Pilate's wife in order thereby to manifest Christ's innocence. We have similar examples [of God's use of dreams] in other places in Scripture: In Gen. 20 God the Lord comes to King Abimilech at night in a dream and warns him to give Abraham back his wife. In Gen. 31 God once more comes to Laban the Syrian [Aramean] in a dream at night and says to him: **Be careful that you do not speak with Jacob in any other way than friendly.** In Dan. 2, Nebuchadnezzar sees the four monarchies or chief kingdoms of this world in a dream. Thus it is not implausible that this wife of Pilate had previously heard much about the miracles of Christ, had deeply thought about them, and thus such a dream later came to her through the marvelous providence of God.

In addition, we here see how the Lord Christ was given testimonies of His innocence from all kinds of people, and also how God had sufficiently warned Pilate about future disaster—as sensible wives are often able to impart good advice to their husbands. There are other lessons we here need to take note of considering how to regard dreams, even though Sirach, chap. 34, rightly states: **Anyone who puts stock in dreams is grasping for a shadow and will snatch the wind; dreams are nothing more than images without substance** (which is to be applied to vain, useless dreams). Nevertheless, not all dreams are therefore to be despised. For to begin with, there are such dreams which God the Lord reveals to men either by Himself, without means, or through the holy angels—as these are related in holy Scripture in Gen. 20, 28, 31, 41; Num. 12; Mat. 1, 2; etc. Since God the Lord then at various times spoke with the prophets and revealed Himself in such dreams, Num. 12, such dreams are not to be disregarded. Also, God still today at times sends such dreams to men, wherein He instructs them about future matters. (There then are many examples of such dreams in the history of the Church.) When the Arian persecution was going on, Antonius saw in a dream that jackasses and mules were uprooting the Church. When the apostate Julianus was about (destined) to die, the pious Bishop Didymus Alexandrius saw this in a dream. In a dream, Alexander the Great saw the high priest Jaddum, who urged him to advance into Asia. The dream which Pilate's wife had was also such a divine dream.

In addition, there are those dreams which come from the Devil, of which we are reminded in Deu. 13, Jer. 29, Zec. 9*. For just as in other matters the Devil is constantly trying to "ape"(mimic) God, so also with dreams. He gives dreams to false prophets, so that they rely on them and turn away from divine truth. He also frequently give men shameful dreams, disturbs them with oppressive dreams, and frightens and plagues them with dreams—as is attested to by experience. In opposition to this, we should then know that no new doctrine should or can be revealed from dreams which is not already revealed in God's Word. Thus, in such cases we should set more store on God's Word than on dreams. So that we are also protected from shameful and disturbing dreams, we should with eager and zealous prayer commend the evening to God, lead a chaste and decent life, and avoid all impure thoughts. Finally, there are the kind of

---

* I.e., Zec. 10:2—a rare memory lapse by Gerhard.

dreams which arise from natural causes, that is, various dreams which occur according to each person's temperament and which are dealt with by the physician. If we then go about with holy thoughts, lead a temperate life, and pray diligently, then we will most certainly have gentle and spiritual dreams. However, since we more often attach our hearts to temporal things, go around most of the time with worldly thoughts, and frequently burden the heart with eating and guzzling, with worries about sustenance and other worldly matters, we therefore also have restless, useless, and often times shameful dreams. Pro. 3: **Whoever finds wisdom, slumbers sweetly slumbers.** Sirach 31: **If the stomach is treated moderately, one will sleep softly.** Psa. 4: **I lie down and sleep in total peace, for the Lord sustains me.**

III. When the people heard how Pilate's wife had sent for her lord [husband], they thought that they should plead for Christ's freedom so that He might be released; but, when the high priests and elders noticed this, they stirred up the people and persuaded them to ask for Barabbas and do away with Christ. They undoubtedly pursued the same argument which they had used in John 11. If they would ask for Christ's release, then the Romans would come and take away their land and their people. With such a perspective and threat by the high priests, the people let themselves be persuaded. That's why when the governor, Pilate, asked: **Which of these two do you want me to release to you?** they all shouted in unison: **Away with Him and release to us Barabbas.** They became so hostile to Christ that they no longer were willing to say His name, and requested that Barabbas be released to them. Pilate shouted out once more, wanting to release Christ, and said: **What should I do with Jesus, Who is called the Christ?** They shouted in unison: **Crucify Him! Crucify Him!** Pilate spoke for the third time: **What kind of evil has He done? I find no cause for death in Him. Therefore I will chastise Him and release Him.** The Jews, however, repeated their previous cries and dinned it into Pilate's ears so that he would thus be drowned out by their shouting.

At the proper place, instruction will follow regarding what a mystery is presented to us in that Barabbas was asked to be freed, whereas Christ was crucified, and also that we should take heed that we do not free Barabbas and crucify Christ. At this time, though, we must take note of:

1. The example of the fickleness (inconstancy) of people. When Christ performed miracles and fed many with very few provisions, they all ran up to Him and wanted to make Him a king. Indeed, it had been no more than five days since they, with great rejoicing, had received Him as He made His entry into Jerusalem. But now, not only did they fall away from Him, but they shouted that He should be crucified. In the contrast of these two contradictory actions, the great fickleness in regard to honor among mankind is exposed. As Christ entered into Jerusalem, they shouted to Him: **Hosanna! Blessed is He who comes in the Name of the Lord**; but now they shout: **Crucify, crucify Him!** There they shouted: **Blessed is the King of Israel**, John 11; here it is much different: **We have no king other than Caesar.** There they carried olive and palm branches before Him; here they see to it that He is crowned with thorns. There they spread their own garments before Him; here they demand that Christ be stripped of His garments and that He be crucified. There they cheered with Christ's apostles and ran with joy around the Lord Christ; here they placed Christ between two murderers and with violence led Him out of the town. Is it not a wonder that in such a short time their hearts changed so dramatically and that, with such wrathful outcry, they strike Him whom they had previously received with such joy? Therefore, no one should rely on human favor and honor. Nothing is more fickle than it. Just as the ocean can rapidly become violent, even though it had previously been beautiful and clear, so it also happens with the children of men. All of a sudden their favor and honor are gone.

From this it is to be seen how utterly foolish are those who, for the sake of honor before men, deny divine truth or refuse publicly to confess it. Some of the authorities among the Jews were the kind of people about whom it is written in John 12: Many of them believed on Christ, but on account of the Pharisees would not confess it, since they rather would have honor before men than honor with God. But Christ testifies that such faith is merely a dead, worthless faith, John 5: **How can you, who receive your honor from each other, believe, and yet not seek the honor which is from God alone?***

2. That Christ here allows this hue and cry to be directed at Him, suffering it for our sakes, because in His own Person He was completely guiltless. All of us have deserved, on account of our sin, to come to that place of the eternal hue and cry, wailing, and gnashing of teeth, Mat. 13. We deserve to wail eternally with anguished hearts: **You mountains fall on us, and you hills cover us**, Rev. 6. [Instead] Christ here stands in our place [and] allows the clamor of the people to be directed at Him so that He might rescue us from the eternal wailing and screaming and bring us to the place where there is no longer any suffering or crying, Rev. 21. Rather, there a person will sing a new song before the throne of the Lamb, Rev. 14, and praise God the Lord forever with a joyful, lovely voice. God help us, through Christ, to join this [heavenly] host. Amen.

---

* It is appropriate to note here that Gerhard's point about the fickleness of the people may be somewhat overstated. Paul Maier has observed, for example, that because the betrayal and trial of Christ took place largely at night, many of those who welcomed Christ into Jerusalem on Palm Sunday could very well have been at home asleep and that Christ's accusers were likely to have been sympathizers and dupes of the scribes and Pharisees, and not representative of the population at large. Nevertheless, some of the same people may well have been present at both occasions. Ed.

O Lord Jesus Christ, let Your holy, innocent suffering be a medicine [cure] for my great debt of sin; may Your holy patience, whereby You bore the violent screams of the Jews, become for me a help and a comfort when my conscience screams against and over me. Protect me, my Lord and God, that I indeed never come to the place were there is eternal screaming and wailing; instead, take me to You in Your Kingdom so that I may eternally praise You with a joyful voice. Amen.

———————

The Fifth Sermon

How Christ was scourged by Pilate, clothed with purple by the soldiers, crowned with thorns, and mocked.

Then Pilate took Jesus and had Him whipped. The governor's soldiers called together the entire troop and undressed Him. They laid on Him a purple mantle and braided a thorn crown and set it upon His head; they gave Him a reed into His right hand, bowed the knee before Him, and mocked Him. Then they began to greet Him, saying: Greetings to You, King of the Jews. And they slapped Him in the face and spit on Him; and they took the reed and hit Him on His head with it; and they fell to their knees and petitioned Him.

In Exo. 12 God the Lord commands that the little Passover (Paschal) lamb should be slaughtered in such a way that the blood flow freely from it. For the Hebrew text uses the word *Schachath**, which actually means "to slaughter [in such way] that from the stretched out and extended body the blood would flow forth abundantly." Since Christ is the true Passover Lamb, to whom this passage points, 1 Cor. 15, He thus did not want to let Himself simply be killed, but rather to suffer death in such a manner so that with all His members stretched out He would freely (copiously) pour out His blood. Indeed, He wanted to pour out His blood abundantly not only on the Mount of Olives and on the timber-trunk of the cross, but also in the judgment hall of Pilate. Here He was gruesomely scourged, mutilated

---

* German for the Hebrew letters *shin* (with a *qamats*), cheth (with a *patah*), teth.

with thorns on His head, and also was despised, spit upon, and mocked, so that He indeed might suffer sufficiently and pour out His blood with ample abundance for our sake. This scourging of Christ, as well as the shame (humiliation) which was laid on Him in the judgment hall, is described to us in the text just read. With the granting of divine help, we intend now briefly to consider these matters.

Since Pilate had, on the basis of much evidence, perceived Christ's innocence, he also in various ways endeavored to release Him. He gave the Jews the authority that, if Jesus had sinned against their Law, they would be permitted to deal with Him at their own risk. But they would not accept his offer. He had sent Jesus to Herod, but he also did not want to condemn Him to death. He had placed Him next to Barabbas, the murderer, and gave the Jews the right to choose one of them to be released on their Passover. But they asked for Barabbas. Since, now, Pilate found it difficult to condemn an innocent man to death against his conscience, yet at the same time saw that the tumult among the Jews was ever increasing, there occurred to him yet one more means by which he might keep the Lord Christ alive; namely, he would recommend that He be whipped, and as He would be pitiably disfigured by the scourging, the hatred of the Jews would thereby most assuredly be assuaged and they would indeed demand no further [punishment for Jesus]. He thought that even though the Lord Christ would innocently suffer, that still would be better than if He were actually sentenced to die. If, then, the intention of this scourging was that the Lord Christ's body should be so severely disfigured that the Jews would then ask that He be set free out of sympathy, then it is proper to conclude how horribly and unmercifully Christ must have actually been scourged.

In Deu. 23 God gave the Jews a law which stated that if someone was to be scourged because of an offense which was not actually worthy of death, then such a person was not to be whipped with more than forty stripes or lashes. However, with the Romans this mitigation was not taken into consideration. Instead, they took the person they were going to scourge and tied him to a column (post). They stripped him of his clothes and, with whips made of braided cords, dealt with him horribly. According to such a Roman practice was the Lord Christ scourged. From this [description] then is once more to be seen what kind of scourging this was. We can understand it even better if we meditate on who it was that scourged Him. The text states that Pilate did it—not that he personally administered it, but rather that he commanded his soldiers to do it, who then, inasmuch as they frequently performed this business, called together the entire troop. This troop was not perhaps composed of ten or twenty men. Rather, it consisted of a host of godless scoundrels, all of whom began to whip the Lord Christ so that His entire body became streaked with stripes, wounds, and welts. Also, since they had heard that Christ called Himself a king, they thought that they should attend to this poor king in such a way that He never again would call Himself a king. Thus, they wove a crown out of the huge, spiny thorns which grew in this hot land, and they pressed it into His head so that the blood flowed down copiously. Furthermore, since they saw lying in the judgment hall an old purple mantle, which may previously have been worn by a Roman prince, they put it on Him and pressed it onto His fresh, bloody wounds. They also gave Him a reed into His hand. With it they mocked His poor, weak kingdom and scepter. In disdain and mockery they fell down before Him, saying: **God be hailed, beloved King of the Jews.** If You still have the desire to be a great king, how does the kingly crown suit You? And out of wrath and impatience over the fact that He let Himself be called a king, they struck Him in the face with their fists and with the reed. They spit in His face, and, to sum up, did whatever they could think of outwardly to mock and plague the Lord Christ.

Here we now see how richly fulfilled are the words of the prophet Isaiah, chapter 50, about the Lord Christ: I held up [exposed] **My back to those who beat Me, My cheeks to those who pulled on Me** [My beard]. **I did not hide My face from their shame and spit. I presented My face there like a flint stone.** But why did all this have to happen? In Isa. 53: **He was wounded for the sake of our transgression and was beaten on account of our sin; the punishment was laid on Him, so that we might have peace; and through His wounds we are healed.** That's why St. Bernhard says: "He was whipped for you, so that He could free you from the whipping of eternal wrath; He was crowned with thorns for you, so that He could crown you in heaven; He was wounded for you, so that He could heal you." For we must well take note of the fact that Christ said to Pilate: **You would have no authority over Me, if it had not been given to you from above.** That's why we must view this in no other way than that God Himself had the whip in His hand and so pitiably whipped His own Son—not as if He deserved it or as if God was at enmity with His Person, but because [Christ] took upon Himself all sin. In Luke 12 Christ says: **A servant who knows the will of his Lord, but makes no preparation to act according to His will, such a one must suffer many stripes.** Adam was such a disobedient servant. He knew God's will, and at the same time he refrained from doing it. Therefore, he should have eternally suffered many stripes—and we along with him, because we inherited such guilt and indeed are likewise often disobedient servants. In Isa. 1 we are described in this way: from the soles of our feet to the top of our heads there is nothing healthy about us. Rather, [we are covered with] wounds, stripes and boils which are not treated or bandaged, nor soothed with oil. In order, then, that such pathetic soul-wounds of ours might be healed, behold how Christ endured such stripes and wounds. In Rom. 7 St. Paul testifies of himself and of all the re-born that nothing good resides within our flesh and that evil lusts break out through every member and strive against the Law of God. Thus, we did not just deserve a gentle spanking with a switch, but a severe scourging. So that we, then, might be rescued from such, Christ here is pitiably scourged on every member of His body. In Psa. 2 and Acts 19 it is recorded that God will rule the disobedient with a rod of iron. So that such a rod might be lifted from us, Christ was willing to let His body be scourged. As we trust in Him in true faith, He is willing to receive us as His people. In Lam. 3 Jeremiah says: **I am a wretched man who must see [experience] the rod of His wrath.** Such a rod of divine wrath and rage would have swept over us and plagued us into all eternity had not Christ suffered this scourging. If our hearts were not so completely cold, we would contemplate the trouble we made for our Lord with our sins and how each of us individually helped to braid this whip and scourge Christ. And since Christ took upon Himself a severe whipping (the harshest punishment for our sins) we would also [if we were not so cold-hearted] patiently accept the chastisements with which God at times afflicts us, Heb. 12. But, since God punished His own dear Son in this manner for sins [not His own] which He has taken upon Himself, those upon whom the scourging of Christ is lost [who do not appreciate its meaning] and those who also by their deliberate sins continually inflict new scourgings on Christ should see in this mirror how God the Lord will someday harshly visit upon the unrepentant sinners [the just deserts of] their own sins.

2. What have we now to contemplate concerning this purple mantle with which the Lord was cloaked? That is indeed beautifully portrayed for us in Rev. 19, where John sees that the Son of God is clad with a garment which was sprinkled with blood. For this purple mantle was dyed on the exterior with the blood of a little worm from which the purple color was generally made; and on the inside, it was colored with the deep red blood of Christ; and thus, this mantel was red on the outside and the inside. And what has Christ won for us with [His blood]? That immediately becomes apparent in the text cited, for here John sees that this One who was clad in red, bloody garments, is followed by the heavenly host upon white horses, clad with white and clean silk; that is, with the garments of innocence and purity. For with this red, bloody robe the Lord Christ purchased for His Church the white cloak of salvation and the pure robe of righteousness, Isa. 61.

Previously Herod let the Lord Christ be clad in a white garment, thereby to indicate His innocence. Now the soldiers dress Him in a purple garment, therewith to announce that for our sin He trod in the winepress of God's wrath and that therefore His garment was red, Isa. 63. Thus, we now see that this our heavenly Bridegroom is white and red, Song of Solomon 5*. He wears the white garment on behalf of His own Person, according to which He is holy and innocent. He wears the red, bloody garment for our sake, because He shed His blood for our benefit. He wears the white garment on account of His eternal Priesthood, the purple garment on account of His Kingdom; and herewith also He has made us into kings and priests before His Father, Rev. 1. When Zipora, the wife of Moses, had to circumcise her child, she said to Moses: **You are a blood bridegroom for me**, Exo. 4. That is to say, it cost blood for you to be my husband because I had to circumcise the child; but Christ would rather say to us that we are a true bride of blood to Him, since it cost so much blood for Him to win us as His spiritual Bride. Not only did He shed tears; rather, out of every member of His body the blood flowed freely because He wanted to wash His spiritual Body, the Church, clean of sin.

In Psa. 22 Christ speaks of the time of His suffering, in which He was a worm. In the holy language [the original Hebrew] the word actually refers to the kind of worm which,

---

* Possibly v.1 "... my wine and my milk" or vv. 10-16. Tr.

when squashed with the feet, squirts out blood in all directions—blood from which purple dye is made. Even as Christ was thus smashed to pieces before's God's judgment and was crushed like a poor little worm, behold, He has also allowed Himself to be clad with a mantle dyed with the blood of such a worm, whereby He then redeemed us. Although our sins are blood-red, Isa. 1—the color of deep red roses (here the very same [Hebrew] word is used [regarding the worm])—they still shall become like wool. When the Scriptures want to describe our sins correctly, they call them blood-debts, Psa. 51, which thus also stain our righteousness, so that it is a soiled rag, Isa. 64.* And in Eze. 16 we are, on account of our sin, likened to a newborn child which still lies in its blood and has not yet been cleaned up. So that we might be washed clean of our blood-red sins, Christ thus dyed this purple mantle with His blood so that He could earn for us the beautiful white garment of righteousness. For in this blood we can wash our garments and make them bright, so that hereafter we can be clothed with white garments, as it is recorded in Rev. 7, where John sees many who have put on white garments. About these he is informed that they are those who come out of great tribulation and have washed their garments and have made them clean in the blood of the Lamb. That is why they are before the throne of God and serve Him day and night. In Num. 4 God had commanded that if the children of Israel wanted to break camp and take along the sanctuary, they had to spread a purple covering over the golden altar. Christ is the true golden Altar, to whom alone all our prayers and other spiritual offerings to God must be presented if they are to please God. Here [Christ] also is covered with a purple mantle for the benefit of all.

---

* The reader is reminded that Isaiah uses a word which means "menstrual cloth or rag." Tr.

3. Of what does Christ's crown of thorns remind us? When Adam sinned along with Eve, he had to hear in Gen. 3: **Cursed be the land on account of you; it will bear/yield thorn and thistle.** Because Christ was atoning for the fall of Adam in His suffering, He allowed a crown of thorns to be placed upon Him. In Judges 8 it is recorded that Gideon wanted to thrash the elders of Succoth with thorns from the desert and with briar hedges, because in their unmercifulness they did not want to give any bread to his weary warriors so they could pursue their enemies. We too, with our unmercifulness, often deserve such thorns and briar hedges. Christ here allows His head be ripped by thorns to save (redeem) us from such punishment. In Isa. 5 God the Lord laments that He had done everything possible that He could do for His vineyard; but it produced "late grapes," while it should have produced [mature] grapes.* Therefore, He wanted to remove the fence from the hill [vineyard] and let it go to waste, so that only thorn and thistle would grow in it; and He would command the clouds not to rain upon it. God the Lord gave our first parents everything that was necessary for complete righteousness and glory. Along with their descendants, they were to be a spiritual vineyard, a spiritual Church of God, and were to bring forth lovely fruits of righteousness. However, since they turned away from God and brought forth the evil fruits of disobedience, behold, God rightly removed from them (and us all) the fence of angelic protection and let us lie in a wasteland. Thus, we would have been able to produce nothing else but the thorns and thistles of disobedience and evil deeds, on account of which we would also have had to be cast into the furnace of hellish fire. However, Christ had mercy on us and

---

* Gerhard here uses the ancient word *Herlinge* (late grapes). In his day, my father-in-law used to cultivate a vineyard on his farm in West Texas; my wife informs me that "late grapes" were immature, would never ripen or attain full size, tasted bitter, and would usually shrivel on the vine. Tr.

allowed Himself to be pierced and ripped with thorns so that through such blood the very same vineyard would again become fruitful.

In Pro. 15 it is written: **The way of the fool is prickly and thorny.** When Christ was crowned with thorns, He found how painfully our foolishness affected Him, Heb. 6. The earth, which yields thorn and thistle, is unfit and near [infected by] the curse, and they are ultimately burned up.* By nature, we are all such unfruitful thorns, from which one never again could gather lovely grapes and good fruit; for on account of sin, the curse devolved upon us, and we all belonged in the fire of hell—even as chopped down thorns are ignited with fire, Isa. 33. Christ, however, rescued us from this [fate] in that He here allowed Himself to be crowned with thorns and thereby won for us the crown of righteousness, 2 Tim. 4. For the sake of His innocence and according to His Person, He was crowned with honor and glory, Psa. 8; and He rightfully could have worn a golden crown, Rev. 14. However, for our sake He here let Himself be crowned with thorns so that God would crown us with grace and mercy, Psa. 103, and with the imperishable crown of glory in eternal life, 1 Pet. 5, James 1. Also fulfilled with this crown of thorns is the type in Gen. 22, where Abraham saw a ram ensnared in the thorns, which he sacrificed at the command of God. Thus, when Christ wanted to offer up our sins in His body upon the tree, 1 Pet. 2, He first allowed the brier to be fastened when the crown of thorns was placed on Him.† Just as at times the thorns of riches, greed, and the cares of this world crush the seed of the divine Word to the extent that it does not always fully produce the fruits that it should, behold, Christ therefore wanted to endure these thorns, so that we might not be punished eternally. In sum, "Christ's thorns heal all of the piercing wounds of our hearts."

---

* We are reminded by St. Peter, "... burn with fervent heat" (2 Pet. 3).
† Thus He was sacrificed in place of us "Isaacs."

4. Also Christ here endured being struck in the face with fists and with the reed, which the soldiers had first placed in His hand to despise and mock Him, so that we would not have to endure the beatings of Satan's angels in eternity, 2 Cor. 12. He was beaten with the reed which had been put in His hand in place of a scepter, thus showing that He suffered for the sake of His kingdom and took all this upon Himself so that He might assemble for Himself a kingdom in this world. Therefore, it is written in Zechariah 13: **But if then a man will say to Him: What kind of wounds are these in Your hands? He will answer: That's how I was beaten in the house of those who love Me.** Had Christ not endured these beatings, He could not have assembled a spiritual gathering of those who love Him. We should, however, take care not to join these soldiers in hitting Christ in the face with His scepter. The scepter with which Christ rules His Church is His divine Word. Those who then malign or slander His holy Word, in a deliberate manner falsify it, and interpret it contrary to Christ's meaning, such people are doing none other than striking Christ in the face with His scepter. Lord God, preserve us from this. Amen.

O Lord Jesus Christ, may Your scourgings and stripes be a healing medication for my soul; may Your holy blood wash me from all my sins; may Your crown of thorns cut my heart so that with a penitent heart I fruitfully contemplate Your holy suffering. Amen.

The Sixth Sermon

How the high priests and the leaders of the Jews unrelentingly demanded that Pilate condemn Christ to death on the cross.

Then Pilate once more came out of the judgment hall and spoke to the Jews: See, I am bringing Him out to you so that you may know that I find no guilt (fault) in Him. Thus, Christ came out wearing a crown of thorns and a purple cloak. And Pilate said to them: Behold, what a Man! When the high priests and servants saw Him, they shrieked and said: Crucify! Crucify Him! Pilate said to them: You take Him away and crucify Him, for I find no guilt in Him. The Jews answered him: We have a law, and according to that law, He must die, for He has portrayed Himself as God's Son.

When Pilate heard that word, he was even more afraid. And he again went into the judgment hall and spoke to Jesus: From whence do You come? But Jesus gave him no answer. Then Pilate said to Him: Do You not speak to me? Don't You know that I have the power to crucify You and that I have the authority to let You go free? Jesus answered: You would have no authority over Me if it had not been given to you from above. Therefore, those who have delivered Me up to you have the greater sin. From then on Pilate concentrated on how he could let Jesus go free. The Jews, however, cried out and said: If you let this One loose, then you are no friend of Caesar; for anyone who makes Himself out to be a king is against Caesar.

When Christ in Psalm 22 pitiably complains about His enemies and persecutors—the high priests, scribes, Pharisees, and elders—He says, among other things: **Huge young bulls have surrounded Me, and fat oxen have encircled Me; their yawning jaws spread open against Me like a roaring and rapacious lion.** And soon thereafter: **Dogs have surrounded Me, and the wicked rabble have accosted Me.** In these words Christ compares His persecutors to three kinds of vicious animals—first, to big young bulls and fat oxen, since they gobbled up the people in order to nourish themselves, Psa. 53, and devoured widow's houses and feigned long prayers, Mat. 23. Next, He compares them to a roaring and rapacious lion, because they roared against Him and lurked in secret ambush to kill Him, as a lion lurks in a cave, Psa. 10. Finally, He compares them to biting dogs, because not only did they unashamedly yelp at Him with their lies, but they also pounced on Him like hunting dogs of the very Devil, which he leads on his leash. They attacked Him from one place to another, and finally they killed Him. How the religious authorities of Jerusalem accomplished this we can observe from this text, as we now hear:

First of all, how the high priests, scribes, and elders showed themselves to be like fat, enraged oxen [bulls], inasmuch as when the bloody Lord Christ was led out to them, they shrieked: Crucify! Crucify Him!—not unlike the way that oxen [bulls] become enraged when they see blood.

Secondly, they show themselves to be like roaring and raging lions, in that they roar: We have a Law according to which He should die, for He has made Himself out to be God's Son.

Thirdly, they show themselves to be like rabid dogs, in that they would not cease pursuing this Hind, which is hunted in the early morning, ([that is,] the Lord Christ) until they had felled Him. Because they could not achieve this any other way, they finally threatened Pilate with Caesar's disfavor.

With the gift of divine help, we want to deal briefly with these three topics.

I. Pilate had allowed Christ to be dealt with pitiably by the executioner's lackeys and the soldiers. He let them scourge Him horribly. He also allowed Christ—with disdain and mockery—to be cloaked with a purple mantle, crowned with thorns, slapped in the face, spit on and despised. [This Pilate did] for the sole purpose of assuaging the Jews' terrible hatred of Christ. He knew very well that Christ was not guilty of anything. Nevertheless, He permitted Christ to be dealt with so miserably in the hope that hereafter the Jews would desist from their charges and hatred. Therefore he led Jesus out to them and said: **Behold, I bring Him out to you so that you may know that I find no guilt in Him.** On account of your blatant charge, contrary to all that is right and just, I allowed this poor man to be scourged so that you might be satisfied and then release Him, since I can find in Him no criminal offense or guilt that is worthy of death. When he had also cloaked the Lord Jesus with a purple mantle and crowned Him with a crown of thorns, he led Him out to the Jews and said to them: **Behold, what a Man.** This poor Man has obviously been so pitiably dealt with so that He is no longer looks like a man. Are you still not satisfied with that? However, the high priests and scribes together yelled: **Crucify! Crucify Him!** With the presentation of the bleeding and pitiably disfigured Christ, Pilate wanted to move them to pity, but they became all the more furious and zealous. They expressly desired that Christ should and must be crucified.

Beside the fact that we should take note of the testimony of innocence which the Lord Christ is here again given by Pilate, we should mark especially these words which Pilate, in view of the bleeding Christ, speaks to the Jews: **Behold, what a man!** For from these words it is easy to conclude what kind of horrible scourging this must have been, which Christ had endured and by which he had been disfigured, that it also moved a heathen heart to mercy. Without doubt, the blood from the crown of thorns must have flowed down over the purple mantle, because they beat those huge, pointed thorns down on the head of the Lord Christ with force so that the bloody streams stuck to the purple mantle, which was soaked with blood outside and inside—a most wretched and pitiful spectacle. We should set this sad picture of Christ before the eyes of our heart whenever the great anguish of conscience over sin would overwhelm us; for through these wounds we are healed. Whenever the Devil says to us in our vexation over our sin: Look, man, you have sinned so much and so severely that you have painted yourself as a detestable portrait before God's eyes—at that moment we should answer him: See, there in Pilate's judgment hall stands another Person. He took my place. He took upon Himself the punishment of my sin. He was disfigured by the scourging and streaming of blood for my sake, so that He would be seen as a squashed, bloody worm and no longer be recognized as a Man, Psa. 22. When the first Adam stumbled into that sad Fall into sin and had made himself (along with all his descendants) into a shameful Devil's larva (grub), God the Lord then spoke out of righteous, zealous wrath and said: "See, Adam has become like one of Us." [That is], see, is this not an Adam—is this not a man—who wants to be like God, and has thereby become a horrible likeness of the Devil? In order then for this sin of the first man to be atoned for, the Lord (the second Adam) allowed Himself to be thus mutilated in Pilate's judgment hall, to the extent that the Gentile judge said out of pity: See, is not this a Man? Is He not so pitiably disfigured that a person looks at Him with sheer loathing? Here was fulfilled what is said of Christ in Isa. 53: **He had neither form nor beauty. We saw Him,** but there was no form which could have pleased us. He was completely despised and worthless, full of pain and sickness. He was despised so much that one hid his face before Him. Therefore, we took no note of Him.

Furthermore, the fact that the Jews thereupon urged that Christ be crucified—not allowing themselves to be dissuaded by the fact that He was so pitiably scourged in Pilate's judgment hall—should not be viewed by us as being caused solely by their terrible, insatiable hatred. Rather, underlying all this we should consider the counsel and hand of God; for the holy apostles expressly proclaim in Acts 4 **that in this matter the Jews did what God's hand and counsel had previously intended to happen.** Thus, we should view this account in this way: Pilate himself recognized that it was far too severe a punishment for Christ as an innocent, righteous Person to be so pitiably scourged. But God the Lord answered: It is still not enough. This Christ still has to go to the cross. He has to become a curse for the sin of mankind. As St. Paul also very reassuringly writes in Gal. 3: **Christ has rescued (redeemed) us from the curse of the Law in that He became a curse for us. For it is written** (Lev. 18): **Cursed is every person who hangs on the tree.**

II. As the Jews then vehemently and horribly shrieked against Christ: **Crucify! Crucify Him!** Pilate answered: **You take Him away and crucify Him, for I find no fault in Him.** He meant to say: If you think that you can justify in your conscience the crucifixion of an innocent Man, then you go ahead and do it at your own peril. I cannot and will not accede to you in this matter. The Jews again did not allow themselves to be deterred. Rather, they replied this way: **We have a Law, according to which He should die, for He has made Himself out to be God's Son.** With their accusations, taken from secular law, they had up to now been unable to proceed against Christ. Therefore, they seize upon the Law of Moses. For since the Roman Caesar had promised them that he would protect them in their religion and law—also, that he would properly punish those who were against him in this regard—they pressured Pilate to sentence Christ to death as a transgressor of divine Law. They held up to him this chief part of divine Law from Lev. 24: **He who blasphemes the Lord's Name shall be put to death.** Deu. 13: **The prophet who teaches you to fall away from the Lord your God shall die.** Since, therefore, Christ had designated and confessed Himself to be God's Son, they thought He had thereby acted contrary to the Law of God; but they should have for once remembered that Christ not only confessed with words to be God's Son, but also demonstrated the same with deeds and with supernatural miracles. Then also, Moses and the prophets had a long time ago proclaimed that the Messiah would be true God, since they ascribed to Him divine works and an eternal kingdom.

    Here we should carefully note that Christ was accused and proceeded against not on the basis of human laws, but rather on the basis of God's Law. How then did that happen? As to His own Person, Christ is innocent. However, God places Him under the Law, Gal. 4; also, Christ, although innocent, allows Himself to be accused by God's Law, so that thereby we (who were under the Law) would be redeemed and freed from the Law's accusations. Our first parents were not satisfied with the honor and glory in which they were created. They wanted to be like God. They did not want to be subject to the obedience of the divine Law; instead, they wanted to be entirely free and without any law. We, too, have inherited this kind of incivility (rudeness); namely, entrenched in the innermost foundation of our hearts we have this very same haughty, pride-filled arrogance, so that we gladly and willingly would be free from obedience towards God and His Law. Indeed, we often transgress the Law of God. So that the Lord Christ then might atone for this our arrogance and disobedience, He, though innocent, allowed Himself to be accused by the Law of God as an evil-doer and a blasphemer of God, just as St. Paul writes to the Philippians (ch. 2): **Christ, even though He was in a divine form, did not regard being equal to God as booty** [to keep], **but emptied Himself, and took on the form of a servant (slave).** Indeed, He not only manifested His divine glory, but He also on that account even allowed Himself to be accused and condemned for confessing to be God's Son—whose Son He of course was, in deed and in truth.

Furthermore, we must also take note of how Christ, the Head of the Church, is treated here: that He is innocently accused as a blasphemer of God and a transgressor of the divine Law. [We should also note] that His members [the faithful] will experience the same. At times, they will be innocently accused as the most wanton evil-doers and sacrilegious transgressors of the divine Law, for we must be formed according to His image, Rom. 8. The scribes, high priests, and Pharisees themselves were the worst transgressors of the divine Law. As Christ often faults them, Mat. 15: **You transgress God's Law for the sake of your writings.** Mat. 23: **You omit the most difficult part of the Law, namely, righteousness, mercy and faith.** Nevertheless, they here accuse Christ, though innocent, as though He had deserved death through the transgression of the Law. So it still is: the worst hypocrites and seducers (deceivers) dare to accuse and condemn the confessors of divine truth as heretics at the first opportunity, and the beloved children of God as accursed people.

III. When Pilate heard that Christ confessed that He was God's Son, it made him worry so that he began to be afraid; he wondered whether also this Christ might indeed not be one of the children of the gods from heaven. For the heathen maintained that on occasion the gods from heaven came down to earth and allowed themselves to be seen in a human form. Such appears to be the response in Lystra, where, when [the people] saw that Paul and Barnabas healed a man who had been born lame, drew the following conclusion: **The gods have become like men, and have come down to us**, Acts 14. In like manner, Pilate thinks this Christ is most certainly one of these same gods; thus, he takes [Jesus] with him into the judgment hall and asks Him: **From whence do You come?** He's not asking about His fatherland, since he previously had heard that He was from Galilee. Rather, he asks Him if He also is one of those gods from heaven. But Christ remains silent since He had already told him enough about the attributes of His kingdom. Pilate wanted to appear disdainful to this silence by Christ; thus he began defiantly: **Aren't You speaking to me? Don't You know that I have the power to crucify You? And I have the power to set You free?** Christ answered with great wisdom and discretion: **You would have no power had it not been given to you from above; therefore, the one who delivered Me to you has the greater sin.** With these words, Christ looks not only to the will and counsel of His heavenly Father—from whom He had been given such suffering and death for the sake of mankind, Rom. 8—but herewith He also wants to remind Pilate of his office (duty), that he should remember by whom and to what end he had been placed in a position of authority; namely, that he had been given such power from God the Lord in order to employ it to protect the godly and to punish the rebellious. This very same Liege Lord over all authority will also someday require an accounting of how Pilate had used his power.

Christ adds yet more meaning with these words: **He who has accused Me before you has the greater sin**; thereby, in a hidden manner, giving Pilate something to think about. Even as the Jews, who wanted to force him into making an unjust sentence, sinned ever more grievously, Pilate in his own person could nonetheless not consent to their unjust desire without himself greatly sinning. These words stirred the heart of Pilate to such an extent that from then on he endeavored to find how he might free Christ and rescue Him from the hands of the Jews. But as the Jews noticed this disposition and intention in Pilate, they shrieked: **If you turn this One loose, then you are no friend of Caesar; for anyone who makes Himself out to be a King is against Caesar.** In essence, they were saying: This One sets Himself up as a King. If you turn Him loose, you will thereby demonstrate that you are not loyal to Caesar. And when we report this to Caesar, it will most assuredly be to your peril. This was the great *Kartaune** with which they struck at Pilate's heart, so that he would rather go against what was right, indeed, go against even his own conscience in order to acquiesce to the desires of the Jews and so as not to lose favor with Caesar.

Here we are to learn:

1. That everything that Caiaphas and the other high priests (as well as also Herod and Pilate) perpetrated against Christ, they did on the basis of an authority which proceeded from [a greater] authority which had been given to them from above. For in the same way that David speaks about Shimei in 2 Sam. 16: **Let him curse [me], for the Lord has bidden him to do so**, even so Christ here also says to Pilate: **You would have no power over Me had it not been given to you from above.** We should then not understand this to mean that God the Lord had inwardly incited Shimei and Pilate to do such deeds; rather, they would not have been able to carry out their mischief against Christ and David apart from God's foreordaining.

We must especially take note of this point, so that we do not see in this only how Christ was so unmercifully and unjustly dealt with by the Jews and Pilate. Rather, we are at all times to remember God's hand and counsel in all this. Neither the Jews nor Pilate would have been able to hurt even a single little hair of Christ had God not previously ordained that He was going

---

* Gerhard uses here an archaic German word for a large caliber cannon. Ed.

to allow all this to happen and be done to Christ. If we then have come this far in our contemplation of Christ's suffering, it will thus be easy to see that God must have had solemn and weighty reasons to permit His only and beloved Son to be given over as *Rappuse** and allow Him to be so pitifully disfigured by them. If we then further inquire about the lofty, vital reasons for which God the Lord allowed all this to take place, the Scriptures report that it all happened solely and simply for our sake—that our sins have thus been atoned for through Christ, and that by [His suffering and death], righteousness, life, and salvation were won for us by Him.

2. We also learn here that the power of [civil] authority is to be viewed and regarded as a power bestowed and entrusted to them from and by God. This power is to serve both the civil authorities and the subjects [citizens]. Indeed, the civil authorities, as feudal lords and underlings of the King of kings in heaven, are to use their power and might properly—as the Book of Wisdom [i.e., The Wisdom of Solomon, from the Apocrypha] admonishes in chapter 6:[3 ff.]: **The authority has been given to you from the Lord, and the power from the Most High, who will ask you how you have performed and will inquire about what you have ordered; for you are stewards of His kingdom.** Alas, O God, how often is this not forgotten! So often one takes the words right out of Pilate's mouth and says to the poor and innocent: Don't you know that I have the power to punish you, and the power to let you go free? But what does the Book of Wisdom [cf. note above] say to such sovereigns who defiantly use their power and misuse it against the innocent? In the place noted [chapter 6] they are warned with these hard words: **The Lord will pass horribly over you, and a very harsh judgment will befall those in high places; for the humble [person] will experience grace, but the powerful shall be mightily punished**, etc. This pas-

---

* Booty, an item of enemy plunder; cf. Jer. 15:13, 17:3, and Eze. 23:46. Tr.

sage also serves to teach subjects [citizens] that they are hereby admonished to render dutiful obedience to the authorities. For because their power has been given to them by God, we should fear and honor God through them. As St. Paul admonishes in Rom. 13: Since there is no authority which has not been ordained by God, one should therefore obey the authorities—not only for fear of punishment, but also for the sake of conscience. This teaching will be dealt with more extensively elsewhere. God give us an obedient heart through Christ. Amen.

O Lord Jesus Christ, You who for my sin were so pitifully disfigured that a heathen heart was also moved to compassion, grant that I may view You with the eyes of a repentant and believing heart. You who were innocently accused by the Law of God, pronounce me free from the legitimate accusation which the Law had against me, so that from now on nothing may be found in me which could condemn me. For I am in You, and You live and rule in me. Amen.

The Seventh Sermon

Pilate acknowledges Christ as the King of the Jews, and as he demonstrates His innocence by the washing of the hands, he condemns Him to death on the cross.

When Pilate heard that word, he led Christ out and set himself on the judgment throne at the place which is called the High Pavement—but Gabbatha in Hebrew. It was the Day of Preparation for the Passover around the sixth hour, and he said to the Jews: Look, this is your King. But they shrieked: Away, away with Him! Crucify Him! Pilate said to them: Shall I crucify your King? The high priests answered: We have no king other than Caesar. However, when Pilate saw that he was getting nowhere, but that the tumult was instead getting worse, he realized he had had enough with these people and decreed that their petition be granted. Taking water, he washed his hands in the people's presence and said: I am innocent of the blood of this righteous Person; you see to Him. Then all the people answered and said: His blood be upon us and upon our children. Then he freed Barabbas for them, who had been thrown into prison for sedition and murder, and for whom they had asked. But Jesus—scourged and mocked—he delivered over to them so that He might be crucified.

In Mat. 20 Christ proclaims to His disciples that He would be delivered up to the Gentiles and that He would not only be despised, mocked and scourged by them, but that He would also be condemned to die on the cross. And so it had also likewise been previously proclaimed in the Old Testament, as the Messiah laments in Psa. 22 that He would thus be stretched out on a cross so that one could count His bones, and that one would pierce His hands and feet with nails on the tree of the cross. A similar type is signified in Num. 21, where it is recorded that as the people of Israel were wounded in the desert by the stinging bites of fiery snakes, the Lord commanded Moses to make a brass serpent and raise it up as a symbol so that anyone who was bitten and looked at the raised up snake would remain alive. He applies this picture to Himself in John 3, where He says: **Just as Moses raised up the snake in the desert, so also the Son of Man has to be raised up** (that is, upon the tree of the cross) **so that all who believe in Him** (all who look to Him in faith and heartfelt trust) **will not be lost, but instead** will be healed and saved from the wounding bites of the hellish snake and from sin, **will have eternal life.**

Since we have up to this point in the Passion story heard how Christ was mocked in the judgment hall of Pilate, was crowned with thorns, and was beaten and scourged, so would we now further hear how He was condemned by Pilate to die on the cross. The evangelists report this in the words just read and show:

I. How Pilate for the last time led Christ out of the judgment hall.

II. How he earlier washed his hands and thereby once more witnessed to Christ's innocence, but then finally freed Barabbas and delivered Christ over to death on the cross.

I. As the high priests, the scribes, and elders noticed that upon their accusation Pilate would not immediately condemn Christ to death, they finally threatened him with the disfavor of the Roman Caesar. **If you let this One go free, they said, then you are no friend of Caesar; for anyone who sets Himself up as a King, such a Person is opposed to Caesar.** They thereby moved the heart of Pilate to think it would no longer be appropriate to defend Christ against their accusations, since it might lead to his being reported to Caesar as one who did not loyally serve him and who was defending a Person who had set Himself up to be a King. Accordingly, Pilate here placed in the pan [on one side] of the scale the disfavor of Caesar which he would experience, and [on the other side] the good will of the Jews for which he could hope. That became the deciding factor, so that in this whole matter he forgot about Christ's innocence and thought to himself: This poor Man will not be able to help me very much if He is set free. Nor will He be able to cause me any harm if He is innocently condemned to death. However, there is great peril in setting Him free. On that account, the Jews would likely bring down on me Caesar's harsh disfavor. Therefore, he decided to defend Christ no longer against these unjust accusations and thus had the throne of judgment carried out and set upon an elevated place, which was called Gabbatha, or High Pavement, so that he could be seen and heard by each and every one. And, he said to the Jews, **Look, this is your King**, as if to say: How are you able to bear such an insatiable hatred against this poor Man and accuse Him of having set Himself up in a rebellious manner as a king, since one obviously can see nothing about Him that is like a king? But Pilate got nowhere with this, for the Jews kept on with their vehement shouting: **Crucify Him! Away with Him!** Pilate mocked them even more and said: **Shall I then crucify your King?** For you have long been heard to say that you were waiting for a King and a Messiah who would once again win your freedom and deliver you from all foreign authority. But now that He is come you want to crucify Him. At this the Jews began to answer impatiently: **We have no King other than Caesar.** Herewith they cast aside their own true King, Christ; and in that they did not wish to be subject to any foreign rule, they forfeited for themselves all divine promises.

1. Here, then, we see how things usually go once one turns away from the path of righteousness: he strays ever farther from the path. Pilate first consented to act against his conscience to the extent that he allowed the innocent Christ to be scourged. Soon afterward he allowed himself to come to the point that, in order to please the Jews and stay in the good graces of Caesar, he was actually willing to deliver Christ over to death. Anyone who just once undertakes to act against right and justice out of hatred, partiality [i.e., to gain favor], fear, or some other affection (passion) may later very easily go further astray. It is the same as when a person once steps off from the right path; he steps ever further into the path of error, until he turns himself around and gives in to the right way. So also, if a person once allows himself to be moved to stray away from the path of righteousness, then he later errs even farther. So, too, it went with Pilate. He thought he might end up in great peril if he continued to defend Christ's innocence. Accordingly, he lowered the hand and held not the level scale.* So it still often happens that judges bend the right (the law) simply to avoid laying any disfavor upon themselves. Thus God also sees to it that it has been written in Pro. 10: **Whatever the godless** [person] **fears, that is what he will encounter.** If a man wants to neglect God's favor and grace in order to maintain human favor, he ultimately loses all of both. Pilate's example testifies to that: he did not warm himself very long by the fire of Caesar's favor. Rather, seven years later he was banished and expelled. Indeed, judges and authorities should zealously take note of this, so that they do not bend the straight scepter of justice. Instead they should remember that they are to uphold the judgments of the Lord. Thus, they also should have in them the just fear of the Lord, 2 Chr. 19. But where there is true fear of God, there one will fear God more than men, Acts 5. And where God is feared more

---

* That is, he did not uphold the even scale of justice. Ed.

than men, there the innocent will not be oppressed nor will the unrighteous be acquitted to maintain the favor of men.

2. At that time the Jews rejected Christ and subjected themselves to Caesar's power. Thus, up to the present time it justly befalls them that they live under a foreign authority (rule) and are deplorably (pitiably) oppressed; and in them is fulfilled what Psa. 59[:6] proclaims: **In the night they howl once more like dogs and run about the city.** God the Lord sent them Christ, who should be their King, to rule and lead them with the straight scepter of His Word. They should have received Him rightly and kissed Him so that He would not be angered, Psa. 2. But here they shriek that they want nothing to do with Him; and just as Christ says in His parable in Luke 19, they cry out: **We do not want this One to rule over us.** Thus God's wrath is now kindled against them, and what is written in Psa. 69 is fulfilled: **Pour Your displeasure upon them, and seize them with Your ferocious wrath. Their dwelling place must become a wasteland, and there is none who will live in their huts (dwellings).** And as St. Paul says in 1 The. 2: **God's wrath is already finally come over** [them] or: until the end **come upon them,** [i.e.,] **because they have killed the Lord Christ.** This has been stated as a warning for us, so that we indeed do not, in keeping with the example of these Jews, cast this King aside and push Him away from us. Ah!, now you say, Who would do a thing like that? Why, all of us Christians confess Christ as our heavenly King! Answer: That may be the case for many with words, but the heart is far removed. If Christ is a King, then one has to let himself be ruled by His Word. Those who no longer want to allow themselves to be reproved by the Spirit of God, Gen. 6—those whose hearts are not stirred and changed through God's Word—the same do not yet confess Christ as their King.

II. Now before Pilate would permit the final sentence to be pronounced, and condemn Christ to death, he had water brought to him while he was sitting on the throne of judgment, and he washed his hands in the presence of all the people and said: **I am innocent of the blood of this righteous One; you see to it.** In olden times this hand washing was a sign of innocence, Psa. 26: **I wash my hands in innocence.** In Deu. 21 it was decreed that if a slain person was found in the field, and the perpetrator was unknown, then the priests and elders from the nearest town should come forth and chop off the head of a young cow [heifer] and wash their hands over the cow and say: **Our hands did not shed this blood**, etc. That's how Pilate now also washed his hands, thus attesting that he intended to be innocent of this righteous blood. Thereupon, all of the people answered: **His blood come upon us and upon our children**; that is, if this blood is innocently shed, then God should punish us and our descendants with the same, [a request] which was at a later time amply carried out against the Jews.

It was thus a foolish plan that Pilate thought that by merely washing his hands—thereby announcing that he intended to remain innocent of Christ's blood—that he had done enough [finished] with the matter. For not only is an innocent person by no means to be condemned, but one should rather also protect such a person against wrong and injustice. But Pilate here forgot about his office and his duty. He freed Barabbas (who had been thrown into prison for sedition), but Jesus he gave over to them to be crucified. Nevertheless, Christ was once more given testimony of His innocence by Pilate in that the evangelists say that he delivered up Christ to be crucified because of the Jews; that is, Pilate had indeed acknowledged Him to be innocent on the basis of worldly justice. But since the Jews were so malicious, to the extent that they were willing to take it on their conscience to claim that as a transgressor of the divine Law [Jesus] rightly should be crucified, Pilate finally conceded at their own peril. All this took place on the Day of Preparation, that is, on the very day just prior to the great Sabbath of the Passover Feast, on which day the Jews used to prepare and get ready for that which pertained to the celebration of the Easter Feast—all by the sixth hour, which by us is the twelfth hour.

1. Here we need to take note that as Christ is condemned to death as a transgressor of the divine Law, He suffered this for our sake. Our first parents had transgressed God's Law, by which they and their descendants were subjugated under the immutable divine judgment, which reads thus: **The day you eat of this tree, you shall die the death.** In order to rescue us from such a punishment, Christ here allows Himself to be condemned to death as a transgressor of the divine Law. That is to say, as St. Paul states in Gal. 4: **that God's Son was placed under the Law so that He might redeem (rescue) those who were under the Law, so that we may receive the status of being children.** Pilate was unable to find a way to condemn Christ to death according to worldly justice. However, God's Law sentenced Him to death, not because of His sin, but because He had loaded upon Himself the sins of others. As a result, the Law has lost its demands upon us in regard to our sin, which means that now **there is no condemnation upon those who are in Christ Jesus**, Rom. 8. Relevant here also is that Barabbas, who was a murderer and seditionist, is set free; however, the innocent Christ is condemned to death. We, then, must view this as St. Peter explains in Acts 4: **that what Herod, Pontius Pilate, along with the Gentiles and the people of Israel, had assembled to do against the holy Son of God, Jesus, the Hand of God and His counsel had already pre-determined that it should so happen.** So, here now before God's judgment stands Barabbas, a murderer and a seditionist; on the other side stands the innocent Son of God, Jesus Christ. The former is going to be pronounced free; this One is going to be sentenced to death.

How did this happen? Pilate couldn't comprehend it; he was astonished by all this. **Shall I let Barabbas go free, he asked, and crucify your King?** However, we will be able to comprehend it if we remember that God had laid all our sin on Christ, Isa. 53, and for us made Him out a sinner, 2 Cor. 5. Barabbas means father and son; he is thus a picture of the first man. Adam, with all his descendants (the entire human race) is now a seditionist and murderer before God's judgment; that is, Adam not only placed himself in opposition to God his Lord, but by his transgression he also brought sin and death into the world. Thus he is the greatest murderer. So then, in order that this "Barabbas" might be set free, that is, so that the sin of Adam and his sons or descendants would be taken away, God lays all this sin on Christ, who is made into sin and condemned to death. For the Law finds lying upon Him the sin of the whole world. That is why it condemns him to death, but Adam and his descendants, as many among them who hold fast to this in true faith, are set free. And thus is fulfilled what is pre-figured in Lev. 16, where God commands that **the high priest should take two billy-goats and place them before the door of the hut [tent] and cast lots for the two goats, one lot for the Lord and other lot for the live billy-goat. And the billy-goat over which the Lord's lot falls he should sacrifice for a sin-offering; but the billy-goat over which the lot of exemption falls he should present alive to the Lord so that He appeases him and sends the exempted billy-goat into the wilderness.** This [type] is here fulfilled by Christ. He, as the true Lamb of God, allows the sin of the world to be laid upon Him and permits Himself be condemned to death, so that He may offer Himself to His heavenly Father and so that we, on the other hand, may go forth exempted.* Psa. 16: **A lot has fallen lovingly to Me**, says Christ, **I have obtained a beautiful portion.** Since the lot

---

* Lev. 16:7–10 is a difficult passage. Cf. alternate translations in the NIV and AAT. Note also the *Concordia Self-Study Commentary* (CPH, 1979), p. 96, in which the goat released into the wilderness is cited as the one vicariously bearing the iniquities of the people. Ed.

has fallen to Me, because it has been determined in the counsel of the Holy Trinity that I should be a Sacrifice for sin, I then am able to obtain a beautiful portion (inheritance); I can accept the believers as heirs and as My own; I can also impart to them eternal life. Therefore, all this also had to take place precisely on the Day of Preparation, because through His death on the cross Christ, for our good, accomplished and prepared everything necessary for our salvation. **Each individual priest**, i.e., in the Old Testament, **is appointed to attend to the worship of God every day and often to perform the same sacrifice—which can never remove sin. But this One, who made one sacrifice for sin which avails for all eternity, now sits at the right hand of God; for with one sacrifice He eternally accomplished perfection for those who are being sanctified**, Heb. 10.

2. Here, however, we should zealously be on guard that we do not blame Barabbas as the murderer of Christ. You then say, Why! God forbid! Who would do a thing like that? If I had been judge in Pilate's place, I would have indeed set Christ free and not have allowed Barabbas to take preference! However, the Scriptures testify that Christ still today must often stand at the end of the line, and the murderer Barabbas is given preference. How this happens we learn in Hebrews 6. Namely, when those who once were enlightened and have tasted the heavenly gift and have partaken of the Holy Spirit later—against the conviction of their hearts—deny and slander the truth, and also persist in it to the end of their lives, such people themselves crucify the Son of God all over again. What is false doctrine other than a murdering of the soul, since the ungodly shall not see the kingdom of God, Rev. 21? On the other hand, Christ's Word and doctrine give eternal life, John 8. Those, then, who deny Christ and His teachings against the testimony of their own heart, prefer the murderer Barabbas over the Prince of Life. Precisely the same occurs in those who follow the temptation of the Devil, the temptations of the world, and the lusts of their

flesh, and who knowingly and deliberately persist in sins against conscience. For what is such knowing, deliberate sin other than a "Barabbas," a murdering of the soul, as it is written in 1 Cor. 6: **Neither whoremongers, nor idolaters, nor adulterers, nor the effeminate men, nor boy-molesters, nor thieves, nor the greedy, nor the drunkards [sots], nor slanderers, nor robbers shall inherit the kingdom of God.** Anyone who desires to sin against conscience, and prefers to follow his lusts rather than Christ, such a person prefers the murder of his soul before Christ. Thus it is written in Hosea 13: **Israel, you bring on your own destruction, for your salvation is only in Me.** Whoever disregards the admonition of the Spirit and willingly follows the sinful flesh, brings on his own destruction; for in Gal. 5 St. Paul says of the works of the flesh: **that those who do such things will not inherit the kingdom of God.** On the other hand, whoever follows Christ and His call, Mat. 11, **Learn of Me, for I am of a gentle disposition and humble of heart, and whoever sows in the Spirit, will from the Spirit inherit eternal life.** Therefore, in the regenerate person, when the flesh lusts against the spirit and the spirit after the flesh, we once more find ourselves in [the position of] Pilate and must judge. If the lusts of the flesh are dampened, and the flesh along with its lusts is crucified (as St. Paul writes to the Galatians in chapter 6) that is the proper action to take. However, when one follows the incitements of the flesh and sinfully goes against conscience, there Christ is slighted and "Barabbas" the soul-killer is given preference. God wants to give us the power to become strong in the inward man through Jesus Christ. Amen.

  O Lord Jesus Christ, You who were innocently condemned to death, [may] Your unjust suffering of condemnation be my ransom payment. You who were innocently sentenced to death, while that murderer Barabbas was set free, give grace so that before God's throne of judgment I may be absolved of my sins, which are the murderers of my soul. Grant to me also the grace of Your Spirit, that I may crucify my sinful flesh with its lusts and desires, so that I myself do not become anew the murderer of my soul. Amen.

230

The Fourth Act

Encompassing the history of the crucifixion of Christ.

The First Sermon

Christ is led out from the city of Jerusalem to be crucified and preaches to the sorrowing women about future misfortune.

Then the soldiers took Jesus, pulled off His mantle and put back on His own clothes, and led Him away to crucify Him; and He carried His own cross. And as they were going out, they found a man passing by from Cyrene, by the name of Simon. He had come from the field and was the father of Alexander and Rufus. They compelled him to bear the cross and laid it on him so that he could carry it behind Jesus. However, a great crowd of people followed after Him, including women, who wailed and mourned. But Jesus turned to them and said: You daughters of Jerusalem, do not cry over Me; rather, cry over yourselves and your children. For take note, the time is coming when a person will say: Blessed are the barren and the bodies that did not give birth, and the breasts that have not suckled. Then they will begin to say to the mountains: Fall on us! and to the hills: Cover us! For if one does this to a green tree, what will become of a dry one?

We read in Genesis 22, that when God the Lord commanded Abraham to sacrifice his only beloved son, Isaac, as a burnt-offering on Mt. Moriah that Abraham arose and laid the wood for a burnt-offering upon his son Isaac. And thus both of them journeyed together to Mt. Moriah so that God's command might be satisfied [obeyed]. This [act] is a type of how the heavenly Isaac born from Abraham's seed, [that is,] Jesus Christ, would personally carry the wood of the cross on which He would allow Himself be slaughtered. The circumstances indicate that it even occurred at the very same place. For Moriah is indeed the mountain upon which the temple at Jerusalem was later built. Just as Isaac, as he came near to Mt. Moriah, carried the wood upon which he was to be sacrificed, so also Christ carried upon his back the wood of the cross as He came down from Mt. Moriah, upon which the city and temple of Jerusalem had been built. In this portion of the Passion story is held before us the leading of Christ out of the city of Jerusalem to the place of crucifixion. And herewith we begin the Fourth Act of Christ's suffering, in which is described the crucifixion. We intend to expound this text in two parts:

I. First, since Christ had now received the sentence of death on the cross, how the soldiers led Him out of the city.

II. Second, what sort of conversation Christ carried on with the mourning women as He was being led out.

I. First of all, the evangelists record that as Pilate had now at the stubborn insistence of the high priests condemned the Lord Christ to death on the cross, the soldiers—or jailer's assistants*—seized Him, [an act] which without doubt occurred violently, in that they bound Him up once more, hit Him, and spit on Him. For He was completely delivered into their hands and into their power as a Man condemned to death. Christ

---

* *Steckenknechte*, lit. "spear servants."

Himself had proclaimed this in Mat. 26, where He states: **The Son of Man will be delivered up into the hands of sinners**; that is, He would be delivered into the hands of the godless guards and led out to the cross like a vile evildoer. The fact that Christ not only was rejected and falsely accused by the Jewish people, but rather also wanted to suffer at the hands of these Gentile guards, implies that He not only wanted to suffer for the sake of the Jews but also for the sake of the Gentiles. For just as all people in the Scriptures are usually divided into Jews, Greeks or Gentiles, so also Christ here intended to announce (since He suffered not only under the high priests and elders of the Jewish people, but also under the Gentile governor and His guards) that He suffered for all people, and that they all contributed to His suffering.

Accordingly [and secondly], the evangelists report that these soldiers took the mantle off the Lord, that is, the purple mantle, which they had earlier placed on the Lord to ridicule and mock Him in the judgment hall, firmly pressing it deeply into His wounds and stripes. As they once again took it off of the Lord Christ, it ripped open His wounds, causing Him great pain. And they again put on Him His own clothes. The crown of thorns, however, they left on His head. The reason that this was done by the soldiers was so that Christ, being in His own customary attire, might indeed be recognized by everyone, and might be all the more despised by each and every one. We must, however, remember what the hand and counsel of God actually had accomplished by all this, Acts 4; for herewith was fulfilled the type of the patriarch Joseph in Gen. 37. When his wicked, spoiled brothers tossed him into a pit, intending to kill him, they took off his colored coat and dipped it into the blood of a kid and sent it back to his father, Jacob. Thus Christ, the heavenly Joseph, who was to fall into the deep pit in which there was no water, Zec. 9, had to suffer having His purple mantle stripped from Him—[a mantle] which He had colored with

His own blood as the innocent Lamb of God. However, by the Lord Christ's once more being dressed in His own clothes, God would have us understand that the Lord Christ Himself—and no one else—was being crucified for us. For St. Peter refers to this in his First Epistle, ch. 2: **Christ offered Himself for our sins in His own body.** And in Heb. 1: **He accomplished our cleansing from sin by means of Himself.** Previously He had been dressed with a white robe as our High Priest, later with a purple cloak as our King and Prophet. Now His own customary clothes, in which He had taught and until now conducted His office, were placed before Him to be put on, so that as our High Priest, King, and Prophet He might allow Himself to be nailed to the cross, and of the cross not be ashamed.

Thirdly, the evangelists report that the soldiers led Christ out of the city; such was the customary practice of the jailer's assistants because the evil doers were done away with outside the city. However, we here must again take note of God's counsel and hand; for with this leading of Christ [out of the city] certain types of the Old Testament were fulfilled. In Gen. 4 it is reported that Cain spoke in a friendly manner with his brother Abel and led him out into the field, where he intended to strangle him. Thus also does this Cainish troop of murderers, as they lead the Lord out into the field where they intended to crucify Him. In Num. 19 God had commanded that the livestock for offerings had to be slaughtered outside the camp. Thus Christ, because He wanted to sacrifice Himself up as a sweet-smelling incense to the Heavenly Father, Eph. 5, allowed Himself to be led out of the city of Jerusalem, just as this type is explained in Heb. 13: [The] **animal blood was carried into the Holy Place by the High Priest for a sin offering, but the animal was burned outside the camp. Therefore, Jesus, so that He might sanctify the people through His own blood, suffered outside the gate.** Furthermore, Jerusalem was also called the Holy City, Mat. 4; the City of God, Psa. 87; the place where God kept His flock and His fire, Isa. 31; and the Holy Place of the Most High, Psa. 46. Indeed, Jerusalem is a picture of eternal life in heaven, and hence is called the heavenly Jerusalem in Rev. 22.

Christ is now led out of this Holy City of God as a banned and cursed Person. He has thereby won for us entry into the heavenly Jerusalem, so that we might come to Mt. Zion, to the city of the living God, and enter into the heavenly Jerusalem and join the hosts of many thousands of angels, along with the fellowship of the first-born—those whose [names] are inscribed in Heaven, Heb. 12. When our first parents had sinned, they were driven out of Paradise, Gen. 3, so that neither they nor their descendants could regain entry. So that the way to the heavenly Paradise might once more be opened up for them and us, Christ allowed Himself to be led out of the Holy City of Jerusalem, which had been an image of the heavenly Paradise. Finally, Christ wanted to be crucified outside the city of Jerusalem to announce that He suffered there not only for the Jewish people as an inhabitant and a parishioner, but for the entire world. Since Christ now allowed Himself for our sake to be led out of the city of Jerusalem in such disgrace, let us then go out to Him from our place of rest and bear His shame, even as we are admonished in the Epistle to the Hebrews, chapter 13. That is, we should willingly and gladly take upon ourselves the disgrace and contempt of this world.

Fourthly, the evangelists set forth this unique detail, that Christ Himself carried His own cross, which is not reported about the two evildoers who were led out with Him. Thus, it may be concluded from this that only in the case of the Lord Christ did the soldiers undertake to lay on Him the heavy, huge cross upon which He was to be nailed, disregarding the fact that during the previous night and into this entire day He had been pitifully worn out with sleeplessness, blows and stripes. Thus this King of Heaven carries His kingdom upon His shoulder, Isa. 9. He carries His cross on which He later died, thereby purchasing us as subjects for His Kingdom. Now it is easy to imagine what kind of huge burden this must have been, since Christ later was nailed to it. However, His burden became even heavier and greater because, along with the wood of the cross, Christ at that moment was also carrying the burden of our sins and of God's wrath [against them]. This was a burden such that no angel in heaven could otherwise have carried. Because He took this, our heavy burden, upon Himself, Christ accordingly promises in Mat. 11 that He wants to refresh the troubled and the heavy-laden persons. He wants to take their burdens from them because He already has carried their burdens and taken them upon Himself. Behold, when we thus consider this burden of the cross, it gives us a glorious comfort; namely, that Christ, as the little Lamb of God, took upon Himself, in addition to the tree of the cross, our sin, carrying it along with Him to the place of crucifixion, John 1. Accordingly, He offered Himself in His own body, 1 Pet. 2. At all times this is how the saints of God have embraced in their hearts the picture of Christ bearing the cross, as can especially be seen in Taulerus.*

  Fifth and last, it is reported that as Jesus was led out He was met by Simon of Cyrene, the father of Alexander and Rufus. The soldiers forced him to carry Jesus' cross behind Him. This Simon was a good and pious man, a disciple of Christ. This may be concluded from the fact that both his sons later associated with the apostles, as can be seen from Acts 19 and Rom. 16. He was a native of Cyrene in Libya, and so was not a born Jew. Rather, he had come to Jerusalem for the sake of the true worship of God, and he had actively committed himself to the Lord Christ. As this good man came in from the field, the soldiers ordered him to carry the cross after Christ, indeed, not

---

* Gerhard is referring to Johann Tauler (14th century) and his *Book of Spiritual Poverty*. He was the greatest preacher of his time in Strassburg, and greatly admired by Luther, and very likely also by Gerhard. Tr.

because they had any sympathy for Christ, but rather because they saw that Christ was utterly exhausted. They were worried that if He carried the cross much longer, He might even give up His spirit [i.e., die on them]. This Simon, then, is a portrait of all true disciples of Christ, who also must bear Christ's cross after Him, as He Himself says in Mat. 16: **Whoever wants to be My disciple, he is to take his cross upon himself and follow after Me.** And in Mat. 11: **Come here to Me all of you who are weary and loaded down, and I will renew (refresh) you; take My yoke upon you.** These, then, are called partakers of (partners in) Christ's suffering, 2 Cor. 1, Rev. 1. Yet there is this marked distinction: Christ carries His cross in Jerusalem all alone, so that all sacrifices are accomplished; also, He takes it upon Himself again when they arrive at the place of crucifixion. It is thereby signified that only Christ's suffering is the sin offering, symbolized by all the Old Testament sacrifices; and in this the saints do not assist; He does it by Himself, Isa. 63. The saints indeed bear the marks of the Lord Jesus in their own bodies, Gal. 6. And they compensate (make up for) in their flesh what is still lacking in Christ's afflictions for the sake of His body, which is the Church, Col. 1[:24]. However, unlike Christ's suffering, such suffering of the saints is not an atoning sacrifice or any satisfaction [reparation] for sin. Instead, the patience of the saints in suffering is a spiritual thank-offering; eventually they will, through tribulation, be made over into the likeness of Christ, Rom. 8.

Accordingly then, Christ leads the way and carries the heaviest end. Even though Simon here follows behind and does his utmost, yet Christ still carries the heaviest [load, i.e., of our sin]. It is thereby signified that our cross and suffering are indeed to be regarded as nothing compared to the sufferings of Christ. Whereas we end up bearing a little splinter, He had to carry a great, immense timber-trunk. Indeed, He goes before; we follow at a distance. He also helps us carry our load of temporal and insignificant suffering so that it does not become too heavy for us, 2 Cor. 4. Indeed, our flesh and blood regard even an insignificant cross as heavy. Such [an attitude] is also portrayed for us here by Simon, who wanted no part in carrying this cross. He saw that all the rest were ashamed to do it. Indeed, the jailer's assistants (guards) shied away from it. Therefore he was forced to do it. So also does our unwilling flesh react, because nobody is willing gladly to carry Christ's cross after Him. Thus one also shies away from it until he is won over by God's Spirit. In this Simon, by birth a Gentile, we also have a type of the pagan world being converted to Christ and following after Him, and also bearing His cross after Him in this world. On the other hand, the high priests and the Jewish people would find His cross offensive, 1 Cor. 1. Nevertheless, the heathen world gladly takes on Christ and His cross and thereby obtains eternal glory, just as in this pilgrimage [lit."cross journey"] Simon obtained an eternal name in all of Christendom, while otherwise he would have remained unknown. Finally, this Simon is a portrayal of each and every Christian, for Simon means a "hearer." Thus the faithful little sheep of Christ hear His voice, John 10. Cyrene means "stranger"; and so also are the believing pilgrims in this world, 1 Pet. 2. Simon went from the field up to Jerusalem; thus the believers hasten to the heavenly Jerusalem. On the way, Christ meets them and makes them partakers of His cross, in that they must follow Him on His sorrowful pilgrimage (sojourn of the cross). He thereby leads them to eternal glory.

II. The second part of this text reports the conversations which took place along the way as Christ was being led out. The disciples had altogether forsaken Him. Moreover, Peter had denied and forsworn Him, and the dear Lord was completely forsaken, pitiably disfigured with spit and stripes, and totally exhausted. Thus, matters were completely reversed and quite the opposite of what they were four days earlier, namely on Palm

Sunday. For then they had cried out with jubilant voices: **Praise to Him who comes in the Name of the Lord; hosanna in the highest.** But now they were all screaming: **Away with Him, crucify Him.** Then they had carried palms and olive branches before Him; but now they lay upon His back the immensely heavy wood of the cross. Then they had set Him onto an ass in order to celebrate His entry; but now they deplorably haul and drag Him out of the city. Then they had spread out their own garments for Him; but now they take off His mantel so that this leading Christ out [from Jerusalem] indeed takes place in a miserable and wretched manner.

Yet at the same time, God the Lord awakens certain hearts so that they have sympathy for Christ. For the evangelists report that certain women lamented and cried over Him; they recalled His glorious preaching and divine miracles. One should not be surprised that these women with their lamenting and weeping indict the unrepentant acts and tyranny of the high priests, whereas the disciples of Christ had disappeared and had, to a man, let their mouths be stopped up. However, God's power is marvelously powerful in the weak, 2 Cor. 12; and through such power of God, those whom we regard as being the weakest are regarded as the greatest. The Lord Christ now addresses these sorrow-laden women and says: **You daughters of Jerusalem, don't cry about Me; rather cry about yourselves and your children. For behold, the time is coming in which a person will say, blessed are the unfruitful, and the bodies that have not given birth, and the breasts which have not suckled. At that time they will look up and say to the mountains: Fall on top of us; and to the hills: Cover us. For if one does this to a green tree, what will become of a dry one?** With these words Christ did not intend to reject the sympathy of these women. Rather, He wanted to instruct them about future events that were presently hidden from them; namely, that they had great cause to cry over themselves and their children. For since the

Jews had sacrilegiously cried out that the innocently shed blood of Christ should come over them and their children, Christ thus here proclaims to them that God will not remain perpetually silent over the fact that they had at this time treated His Son so wretchedly. Instead, He will send over the Jews such misfortune that one will consider as blessed those who were not born and who never nursed, because they would not want to see such misfortune come upon their children. Likewise, even as Christ uses this same manner of speaking in Mat. 24—**Indeed, at that time there will be such a disaster,** the Lord further states, **so that they will cry out to the mountains and hills: Fall on us, and cover us**—so also was this [prophecy] abundantly fulfilled in the siege of Jerusalem, when the Jewish housewives hid themselves in caves and cliffs from the Romans and when, as Josephus reports about the Jewish war, because of their hunger, mothers were reduced to devouring their own children. Christ thus concludes His prophecy: **For if one does this to a green tree, what will happen to the dry?** Christ likens Himself to a green tree, but He likens the unrepentant Jews to dry trees, which bear no good, God-pleasing fruit and are consequently cast into the fire of temporal and eternal punishment.

Here we have:

1. A glorious explanation [epitome] of the whole Passion story, dictated by Christ Himself; namely, we should not stop with weeping over Christ, over how badly He was treated. Rather, we should all the more weep over ourselves, since with our sins we caused Him such extreme suffering. And we should at all times remember that if this is happening to a green Tree (Christ), what actually could we dry trees have experienced if Christ had not taken our place and made payment for us? [For example], if this happens to a green Tree, what will happen to the dry one? What will those experience who persist in their sins, who are not—through true faith planted in Christ, the green

Tree—bringing forth good fruit, but who instead constantly remain dry trees... what will be their eventual fate? Since Christ was beaten and tormented like this by God on account of alien sins [not of His making or doing], how immeasurably more severely will not unrepentant, godless persons be punished on account of their own sin!

2. The punishment which Christ here proclaims to the Jews is a picture of eternal punishment, which eventually will befall all unrepentant, unbelieving and godless people. For just as the Jews crucified Jesus, thus bringing severe punishment upon themselves, so is it also written about the wanton, wicked sinners in Heb. 6, that they themselves once again crucify the Son of God and hold Him in derision. Just as the Jews are afflicted with such severe punishment because they remain dry, rotten, and unfruitful trees to the end, so it is also written about the godless in Mat. 3: **Each individual tree which does not produce good fruit will be chopped down and heaved into the fire.** Even as it is here stated that the Jews will cry out in their punishment: **You mountains, fall on us, and you hills cover us**, so is it also written about the damned in Acts 6, that on the Day of the Last Judgment they will say to the mountains and rocks: **Fall on us and hide us from the face of Him who sits on the throne, and from the wrath of the Lamb.** However, this screaming and these wishes will be in vain, because no mountain nor boulder can hide one from God's wrath (mountains melt before Him like wax, Psa. 85) and also because they carry in their hearts a gnawing worm which no mountain nor boulder can kill with its earthquake. This we should ponder, so that we indeed not be found to be unfruitful trees and be hurled into the hellish fire.

3. Finally, Christ here calls Himself by a delightful name: a green Tree. He herewith gives us the following to think about: Adam was originally thus created by God as a green, fruitful tree, planted by the well-watered brook of divine grace, and was able to produce truly pleasing fruits for God, Psa. 1. However, as he turned away from God through sin, he became a dry tree; he lost the sap of divine grace and the Holy Spirit. Consequently, all his descendants are now dry trees by nature, serving no other purpose than to be tossed into the fire of eternal damnation. If we were to be helped, God's Son had to be ordained as our Mediator. He is the green Tree of Life, as He is called in Acts 22, who produces His fruit every month, that is, constantly; and, the leaves of this Tree serve for the healing of the Gentiles. We must be grafted into this Tree of Life through true faith if we are to bear any good fruits, just as the Lord indeed so comfortingly describes in John 15: **I am the Wine-stalk (Vine); you are the tendrils. Whoever remains in Me and I in him, such a person bears much fruit.** Apart from Christ all men are dry, rotten trees; but when the believers are grafted into this green Tree of Life, they green up like a palm tree and grow like a cedar of Lebanon. They are planted into the house of the Lord and green up in the vestibule of our God, Psa. 92. They bear fruits which last forever, John 15. God, through Christ, help us to that end. Amen.

O Lord Jesus Christ, You evergreen Tree of Life, allow us who are by nature dry, unfruitful trees to be engrafted into You through true faith, so that we may receive sap and power from You and may bring forth such fruits as are acceptable to God and last forever. Amen.

The Second Sermon

As He first tastes the bitter wine denatured with myrrh, Christ is crucified, and prays for those who crucify Him.

However, two other evildoers were also led forth to be executed with Him. And they brought Him to the place which in Hebrew is called Golgatha, which is translated (interpreted) "place of a skull." And they gave Him a drink of vinegar and myrrh in wine, mixed with gall; and, when He tasted it, He would not drink it. And they crucified Him at the place of Golgatha, and two evildoers along with Him—one on the right, the other on the left, and Jesus between them. Thus the Scripture was fulfilled which said: He was judged along with the evildoers. And it was about the third hour when they crucified Jesus. However, Jesus said: Father, forgive them, for they don't know what they do.

Just as the high priests in Old Testament times carried out their threefold duties of office, first with teaching, next with praying, and third with sacrificing (as can be seen in the fourth Book of Moses [Numbers] and again in the Epistle to the Hebrews), so also did Christ, since He is the only High Priest of the New Testament, Psa. 110, Heb. 5. Thus He wanted to carry out these three duties of office during His days in the flesh. As pertains to the first office, Christ not only taught over a period of three whole years in many and various places, but, even as He was led to the place of His suffering, He also advised the women as to how they were to regard His suffering; namely, they were above all not to weep and lament over Him but over themselves. Accordingly, regarding prayer, not only did

He commend His disciples and all believers to His Heavenly Father with zealous, active prayer, when in the Garden He was about to embark on His suffering, John 17, but also on the timber-trunk of the cross He prayed for His crucifiers. Finally, He gave Himself up for us on the tree of the cross as a gift and as a sacrifice for a sweet fragrance to God, Eph. 5, and offered up Himself as a sacrifice for sin which would avail forever, Heb. 10.

Since, therefore, one aspect of Christ's high-priestly office was dealt with in the previous text, namely how He instructed the sorrowing women about the true and blessed contemplation of His suffering, we will now consider the other two aspects, namely:

I. concerning His sacrifice and prayer, that is, how on the tree of the cross He presented Himself to God as a pleasing Sacrifice, and,

II. furthermore, offered up prayers and petitions with intense weeping and tears, Heb. 5,

with which we intend to deal briefly.

I. In describing the crucifixion of Christ, the evangelists at the outset report that at the same time two other evil-doers were led out with Him. Later they were crucified next to the Lord in such a way that Christ was placed between them. By so doing the guards intended to draw down even more shame and disgrace upon Christ, as if He were as guilty as those [other two] who were receiving this same punishment. But the evangelists further state **that this happened so that the Scripture might be fulfilled: He was counted among the evildoers**, Isa. 53, thereby reminding us that also this part did not take place apart from God's counsel and will. All of us to a man were gross evildoers in God's eyes, and we had rightly deserved to be eternally accursed. However, Christ here comes to us, places Himself in our midst, is reckoned as one of us evildoers, and extends His open hands to us so that He can draw us to Himself. It is also relevant to note that Christ did not want any of His apostles to be crucified with Him at this time, so that one would not think that they in any way had contributed something towards His atoning sacrifice. However, there is no way that one could make such an assertion or even think such about the evildoers [who were crucified with Him].

Later the evangelists report concerning the place of crucifixion, that it was a little mountain outside of Jerusalem, called Golgatha or "Skull-place," where the evildoers were usually executed, a name the place acquired because many skulls of murderers and evildoers lay there. [This fact], moreover, was intended by His crucifiers to be a greater humiliation for Christ. However, we must once more contemplate a divine mystery: After the Fall from God the Lord, each and every one of us is from that time forth nothing but a murderer. We are descendants of the first arch-murderer, Adam, and thus before God are cast-off, dried-up death heads [skulls]. But here Christ comes to us, sets up His cross, and on it allows His holy blood to flow down onto us so that we dried up skulls (death-heads) are once more made alive, even as the [Church] fathers for that reason likened the Lord Christ to the pelican bird, who, by sprinkling its own blood on its dead chicks was said to be able to bring them back to life. Augustine, Hieronymus, Epiphanius, and others of the fathers were of like mind that Adam supposedly lay buried at this very same spot. If that were the case, then it would also give us agreeable thoughts that the second Adam wanted to die at the precise place where the first Adam had brought sin and death into the world. Otherwise, this much is certain: This place of the crucifixion is the exact location where Isaac was to have been offered in Gen. 22, and also the site where David later built an altar at the time of the pestilence and there made an offering to God so that His wrath might be turned away, 2 Sam. 24. It is herewith announced that Christ had fulfilled all these types of the Old Testament and that this His Sacrifice was the only, true atoning sacrifice by which the wrath of God is appeased.

In the third place, it is recorded that the wicked knaves, even before Christ had been crucified, offered Him a drink of vinegar and myrrhed wine mixed with gall, which Christ nevertheless would not drink. With this they intended to hasten Christ's death, for they had heard what a sharp-edged sermon He had proclaimed to the dear women as He was led out [of Jerusalem]. Thus they thought it most advisable to do Him in quickly with such a bitter, deadly drink so that He would not preach a similar sermon from the cross. For it is here written in the text that the Lord Christ was given some nearby vinegar and bitter myrrh, also gall, so that it be fulfilled what is proclaimed in Psa. 69: **They gave me gall to eat, and vinegar to drink in my great thirst.** In the holy language [original Hebrew] the word here used is the little word *Rosch**, which supposedly was a poisonous herb, whose sap, when mixed in a drink, would quickly kill a man. The same can be understood from other places where the word is used in a similar way, as for example Deu. 32, Jer. 8, Hos. 10. That's why the Lord Christ also did not wish to drink it, for He did not wish to die by poisoning, but rather on the cross.

We herewith ought to remember, however, that from the Fall on we are poisonous trees; our wine-vine is the wine-vine of Sodom and from the fields of Gomorrah. Our clusters of grapes are gall; they produce bitter berries. And our wine is the poison of a dragon and the raging [venomous] gall of an adder, Deu. 32. And when God the Lord waits for us to bring forth good clusters of grapes, behold, we bring forth *Heerlinge* (late grapes), Isa. 5. We have sucked the poison of sin from the *Rosch*, or head, of the hellish snake, and that is the reason Christ had to suffer and that

---

* Psa. 69:22 in Biblia Hebraica: *Rehsh Ahleph Sheen = a poisonous plant.*

such a bitter, poisonous drink was set before Him, so that this poison of sin might be removed from us. Moreover, God the Lord had commanded in Pro. 31: **Give strong drink to those who are to perish, and wine to the distressed soul, so that they drink and forget their sorrow, and no longer remember their misfortune.** But it cannot be this good for Christ, who instead receives a libation of a bitter, poisonous drink of vinegar and, indeed, from those whom He had led into the beautiful, fruitful land which flowed with milk and honey. Thus was our first father, Adam, established in beautiful Paradise, where he had pure, delicious fruits for food and drink. But he turned away from God and took a poisonous drink from the snake. Thus it came about that when God the Lord had wanted a drink (as He had hoped) of sweet wine from this noble wine-vine which He had planted with His own hand, behold, it was as sour as vinegar and more bitter than gall. Instead, to atone, Christ here receives this evil drink. Nevertheless, Christ did not swallow this drink; rather, He only tasted it and gave it back again. It is thereby indicated that God the Lord would disown the Jewish nation on account of their late grapes and bitter grape berries; just as in Psa. 69 it immediately follows that, as Christ laments over this drink, He additionally states: **Their table before them will be a rope** [i.e., a hangman's noose, a snare] **against them for a retribution and for a downfall.**

Fourthly, the evangelists describe the manner of death, namely, that Christ was crucified; and, indeed, they do so with brevity of words, because it was a customary deed with which everyone was familiar. It was done in the following manner: They first of all took off the clothing of those who were to be crucified. It is to be concluded from this that such now also happened to the Lord Christ, for the evangelists report in what follows that the soldiers divided His garments among themselves. The reason that Christ's clothes were taken off Him was that He might thereby win for us the Garment of Righteousness in which we are enabled to stand before God. Our first parents were created by God holy and pure. They were dressed with the beautiful garments of innocence and righteousness. But then the hellish murderer overcame them and pulled this beautiful coat off them, Luke 10. From that time forth all their descendants were naked and exposed, Eze. 16, Rev. 3. So that we might once more be clothed with the Coat of Salvation and the Garment of Righteousness Isa. 61, and [so that] the shame of our nakedness not be exposed, Christ was willing to let Himself be stripped naked. After that, people who were to be crucified had all their members stretched and pulled from one another, as perhaps one might have done to Him in our day on the rack. That Christ also experienced [such an ordeal] is testified to in Psalm 22, where He prays thus: **All My bones have been torn apart; My heart is like melted wax in My body; I'm able to count all My bones.** All of us deserved to suffer eternal torture, to be beaten with fists by Satan and his angels, 2 Cor. 12. So that we might be freed from this [fate], Christ here allows Himself to be pitifully tormented and tortured. Thirdly, when [crucifixion] was carried out, they also sank a huge timber into the ground, on top of which they horizontally erected a long beam. To this they attached with nails the hands and feet of such an evildoer. Once again Psa. 22 testifies to the fact that Christ also endured this: **They have pierced my hands and feet.** (Also germane here is the fact that after His resurrection Christ showed the disciples His hands and feet, John 20.) If we will now look at this portrait of the hanging and bleeding Christ on the Cross, we will find therein some great mysteries. For,

    1. Crucifixion was a horrible way to die. Cicero, 5. *contra Berres*, calls it "most gruesome and terrifying;" Paulus Ictus, 5. *Sent. Tit. 21*, [refers to it as] the "most severe punishment by death." Indeed, it is written in Deu. 21: **Anyone who is hung is cursed by God.** Paul applies [this passage] thus in Gal. 3: **Christ has redeemed us from the curse of the Law, in that**

He was a curse for us. For it is written: Cursed is anyone who hangs on a tree, so that the blessing of Abraham might come among the Gentiles. "The shame of the cross becomes the glory of faith." Bernhard, *Serm.* 4.

2. We should interpret the fact that Christ was willing to give up His spirit on the wood of the cross as an announcement of His intention to restore what Adam had broken on the wood of the forbidden tree. There the first Adam had stretched out his arm to the forbidden tree-trunk, thereby bringing death upon all his descendants. Here the second Adam stretches out His arms on the timber-trunk of the cross and brings to us life and salvation. Here the fathers draw upon the fact that Noah, along with his [family], was sustained in the ark during the time of the flood, Gen. 7, and the Wisdom of God had thus helped him by means of an ordinary wood timber, Wisdom of Solomon 10.* Thus is the wood of the cross given to us as a secure little ship in which we can be preserved from the flood of divine wrath. The Lord God directed Moses, Exo. 15, to a take a tree or timber and place it in the bitter water so that it might become sweet. Thereby it is signified that Christ's cross is able to take away the bitterness of death and every misfortune. 2 Kings 6: As the children of the prophets wanted to fell some trees, the iron [head of the ax] fell into the water. Then Elisha cut off a piece of wood and plunged it into the water; thereupon, the iron floated to the top. The entire human race had fallen into deep, eternal damnation and was unable to rescue itself. Christ, the heavenly Elisha, came with the wood of His cross and lifted us up again. In Exo. 14 Moses struck the Red Sea with his staff so that it would divide and the Israelites could escape from Pharaoh. With the wood of His cross, Christ made it possible for the spiritual Israelites to travel through the Sea

---

* Gerhard may be referring to v. 4 of this book from the Apocrypha: "und regierte den Gerechten durch ein gering Holz."

of Tribulation and to be rescued from the hand of the hellish Pharaoh.

3. That Christ was affixed [to the cross] with nails by the hands of unrighteous people, as the apostle states in Acts 2, is explained by St. Paul in Col. 2: Christ herewith wiped out (obliterated) the handwriting that was against us, which originated in the Law and was in opposition to us, and has taken it out of the middle [i.e., the way] and affixed it to the cross. We all were in debt to God; of that the testimony of our hearts, like an undeniable handwriting, convinces us. As He is fastened with nails [to the cross], Christ now pierced through this very same handwriting so that it was no longer valid, just as a cut-up and pierced-through handwritten document is usually no longer valid. From Christ's split hands flows forth the fountain of our salvation and divine grace. There are also ancient paintings [which depict] how one nail on the cross nailed God's righteousness, the second God's mercy, and the third the peace of God. Thereby the beloved ancients wanted to indicate that the mercy and peace of God could not have come over us, nor His righteousness have had any satisfaction, had not Christ through the death on the cross reconciled us with God.

4. Also, that on the cross Christ was wounded in both His hands and feet as well as in His side, and thus was pierced with five wounds, fulfills the type in 1 Sam. 17, where David took five smooth stones from the brook and with them killed the huge Philistine giant. For when Christ in His suffering drank from the brook along the way, Psa. 110[:7], He killed the hellish Goliath with His five holy wounds.

5. By the fact that Christ from His wounds liberally poured out His blood and hung bleeding on the cross, He thereby declared that He was actually giving satisfaction for our sins, which were blood-red, Isa. 1; that He was actually offering up our blood-guilt and sins in His own body upon the tree, 1 Pet. 2;

and that from now on His blood should cleanse us from sin, 1 John 1.

6. That Christ hangs in the air—in the same way that a poisonous worm is speared and hung in the air so that no one be poisoned by it—proclaims that Christ Himself hung there as the greatest sinner, upon whom the poison of all mankind's sin was laid, as He speaks of it in Psa. 122: **I am a worm and no man.** And in John 3 He applies to Himself the type of Num. 21: Just as Moses in the wilderness raised up a snake so that those who had been wounded by the poisonous serpent-sting would look at this same snake and thus be healed, so also must the Son of Man be lifted up so that all who look at Him with the eyes of a believing heart would not on account of the poison of the hellish snake be lost, but rather have eternal life.

7. That Christ was lifted up on a cross thereby fulfills what is proclaimed in Isa. 53: **Behold, My Servant will be lifted up and will be highly regarded.** And Christ hereby wants to declare that He actually had to deal with His Father in heaven, to whom He now had presented Himself as a sacrifice. When a heave-offering was brought to God in the Old Testament, it first had to be raised up high and thus be sacrificed. Christ also wanted to fulfill this type and allow Himself to be lifted up on the tree of the cross.

8. By the fact that Christ bowed His head on the cross, He thereby intended to indicate His love towards us; namely, that for our sake and because of His great love toward us He Himself hung there, as He Himself thus explains in John 12: **When I will be lifted up from the earth, then I will draw all of you to Myself.**

9. That Christ extended His hands, He did in order to embrace us out of love and to bring to Himself under His cross both Jews and Gentiles so that they might be sprinkled by His saving blood and be washed from sin. Hereby has He also redeemed us so that the whole day long God would spread out

His hands to us, Isa. 55, and await our conversion with great patience. Thus, we should not turn our back on Him, but instead gather ourselves under His wing.

10. The cross of Christ also has the form of a sword and spear, which the Lord Christ sticks into the earth. He herewith challenges the Devil (who has his hellish dwelling beneath the earth) to combat; and He threatens that with His feet He will crush [the Devil's] head, Gen. 3, and destroy his palace, Luke 11. The Devil shivers and shakes over this threat and perceives that from now on will be fulfilled what Hosea proclaimed, chapter 13: **I will redeem them from hell and rescue them from death. Death, I will be a poison to you. Hell, I will be a pestilence for you.** That's why the earth also shakes and quakes at the time of Christ's death; namely, because the Palace of Hell was being seized and destroyed through the death of Christ.

11. Finally, Christ was thus lifted up on the cross so that thereby might be proclaimed how He will be seen by everyone, and that from all the four corners of the world each and every one will be gathered to Him, so that His cross will thus become a banner for the people, about which the Gentiles will inquire, Isa.11. These, and perhaps still more, mysteries are presented to us in the crucifixion of Christ.

Fifthly, [we consider] the time of the crucifixion, namely, that it was the third hour, that is, around noon. Against that there is no conflict in that the other evangelists say it was the sixth hour. For it could have taken place between those two times, in that they began [calling it that] around the third hour. As the Jews then divided the day into four parts, the part between the third and sixth hour was called the third hour as well as the sixth hour. It was, however, at that time formerly maintained by the ancients that that day was actually the same day on which heaven and earth were originally created, thereby indicating that on the cross Christ was actually bringing to completion the work of redemption (which is like unto a Second Creation) thus creating aright what had been corrupted by the Devil in the work of the first creation.

II. In the second part of this text it is recorded that Christ prayed for His crucifiers: **Father, forgive them**, He says, **for they know not what they do**, the first word which Christ spoke on the cross. In the Old Testament, as the sacrifice was being offered, the high priest at the same time had to instruct the people about its true benefit. Christ, the High Priest of the New Testament, also does this; and He teaches that this His sacrifice is intended for the forgiveness of sins. Also, since Christ suffered not for Himself but for us, He does not immediately at the outset lament that He was forsaken by God. Rather, He, as it were, forgets His agony and concerns Himself with us human beings and prays that God would forgive us for what we were doing to Him. He thus here portrays Himself as our true Advocate, 1 John 2, who pleads on our behalf before the heavenly Father with the power of His sacrifice. He holds before Him, as it were, His wounds and petitions that God would allow His wrath to abate. Just as in those times Christ's petition was so powerful that many of those who helped crucify Him were converted and the remainder were given forty more whole years in which to repent,* so now Christ's intercession retains its power to this very day. For we should not think that Christ was praying [only] for the Jews and soldiers who at that timed crucified Him. Rather, this prayer applies to us all. He was crucified for the sake of all of our sins, Isa. 53; and with our sins we caused Him pain and effort, Isa. 43. And if we still at times go forth with confidence (brashness) and don't realize what we are doing—that is, we don't realize the consequence of lying in sin, nor do we consider what a serious matter the wrath of God is—behold, with His intercession Christ presents the very best

---

* Very likely a reference to the destruction of the temple.

and obtains so much that God grants time for repentance and does not so quickly destroy with His wrath. Ponder here also the incomprehensible patience of Christ, how He in His distress also prayed for His worst enemies who dealt with Him so pitiably and horribly. They had affixed Him with nails so that He could do no other good for them. Only His tongue remained, which even so, because of torture, stuck to the roof of His mouth, Psa. 22. Yet, He used it still to pray for His crucifiers. Indeed, how distant are those from this example of Christ who do not pray for their enemies. Even more distant are those who return evil with evil. Farthest away of all are those who deliberately offend their neighbors. From this, God graciously preserve us. Amen.

O Lord Jesus Christ, You are the One who became a curse on the timber-trunk of the cross for us. Make us partakers of this divine blessing. Let Your holy blood flow over us so that we thereby are washed of our sins and are given to drink of eternal life. O You eternal High Priest, let Your intercession redound to our good, so that in the power of the same we may benefit from Your holy suffering and may obtain forgiveness of sins. Amen.

The Third Sermon

Pilate honors Christ's cross with a glorious superscription; the soldiers divide Christ's garments.

Pilate wrote a superscription, stating of what [Jesus] was guilty and the reason for His death, and placed it upon the cross over His head. But it was written, Jesus of Nazareth, the King of the Jews. Many Jews read this superscription, for the place was near to the city where Jesus was crucified. And it was written in the Hebrew, Greek, and Latin language. Then the high priests of the Jews said to Pilate: Don't write, the King of the Jews; instead write that He has said, I am the King of the Jews. Pilate answered: What I have written, that have I written. However, the soldiers who had crucified Jesus took His clothes and made four portions, one for each soldier, in addition also to the coat. The coat, however, was seamless, completely woven together from top to bottom. Thus they said to one another: Let us not divide the coat; instead, let's cast lots as to whose it shall be (so that the Scripture might be fulfilled, which says: They divided My clothing among each other, and over My coat they cast lots). And the soldiers all sat there on guard. And the people stood around and watched.

In Exodus 28[: 36-37] it is reported that, among other glorious ornaments which the high priests of the Old Testament wore by special ordinance of God, they wore a sheet made of pure gold on their forehead. On it were engraved these words: **The Holiness of the Lord.** This plate of gold was tied to the front of the hat of the high priests with a yellow cord, and the high priest at all times wore it on his forehead whenever He entered into the Holy of Holies to perform the sacrifice for the people. Since our Lord Christ, as the only High Priest of the New Testament, intended to perform upon the high altar of the cross the only true atoning sacrifice for the sins of the entire world and, by means of His own blood, wanted to enter into the Holy of Holies, He thus also permitted such a plate to be fastened to the top of His cross, thereby fulfilling this type. For just as upon the forehead plate of the high priests of the Old Testament were inscribed the words, "The Holiness of the Lord," to indicate that the high priest was sanctified to the Lord and was betrothed to His service, thus also was such a title affixed at Christ's head on the timber-trunk of the cross as the sole High Priest of the New Testament: **Jesus of Nazareth, the King of the Jews**, to announce thereby that this was the only Jesus or Savior—the Nazarene, or the Betrothed of God—the High Priest and King of all spiritual Israelites.

I. This superscription on the cross of Christ will be dealt with in the first part of this lesson.
II. In the second part, the evangelists describe for us how the soldiers divided Christ's clothes among themselves.

I. It was the custom of the Jews when some were being executed that the reason for the death was publicly cried out, or also written upon a little placard, so that others would be deterred from [doing] the very same evil deeds. Since Pilate had found no blame in Christ, but allowed himself to be persuaded to crucify Him solely because of the persistent urging by the Jews, he therefore placed such a title over Jesus' cross whereby the Jews were given full blame for allowing this their King—for whom they had hopefully longed—to be crucified. And, because on the aforesaid Feast of the Passover all sorts of folks had come up to Jerusalem, he permitted such a title be written in the three principal languages (Hebrew, Greek, and Latin) and in these words: **Jesus of Nazareth, the King of the Jews.** Such a superscription would have been read by many Jews and the comrades of the Jews at that time, because the place of crucifixion was next to Jerusalem. Thus, the high priests would not permit this. Instead, they petitioned Pilate to change the title to this extent: namely, that Christ merely represented Himself as and claimed to be King of the Jews, while in fact He was not. However, Pilate answered them: **What I have written, that I have written**; [that is,] I will leave stand what I have already written.

From this we must first of all learn, as the evangelist John states, chapter 11, that the high priest Caiaphas had unwittingly prophesied about the result of Christ's death when he said: **It is better for us that One Man die for the people than that the entire nation perish.** Thus, we can also say that Pilate here (through God's special providence, yet unwittingly) proclaims Christ's praise. It had been Pilate's intent to show his faithful allegiance (submission) to Caesar—that he would not allow someone else to represent himself as king. Also, with this superscription, he intended secretly to taunt the Jews, in that they for so long had hoped for a King, and yet now they allowed Him to be crucified. However, God saw to it that Pilate unwittingly wrote a beautiful epitaph for Christ.

[Pilate] calls Christ, Jesus; that is, he calls Him what He actually was in deed and in truth, our Savior and our Bliss-maker, as this Name was given to Him by the angel even before He was conceived in the womb, Luke 1. That precisely this name, however, was inscribed over the cross of Christ, announces thereby that the real reason He suffered death on the cross was so that He might be our Jesus, our Savior and our Bliss-maker.

Furthermore, Pilate calls Jesus a Nazarene, because He was conceived and reared at Nazareth. It was, however, in a veiled manner thereby proclaimed that Jesus is the genuine

Nazarene of the Old Testament and that He also is the true branch or twig that sprouted from the root of Jesse, Isa. 11, among whom [whose descendants?] it would once more become green and grow, Zec. 6. That precisely this Name was now written over the cross of Christ announces that He, as the betrothed of God, now sanctifies himself for us, John 17, so that we, through Him, are made into a people who are the possession of the Lord.

Finally, Pilate calls Jesus the King of the Jews. In truth, He certainly was that, as He also had publicly confessed before Pilate. But even though the kingdom of His power extends over all the world, He nevertheless is the King of the Jews in a special way, because the scepter of His kingdom of grace emanates out of Zion, Psa. 110 and Isa. 2, and because the spiritual Israelites, the true confessors, who walk in the footsteps of believing Abraham and according to the Spirit, are inwardly secret Jews, Rom. 2, and because (I say) such properly belong to His kingdom of grace and are true subjects of His kingdom. One day He also wants to receive them into the kingdom of glory. However, the fact that precisely this Name was thus written over the cross of Christ announces in a hidden manner that Christ carries the power (rule) of His kingdom upon His shoulders, Isa. 9. It cost Him His blood and His death, so that He might gather a kingdom of grace among men. For we all had been under the power of the Devil and were his prisoners. If we were all to come into Christ's kingdom of grace, then He first had to rescue (redeem) us through His own blood. Also, [the sign on the cross] shows that He does not lose His kingdom and His rule while on the cross; rather, it declares that in the midst of death He remained a King. The power and authority of other kings cease to exist at death, but with the death of Christ something entirely different occurs. He even overcomes His enemies by His death. **He has undressed the principalities and the mighty, and publicly showed them off, and by Himself He made them into a triumphant spectacle**, Col. 2.

Secondly, we here note the fact that Pilate fashioned the superscription not only in the Latin language (as the Romans customarily did) but also in the Hebrew and Greek. Indeed, his intention for doing so was to assure that the people who had come to the Feast of the Passover from every corner and place would be able to understand this title. For the Hebrew was known to the Jews and their comrades, and the Greek was in use by nearly all the people in the world. But God the Lord also brought this about to proclaim that Christ's Kingdom would be spread abroad into all the world, just as the heavenly Father said to His Son in Psa. 2: **Request it of Me; thus I will give You the Gentiles as an inheritance, and the ends of the earth as [Your] property.** The use of these three languages also signified that before all the other variations and forms of languages, these three (namely, Hebrew, Greek, and Latin) would serve to spread of the Kingdom of Christ. For the Old Testament is written in Hebrew, and the New Testament in Greek. Now, however, both Testaments of this double witness which speaks of Christ, Rev. 11, are written in Greek and Latin. Also, the best interpretations (expositions) of the holy Scriptures are written in the Greek and Latin languages.

Thirdly, despite the request of the high priests, Pilate refused to change the superscription (responding, instead, that what he had written would remain) because he had previously conceded enough to them by condemning the innocent Christ to a death on the cross at their insistence; and so he no longer wanted to listen to their unjust requests. Underlying this decision, however, we must remind ourselves, is the providence of God. Also, just like Pilate, God the Lord had allowed the high priests, the Pharisees, and the elders such great latitude so that they had brought His beloved Son to the cross. For such was required by the urgent need for our salvation and for the payment of our sin. However, because now the glory of Christ would soon commence, and since the superscription contained the thought that

Christ was a King of the Jews, God the Lord would not allow the high priests further to vent their jealousy against Christ nor to change the superscription on His cross. Accordingly, if even what this heathen (Gentile) judge had written to honor Christ should and could not be altered, how much less, then, may what the holy men of God (the prophets and apostles, moved by the Holy Spirit) have written about the majesty and glory of our Lord Christ and His Kingdom ever be altered or annulled! So also, as the holy Scripture (which refers to authorities as "gods") cannot be broken or undone, how much less shall it be broken or changed when it testifies that Christ is God's Son, that He is the world's Savior, and that He is the King of the Jews, as Christ affirms in John 10.

II. In the second part of this lesson the holy evangelists report how the soldiers who had crucified Christ divided His clothing among themselves, as well as how they cast a lot for His coat. If someone was crucified, his clothes were first removed and given to those who performed the crucifixion. Such now also happened to Christ. The four persons who crucified Him divided His clothes into four shares, each one receiving a part. However, since the Lord Christ's cloak was seamless, woven through from top to bottom, they did not want to cut it up to divide it. Rather, it would become the possession of the winner of the lot. All of this occurred while the Lord Christ still was alive. From the cross, He could see how they were dealing with His garments. The mother of the Lord Jesus, who was standing beside the cross, also saw this and no doubt had ardently pleaded that they not thus divide the clothing of Christ. But the holy evangelists divert [our attention] from this common custom and direct us instead to the prophecy of Psalm 22, wherein it was long ago proclaimed that the soldiers would divide Christ's clothes among themselves and throw the lot over His coat.

Here we should first consider the outward poverty of Christ, in that He hangs naked and uncovered on the timber-trunk of the cross. During His entire life, the beloved Lord was extremely poor. He did not have a place to lay His head, Mat. 8. Thus He also desired that His departure from life would be in keeping with His prior mode of living. The birth of the Lord took place in miserable poverty. He was born an alien in a stall. His life was poor and toilsome. But the most wretched of all was His death, when His insignificant bits of clothing were taken from Him and divided among the soldiers. Through this poverty of Christ we have become rich, 2 Cor. 8. The first man was created by God as a rich lord. He was clothed in soul and body with temporal blessings. His soul was adorned with the beautiful cloak of innocence and righteousness. His body was attired in immortality. Everything upon earth was placed under his charge so that he should be lord over all. However, he allowed the Devil to take from him all this beautiful garb, Luke 10. He let the Devil take this kingdom away from him. And thereby he, along with all his descendants, became poor and naked in body, soul, and temporal blessings to the extent that in God's eyes we are miserably and pathetically poor, blind and naked, Eze. 16 and Rev. 3. To help us out of this outward poverty and nakedness, behold, God's Son thus gives Himself over to external poverty, even though He is a two-fold Lord of both heaven and earth. He allowed Himself to be stripped naked on the timber-trunk of the cross, yea, let Himself be stripped thread-bare naked, even as He clothed the entire earth with grass and fruits. He did all this so that He might regain for us the lost blessings and prepare for us again the robe of righteousness and immortality. Since then, He is able to make our souls rich and to give us white garments to wear, so that the shame of our nakedness will no longer be exposed, Rev. 3.

Accordingly, this poverty and nakedness of Christ should exhort us to love Him, not in a fleshly manner, but according to the Spirit and in Truth, John 4. **Even though we have also known Christ according to the flesh, we nevertheless know Him no longer**, writes St. Paul in 2 Cor. 5. To know Christ according to the flesh means to regard Him as an earthly, worldly King. It means to seek fleshly things from Him. It means to cling to His visible presence, the way the apostles knew Christ while He traveled with them here upon earth. However, we are not to know Christ in this way; for precisely for that reason He let Himself be stripped to the skin and permitted to be taken from Him the only thing He still possessed (His clothes), so that we would not love Him according to the flesh, seek fleshly benefits from Him, nor first and foremost require earthly blessings from Him. Instead, we should love Him in spirit and petition Him for spiritual benefits and riches of the soul. That is the truly blessed fullness which we should receive from His abundance, John 1. Many love Christ in this way: They petition Him solely for bodily health and temporal honor and goods. However, that means seeking only wretchedly perishable clothing from Him. After all, Christ did not regard his own clothes very highly. Rather, He allowed them to fall into the hands of the soldiers. Why would we then want to love Him for the sake of health, temporal honor, and goods; that is, for the sake of squalid clothes? He dispensed Paradise to the repentant criminal on the cross; but His clothes He let fall into the hands of the wicked knaves. We should first of all seek and petition Him for Paradise and the blessings of the Kingdom of heaven; afterwards, the clothes will also be found.

Thirdly, just as Christ here not only shed His blood, but also had the scraps of His clothing taken from Him, so it still sometimes happens to His members. They are attacked by the persecutors of the Church not only for their life and blood, but also for their honor and possessions. Such happens especially to the possessions of the Church, which the Lord Christ has bestowed upon it from the beloved forebears so that His members may clothe themselves therein. These are frequently taken from them as they are swallowed up by war. Just a few days earlier, as Christ celebrated His royal entrance into Jerusalem, some of the people had spread their own clothes upon the way before Him. But now Christ has His own clothes taken away, and they are divided among malicious thugs. So it still goes. Our beloved ancestors had, as it were, stripped themselves bare and spread their clothes before Christ; that is, they gave richly and generously for the maintenance of churches and schools. But these clothes are again sometimes taken away from Christ; and so it happens that Christ's members remain in need for clothes and food. However, the Lord Christ sees all this. His Word is a comfort to those who suffer such robbery; but to the others who undertake such deeds against Him, His Word is a terror. For when Christ sees how also in this respect His members are treated, there will be no distress or want. According to His promise in Mark 10, He will His own their loss richly repay. Also, in the meantime, He will firmly take to task the unrighteous, according to the threat of God in Isa. 33: **Woe to you who rob, for you again will be robbed.**

Fourthly, the ancient teachers have also construed various spiritual meanings from this Passion story. For since Christ's body is called His cloak, Gen. 9*, Cyril of Alexandria in his commentary on John, *lib.* 12, *cap.* 32, ascribes to the passage this kind of allegory: *In quatuor partes vestimenta Christi divisa sunt & tunica sola indivisa mansit, quod mysticae cujusdam rei fignum esse dicerim. Nam quatuor orbis partes ad falutem reductae indumentum Verbi, id est, carnem ejus impartibiliter inter fe partitae*

---

* Noah has his naked shame covered by someone else's garment, just as Christ's robe of righteousness covers our shame and guilt—a passage in keeping with Gerhard's metaphorical-typological mode of thinking, as he, quite possibly from memory, selects an Old Testament text to illustrate his point. The statement regarding Christ's body being called his cloak, however, remains obscure in reference to Gen. 9. Tr./Ed.

sunt.* In essence he is saying that Christ after His resurrection from death on the cross, in the state of His exaltation, is present in all four corners of the world, not only according to His divinity, but also according to His assumed humanity with which He had clothed Himself. Nevertheless, He is not thereby divided or dismembered; rather, His body remains whole and undisturbed, just as His cloak remained undivided.

Furthermore, since the Christian Church is the spiritual body of Christ, Eph. 1, with which He is constantly present (yet attired in Word and Sacrament) St. Augustine, in his *Treatise 118 on John*, thus constructs the following allegory: This dividing of Christ's clothing signifies that the Christian Church is distributed and scattered into all four corners of the world, even as Christ says in Mark 13: On Judgment Day He will let His elect be gathered by the holy angels from the four winds, from the ends of the earth to the far reaches of the heavens, that is, from every end and place in the world. Nevertheless, this Church, which is dispersed into the entire world, is united among itself through the bond of faith and love in the same manner as Christ's seamless cloak was indivisibly woven together. Eph. 4: **Be zealous to maintain the unity of the Spirit through the bond of peace—one body and one Spirit—just as you have also been called to one and the same hope of your calling: one Lord, one faith, one Baptism, one God and Father of us all.** 1 Cor. 12: **Just as there is one Body, and yet it has many members, yet all are members of one Body; even though you are many, yet you are one Body; so also is Christ.** Col. 3: **Love is the bond of perfection.**

---

* "The vestment of Christ was divided into four parts, and His tunic was not divided, something which I may have said was a sign of something mystic. For the four parts of the earth, brought back to salvation as they have been, have divided or shared indivisibly among themselves the covering of the Word, i.e., His flesh." Tr. Richard Dinda. The Latin passage is from the 1622 edition.

We have previously heard that the high priest Caiaphas tore his garment, thereby giving notice of the dismemberment of the Jewish polity and synagogue. Here Christ's cloak remains untorn, thereby signifying the unity of the Christian Church in the New Testament. Furthermore, the dividing of Christ's clothes may be seen as a sign that in this life the embattled Church here on earth is sometimes divided by heresies; however, just as Christ's cloak remained undivided, so also the victorious Church in heaven will remain free of all division and dismemberment. St. Augustine testifies to that with these two stories: In Luke 5, the apostles, at Christ's command, threw out the net and enclosed a great multitude of fish, which caused the net to tear. But following Christ's resurrection, John 21, when the apostles once again cast out the net and hauled in many fish, this time the net did not tear. Since both miraculous catches of fish symbolize the spiritual fishing for men in the Kingdom of Christ—as Christ Himself teaches, Mat. 3, Luke 5—Augustine thus interprets these stories as follows: In this life the Christian Church, before its entry into glory with Christ, is cast into all sorts of divisions and schisms. However, after the [final] resurrection such division and ripping apart will cease; then all the members of the Church will praise God the Lord without any scandals (offenses), hindrances, or divisions. Finally, St. Paul, Eph. 4, describes the heretics as inciting true knavery like some gambling dice-players [referring to v. 14]. From this reference, Ireneus, *lib*.1, *cap*.1, creates the following allegory: Just as the soldiers cast lots for Christ's coat, and no doubt roguishly grabbed the dice, so also the heretics still today deal with the Scriptures. They seize the glorious verses of the Bible so that thus they can misuse them as an excuse for their false doctrine. God the Lord wants to sustain us in the oneness of the true faith against all mischief and deception of the false teacher. Amen.

O Lord Jesus Christ, who wears such a superscription on Your cross: Jesus of Nazareth, King of the Jews, also be my Jesus and Savior, my King and Ruler. Uphold me in Your kingdom of grace, and lead me into the kingdom of glory. May Your poverty make me rich in my soul. May Your nakedness be my covering, so that the shame of my nakedness may never be revealed before the pure eyes of God. Amen.

The Fourth Sermon

How Christ commanded John to take care of His mother, and how He was defamed on the cross.

Standing beside the cross of Jesus was His mother and His mother's sister Mary, wife of Cleopas, and Mary Magdalene. As Jesus looked at His mother and His disciple standing there—the one whom He loved—He spoke to His mother: Woman, behold, that is your son. After that, He said to the disciple: Behold, that is your mother. And from that hour on, the disciple received her to himself.— But those who passed by reviled Him and shook their heads, saying: What a job You're doing of destroying the Temple and rebuilding it in three days. Help Yourself now; if You are God's Son, then step down from the cross. In like manner, the high priests also mocked Him among themselves, along with the scribes and elders and the rest of the people. They said: He helped others, and He cannot even help Himself. If He is Christ and King of Israel, the Chosen One of God, let Him help Himself and step down from the cross so that we may see it and believe Him. He trusted in God; let God now rescue Him, if it please Him. For He said: I am God's Son. The murderer who was being crucified with Him, also confronted Him and reviled Him. The soldiers also mocked Him. They stepped up to Him and brought Him vinegar and said: If You are the King of the Jews, then help Yourself.

In John 13 it is recorded concerning Christ, that as He had always loved His own who were in the world, He thus also loved them up to the very end. Of this, we have an example in the text just read. In it is reported that Christ, as He was enduring His greatest torment and anguish on the cross, for all that still thought of His dear mother. Even before He complained of His own great pain, He assigned her a guardian, whom she adopted. In like manner as Christ patiently endured shame and rejection throughout His entire life, He thus also endured the same to the end. Hence in Isa. 53 He is called the most rejected and the most worthless; and His entire life is nothing but public scorn. Of this, we have an example in this [Passion] story, wherein we perceive that even in the midst of His great anguish on the cross He was still mocked by many. In respect to the first matter, by so lovingly providing for His mother, He let His love shine forth. Regarding the other, in that He was despised by everybody, He let shine forth his patience. Therefore, we rightly say with St. Augustine: From the high pulpit-throne of His cross, Christ proclaimed to us in word and in deed His love, patience, and humility. We now intend to deal with and hear about both of these subjects:

I. How Christ commended John to Mary as her foster son and, in return, directed Mary to be the guardian of John.
II. How He was, by one and all, despised and scorned on the cross.

I. Even though the Lord Christ hangs on the cross in utter shame and scorn, appearing as if He has been forsaken by God and men, even so, some (although few) find themselves steadfastly keeping watch by the cross and awaiting the end. The evangelists particularly remember Mary, the mother of the Lord. What pain and anguish this must have been for her can best be comprehended by a true mother's heart; for here was richly fulfilled what Simeon in Luke 2 had earlier proclaimed to

Mary: **Behold, a sword is going to pierce through your soul.** These words referred to this great pain which would so severely wound her soul—more severely than a real sword might ever have wounded a human body. And one must truly marvel that Mary was able actually to view her own beloved Son (whose wholesome, saving teaching and work she had until now so deeply embraced in her heart) thus being stretched out on the cross, nailed to it, given to drink of vinegar and myrrh mixed with wine, and maligned by all. However, God's might manifests itself in the midst of her weakness, 2 Cor. 12. It gives her strength to bear this overwhelming agony. As the Lord now takes notice of her, as well as of His beloved disciple John, He says to her: **Woman, behold, that is your Son.** The fact that He here does not call her His mother (which, in truth, she was) could well have been because He did not wish to distress her even more by calling her by that most intimate name, "Mother." With this statement He commends her to His beloved disciple John. In the same manner He says to John: **Behold, that is your mother.** With these words He commends His beloved mother to him, so that they might mutually have each other for comfort, protection and help. Christ had no significant possessions in this world; indeed, He had not even a place to lay His head, Mat. 8. The soldiers had divided his clothing among themselves, and they tossed lots for His coat. Thus, there was nothing left for the dear Lord possibly to allot to His mother. Accordingly, He commended her to John, for him to comfort her and provide for her needs according to his ability, which then John also did. For shortly afterwards it is reported that he took her to himself, or, as it properly reads in his language [the Greek]—which indeed by some at that time was understood only in that way—that he took care of her and comforted her. However, the words in Greek read almost as if he had received her into his home. For although he, along with the other apostles, had forsaken everything, John 6, they nevertheless did not so completely disperse their possessions that they never again made further use of them. As Nicephorus reports (1:28), John sold his ancestral possessions in Galilee and purchased a home in Jerusalem, which was located on Mt. Zion, in which he and Mary lived for eleven years before he set out for Asia.

1. Mary is a picture (portrayal) of the Christian Church, through whose service Christ is still born daily in a spiritual manner in the hearts of the believers, as St. Paul says, Gal. 4: **My beloved children, to whom I once more anxiously give birth, so that Christ might gain stature within you.** In this world, this same Christian Church must also stand beneath the cross. If it someday wants to partake of the heavenly comfort and of the eternal glory, then it must first also partake of the suffering of Christ in this world, 2 Cor. 1. Regarding such suffering, this spiritual Bride of the Lord laments, Song of Solomon 5, that she had been struck and wounded by the herdsmen who went about the city. The herdsmen are those who falsely boast that, in keeping with the orderly succession, they alone have been appointed as the shepherds and watchmen over the city of God. However, these very ones are often times the first to strike and wound the members of the true Church, even as Christ was brought to the cross by the Pharisees, scribes, and high priests; who nevertheless boasted with big mouths that they sat on the throne of Moses and that they alone had been appointed as guardians (herdsmen) of the people of God. Whoever would now be a member of the Church and a beloved disciple of the Lord, as John is here, must not be surprised if he also has to step beneath the cross. If Christ is to sprinkle us with His blood, which He shed upon the cross, we must not refuse to follow if He calls us beneath the cross.

2. Since Christ acknowledged His own while in the depths of His outward humiliation, and provided for them, how much more shall He now also acknowledge them in His state of glory, and receive them to Himself. For His love and faithfulness, which He bears towards all His believers, is not diminished by glory. In the life to come, love will be righteous and complete (perfect) among the elect; how much more does not Christ in such a state of His glory have perfect love towards His own, which David indeed highly extols, Psa. 31: **You perceive my soul in its need**, as if to say: Whenever I am in tribulation and need, no man wants to know about it; but You Lord are a true, faithful Friend. You acknowledge me in my need. Christ here demonstrates [this concern] with a comforting example in that He, in such a plain and simple manner, had His disciple and other believers take care of His beloved mother, forgetting [ignoring] His own anxiety about it. In this all poor widows and orphans may take comfort, just as God the Lord in Psa. 68 calls Himself a Father of the orphans and a Judge for the widows. Exo. 22: **If you offend widows and orphans, they will cry unto Me; and, I will hear their cry. Thus My wrath will grow furious, so that I will kill you with the sword; and, your wives will become widows and your children will be orphans.** For that is God's way: Whenever man's help ceases, then is He most ready to help; whenever worldly comfort has fled, then will He send His heavenly comfort.

    3. Here we also behold the marvelous power of God's grace. Who would have thought that the disciples, who were such mighty heroes in their own minds, would forsake the Lord to the extent that only one among them all would follow the Lord to the cross—even though they all had offered that they would go with Him even unto death. It thereby becomes clearly apparent that all good, especially steadfastness, has to be crafted by the grace of God, for our strength is too weak for that. When in our own eyes we are the strongest, that is when in God's eyes we often are the weakest. And when in our own eyes we are weakest, that is when in God's eyes we are the strongest. Thus why St. Paul writes in 2 Cor. 12: **When I am weak, then I am strong.** If we want to conduct our lives properly and securely, one eye of our heart must at all times look to God for His strength so that we do not become discouraged (faint-hearted); the other eye must look at our weakness so that we do not become arrogant. Therefore St. Paul writes in the text already cited: **Best of all, I will boast about my weakness so that the power of Christ may live within me.**

4. Just as Mary is here commended to John, the Lord's apostle, so also should all teachers and preachers remember that Christ has actually at great expense entrusted to them His Church, which He purchased with His own blood. Thus, they are indeed to have a zealous concern for her. For what God the Lord says in Eze. 3: **You child of mankind, I have established you to be a watchman over the house of Israel; you are to hear the Word from My mouth, and then proclaim it**, precisely this should all teachers of the Church have said to them (drawn to their attention). They should hear the Word from the mouth of the Lord, even as John lay his head on the Lord Christ's bosom and dipped heavenly wisdom from His heart. Thereafter, they are to expound anew this Word to the Church. On the other hand, just as Mary was told to take care of John, so should the Church also duly provide for her servants, to protect and assist them, that they thus share in petitions, instruction, comfort, and help, since they stand here under the cross of Christ until they both finally will be taken up into the glory of Christ.

II. As Christ thus takes care of His own, He is for that reason slandered and scorned by many. The evangelists tell of five different kinds of slanderers. First there are the common folks who came by and slandered Him. They shook their heads, spit on Him as it were, and said: **What a fine job You are doing of destroying the Temple and rebuilding it in three days. If You are God's Son, help Yourself now.** They borrowed these words from their father, the Devil, who spoke the same way to the Lord in Mat. 4: **If You are the Son of God, then speak so that these rocks become bread.** They also follow the tune of their father, the Devil, in shamelessly perverting (twisting) the words of Christ; for, Christ had not spoken of the Temple at Jerusalem, but rather of the Temple of His body. When it was destroyed, He would build it again in three days, John 2. The second group is the high priests, even as the third is the scribes and elders. Their hatred was still not satisfied; instead, they spoke from excessively devilish hearts: **He helped others, and yet cannot help Himself.** They are thus offended at Christ's outward weakness, even though He was mighty enough to rescue Himself immediately through divine power, had not our salvation and redemption required something different. They furthermore say: **If He is Christ the King of Israel, the Elect of God, let Him help Himself and thus step down from the cross, so that we may see and believe.** But that was nothing. For when Christ once more arose from the dead, that was an even greater miracle than if He had stepped down from the cross while He still was alive. Nevertheless, these godless people did not believe in Him. Finally they say: **He trusted in God; let Him now save Him, if it please Him; for He had said, I am God's Son.** Herewith they mock the Lord with the taunt that He is waiting in vain for help; and, since He was stuck on such a wretched cross, He dare not try to convince them that He was God's Son.

The Devil, through these tools [dupes], spewed all this forth against Christ to break Him down through distrust and impatience so that He would descend from the cross, thus leaving behind the comforting [words], **It is finished.** Fourth come the murderers who were crucified with Him. They also slander Him. However, one of them is later converted. Finally, the soldiers also do not fail [to slander] Him. They bring Him vinegar and say: **If You are the King of the Jews, then help Yourself.** Such rejection of Christ was proclaimed long before in Isa. 53, and especially in Psa. 22, where are recorded almost the same words which are here used by these slanderers: **I am** scorned by the people and rejected by the nations. All those who see Me ridicule Me, spread open their mouths, and shake their heads. **He complains to the Lord; let Him help Him out and rescue Him, if He so desires.** Thus also in Psa. 31: **I experienced so much evil that I became a great disgrace to My neighbors and an object of aversion to My relatives.** Psa. 35: **They open their mouths wide against Me, and say: There, there, we are glad to see that.** Psa. 109: **They have opened their ungodly mouths against Me. They speak evil against Me everywhere.**

1. Why, then, is Christ thus scorned and maligned in the midst of His greatest anguish? This shame befell Him so that we might not fall into eternal disgrace. Had not Christ stepped in to take our place, and had He not allowed this disgrace to come over Him, then we would have had to be put to shame before God's judgment. One usually is accustomed to having compassion for those who have been condemned to death; however, Christ, who suffered everything innocently, was not able to experience that. He was here forsaken by all human comfort and compassion, thereby making payment for our debt. We should have been punished in eternity on account of our sins without any comfort or compassion. Christ, however, here stepped into our place and allowed Himself to be so pitiably tortured without any sympathy. These poisonous slanders were none other than fiery arrows which the Devil shot into the heart of the Lord Christ, which the dear Lord endured so that these fiery darts of the Devil might not bring us harm. Oftentimes these kinds of thoughts also creep into our hearts: Were God really pleased with you (were you actually His dear child) then He would rescue you and not let you suffer this cross for so long. So that such thoughts might not harm our salvation when we turn to God in repentance, behold, Christ listened to [put up with] such slanderous talk.

2. Just as the Lord Christ was tempted by the Devil at the beginning of His ministry, in that He had to hear: **If You are God's Son, then say that these rocks are to become bread**, so also at the end of His life He had to hear from the instruments of the Devil: **If You are God's Son, then step down from the cross.** Through such means, the Devil intended to bring Him to the point of rejecting His trust in God. And since He had to endure hunger and suffer on the cross, He no longer was to regard Himself as being the Son of God. Thus also must the true disciples of Christ often hear someone remark regarding their crosses: If this person loved God, he would not have to go through this, as David laments in Psa. 42: **My tears are my food day and night because one daily says to me, Where then is Your God?** Such a remark really does cause one much pain, as David immediately adds: **It is as if my bones are being murdered**; that is, I am so distressed over this that my bones dry up **on account of my enemies slandering me, as they say to me every day, Where now is your God?** However, we are to learn here from Christ's example that we are no less children of God even though we are put under the cross and do not immediately find relief. Christ does not throw trust away; rather, He remains steadfast and tenaciously clings to God's promises, knowing that this suffering is a road to glory. So also, to that end should we cling to [His promises].

3. Both malefactors who were crucified with Christ here slander the Lord—though later one of them, through a great miracle and through the words of Christ, is converted. Here we have a type of the two peoples: Jews and Gentiles. At first, both slandered Christ and despised Him; but later one group, namely, the Gentiles, is converted by word and miracle and still reproves daily the other, the Jews, who never cease being offended over the cross of Christ and slandering Him. We, however, give thanks to God that He has brought us to the knowledge of His Son and would uphold us in the same. Amen.

O Lord Jesus Christ, You who also on the timber-trunk of the cross demonstrate care and concern for Your mother and Your beloved disciple, look upon me with the eye of Your mercy. Give grace that I may follow You when You call me under Your cross. You, who on the cross were slandered by one and all, let not the shame and scorn of the Devil take me unawares; and if I be scorned by the godless, then give me grace to bear such with patience. Amen.

The Fifth Sermon

Heaven is opened to the converted criminal*; the sun becomes darkened; Christ laments His being forsaken by God.

But one of the evil-doers who had been hung there reviled Him and said: If You are Christ, then help Yourself and us. Thereupon the other one answered and rebuked him, saying: And you also do not fear God? – you who even are under the same condemnation? And indeed, we are rightly under it, for we received what our deeds deserved; this One however has done nothing wrong. And, he said to Jesus: Lord, remember me when You come into Your kingdom. And Jesus said to him: Truly I say to you, today you shall be with Me in Paradise. And it was around the sixth hour, and there was a darkness over the entire land until the ninth hour; and the sun lost its brightness. And around the ninth hour Jesus cried out loudly and said: Eli, Eli, lama sabachthani, that is translated: My God, My God, why have You forsaken Me? Some who stood there, however, as they heard this, said: He is calling for Elias.

In Gen. 3 it is recorded that the first Adam, after he had transgressed God's command, and had stretched out his hand to the forbidden tree, was soon driven out of Paradise. Instead a cherubim was encamped in front of it with an unsheathed, slashing sword. For since Adam had brought death upon himself and all his descendants by his sin, and thus was the greatest murderer, God no longer wanted to associate with him in His Paradise, which was the land of the living and the place in which

---

* In Gerhard's time Schächer could mean "robber" or "murderer."

stood the Tree of Life. In this Scripture lesson, on the contrary, it is reported that as the Second Adam stretched out His hands on the tree of the cross, thereby making payment for sin, that a repentant murderer had the gates of Paradise opened again for him; and herewith it is affirmed:

I. That at this time grace is purchased anew for the poor human race through Christ's suffering and merit; that the way to Paradise stands open for all those who with prior genuine repentance believe in Christ as the Prince of Life; that they may enter into this blessed land of the living. (The first part of the lesson deals with this matter.)

II. In the second part is remembered the darkness which occurred during the time of Christ's suffering.

III. In the third part is described the ardent (longing) lament of the Lord on the cross, that He was forsaken by God.

I. The evangelists record that at the outset both criminals had maligned the Lord Christ, but later one was converted. For he remembered how each and every one had testified to the Lord Christ's innocence. He recalled the magnificent sermon the Lord had shortly before proclaimed to the mourning women as He was led out of the city. He reflected as well on the great patience with which Christ had endured all the pain and slander, and with what gentle meekness He prayed for His worst enemies. And he saw also the superscription that was attached to the cross of Christ, which testified that He was a King. Through all these reflections the Holy Spirit worked a genuine conversion in his heart, so that he ceases his slander. And, as the other criminal, from a satanic heart and with a blaspheming tongue, blurts out: **If You are the Christ, then help Yourself and us**, he rebukes him, saying: **And do you not fear God, you who are under a similar condemnation? And indeed, we rightly so, for we are** receiving the just deserts for our deeds; however, this One has done nothing wrong. Thereupon he turns to the Lord Christ and says to Him: **Lord, remember me, when You come into Your kingdom**, and immediately obtains from the Lord the comforting declaration: **Truly I say to you, today you will be with Me in Paradise.** Christ gave more than what was asked of Him;"for He who was mute and deaf towards all shame (affront), did not remain mute and deaf to the prayers directed to Him in confident faith."

Here we must now consider, **1.** that by the death of Christ the way to Paradise has once more been opened. The ladder to heaven which had been handed over to the first man for him and his descendants to enter into heaven was broken by him; however, by His death Christ once again prepared it for us, as He accordingly indeed also beautifully portrays Himself as a ladder (standing upon the earth, its top reaching to heaven) upon which the angels of God ascend and descend, Gen. 28; for Christ testifies to such a portrayal of Himself in John 1. Thereby is it announced that Christ once again raises the heavenly ladder for us so that we may draw near to God in heaven. And so it was that He could promise the criminal an entry to heaven.

After the Fall, the way to life had been closed to us. However, Christ has once again found the very same way to life: as it is written, from now on we can enter into life through Him, Psa. 16, and be with Him in Paradise and behold His glory, John 17.

2. Accordingly, we have here an example of true conversion to God. The example of this criminal witnesses to the fact that conversion is purely and simply a work of God's grace. He had carried on for his entire life with evil misdeeds, and yet at the end of life he is converted through the grace of God. Indeed, no one can say that this criminal was converted through his own power, or attained salvation through his own merits. Rather, it is by the pure, unmerited grace of God. Also, we see here of what elements true conversion consists. This thief acknowledged his transgression. **We are receiving**, he says, **the just deserts for our deeds.** If conversion to God is to occur, then the turning away from sin must precede it. He thereupon turns to Christ, for in Him and through Him alone we must again come to the grace of God and forgiveness of sins. [The criminal] not only testifies to Christ's innocence, but he also confesses Him to be his King, [a King] who has prepared an everlasting Kingdom for all those who believe on Him. Thus, along with this contrition and inner faith of heart there was also the outward confession of the mouth, and indeed a marvelous and glorious confession it was. Even though Christ was in outward humiliation (hanging [on the cross] and pitiably treated, slandered by one and all) [this repentant criminal] nevertheless confessed Christ to be a King with an eternal Kingdom. This is a much more glorious faith and confession than if he had confessed Christ as the Son of God while He manifested His power with teaching and miracles.

Along with this confession also came love, as he admonishes the other unrepentant criminal and would gladly bring him to the fear of God, so that while there still was time, he would desist [from his slander], confess his transgression, and turn to Christ. This was a great work of love, for one can show no greater love to the next person than when one with teaching, comfort, admonition, and warning shows him the true Way to salvation. This was thus a true, complete conversion of the criminal. The reason that there was no hindrance to his coming to such a conversion so late is that as long as it is still called "today," Psa. 95 (as long as this life lasts) the portal to grace remains open. Also, the previous magnitude and quantity of sins is no hindrance for this conversion to be righteous (honest, upright). For as it is written in Eze. 18, that **when the godless person converts from all his sin, then all his transgressions which he committed shall not be remembered.** Thus, a great comfort is comprehended in the example of this criminal, namely, that even though the sins are many—and at times repentance is slow to follow—for all that, the door to grace is not obstructed. Rather, it remains open for all sinners for as long as they live, no matter how much they have sinned—just so they do not deliberately neglect (let slip by) the time of grace. Rom. 5: **Where sin is mighty, there the grace of God is even mightier.**

At the same time, so that a person does not misuse this comforting example and deliberately postpone repentance, the example of the other criminal is set along side of this one. He persisted in his sins up to the end [and] therefore fell into eternal damnation. Finally, we may conclude from the comforting answer of Christ that the souls of repentant believers enter into Paradise after death; that is, to such a place where there is fullness of joy and a delightful existence at the right hand of God, Psa. 16, where no excruciating agony can touch them, but rather where they are guarded and kept by God's fatherly hand, Wisdom of Solomon 3, just as in former times the earthly Paradise was a place of joy and the land of the living. And indeed, the soul does not arrive there perhaps after many long years, but rather as soon as it departs from the body, as the Lord here also states: **Today you will be with Me in Paradise.** So that one does not think that this was something very special just for the [believing] criminal, with which other believers may not comfort themselves, it is generally applied in the Revelation, chapter 14: **Blessed** [i.e., Saved are] **the dead who die in the Lord, from now on.** And, Christ speaks of all true believers in John 5, that they immediately pass through death into life.

II. In the second part of this lesson the evangelists recall a darkness of the sun which at that time (around the sixth hour, that is, at noon) occurred over the entire land. It lasted until the ninth hour, that is, for three whole hours. In this darkness of the sun, many strange and distinct elements coincide. First of all, it occurs during the full moon, which can be concluded because the Jews had to celebrate their Passover during the full moon. Darkness [i.e., an eclipse], however, usually occurs during the new moon. Next, it extends over the entire land, whereas the darkness is usually not seen by all the people [simultaneously]. Furthermore, it takes place in bright noon day, when the sun usually shines the brightest. Finally, it lasts for three whole hours. And Orosius even reports (as does also Phlegon, the calculator of the Olympiad) that at that time one could see the stars in the sky, and that it was as dark as night. Dionysius Areopagita records, Epistle 7:11, that he also saw the darkness, and, since he could not find any natural cause for it, he consequently concluded that either the Lord of nature was suffering, or else the world was perishing.

By this darkness then is signified, first of all, that the sun was, as it were, showing sympathy for the Lord Christ, and that the heavens became black because God's Son was made thus to suffer and be maligned on the cross. For if St. Paul dared to say, Rom. 8, that all creation (nature) was in anguish at having to be subjected to the vain and unlawful use of godless [men], even more can we say that the sun was struck with dread and put on, as it were, a black mourning garment [in sorrow] over having to give light for godless men to stretch out their hands and tongues against Christ. Even as Jeremiah dared to say, chapter 2, that the heavens themselves were scandalized, terrified, and violently shaken because of the idolatry of the Israelite nation, how much more are we able to say that the heavens were appalled and darkened over the fact that the Jews had crucified the Lord of glory.

Thus, with this darkness of the sun is fulfilled the threat to the Jews in Jer. 15, that the sun will go down on them at high noon. Indeed, by the sun is also understood joy and well-being, of which the Jews will be robbed when they will least expect it. However, it is nevertheless not incorrect if one interprets this literally to mean that at brightest noon-time the sun set for the

Jews. Also relevant here is the type found in Exo. 10: three entire days of thick darkness throughout all Egypt when God wanted to rescue His people from their slavery. Even so, because God the Lord now intended to rescue His people from their hellish slavery by the death of Christ, there was a darkness throughout the entire land for three solid hours.

Thirdly, the darkness also signified that Christ—the Sun of Righteousness, Mal. 4, and the Light of the World, John 11—intended to walk into the dark valley of death so that His eyes might be darkened in death. However, just as the sun finally, after three hours, came forth again with its previous light, thus is thereby signified that Christ, the Sun of Righteousness, would after three days once again come forth from the darkness of the grave and walk in the light of His heavenly brightness.

Fourthly, the darkened sun at its zenith was (in the language of the astronomers) not far from "the head of the dragon," thus signifying that Christ was at the same time crushing the head of the hellish Snake, the old Dragon, Revelation 12. And since the moon has no light without the sun, it is thus to be concluded that the moon, in the opposite portion of the heavens, was likewise at the same time also darkened by the tail of the Dragon, as the hellish Dragon at that time stung His heel, and as He indeed felt [the Devil's] stinger on the cross, Gen. 3 [v. 15].

Fifthly, it is hereby proclaimed to the Jews that since they had rejected the true Light, Christ, from henceforth the light of godly grace and knowledge would be taken from them and they would thus also in their souls experience pitiable, dreadful darkness—just as they now experienced outward darkness.

Sixthly, darkness in the Scriptures signifies God's wrath, just as, on the contrary, the light of the divine countenance signifies His grace, Num. 6, Psa. 4, Psa. 67. The fact that the sun then became so frighteningly darkened indicates that at that time God looked with wrath upon His Son since the sins of the entire world were laid upon Him. And this wrathful viewing [of Christ] lasted for three whole hours. God viewed the Lord Christ as being so black on account of our sins, even as the time of divine punishment is described as a black day in Joel 2. And through the prophet Amos, ch. 8, as God the Lord proclaims His wrath over the people of Israel, He says: **I will let the sun go down at noon and let the land become dark in broad daylight.** Christ understood this very well. Thus, He soon thereafter cried out in agony: **My God, why have You forsaken Me?**

Finally, in the Scriptures darkness also signifies eternal damnation. In Mat. 22 the king commands that the servants who had on no wedding garment were to be cast into the darkness; that is, into hell. It is used in a similar way in Mat. 8 and 25, 2 Pet. 2, and in the epistle of Jude, while, on the other hand, eternal life is called the inheritance of the saints in light, Col. 1. That the sun is now here darkened signifies that the agony and darkness of hell fell upon the Lord Christ for the sake of our sins so that we might come to eternal light. We had altogether deserved to be cast into the eternal darkness. But then Christ stepped into our place, allowed darkness and the agony of hell to come over Him so that we might be freed from it. This, then, is the second part of this lesson; namely, of what the frightening darkness in Christ's suffering signifies.

III. In the third part [of the lesson], the evangelists report that around the ninth hour, as the darkness had finally ended, Christ began [to say] with a loud voice: **My God, My God, why have You forsaken Me?** These words were taken from the 22nd Psalm of David. The Lord Christ well understood what this darkness signified; namely, how His heavenly Father looked upon Him as so very black and dealt with Him in His wrath for three whole hours. Therefore, He cried out with a pitiful voice and lamented that He was forsaken by God, as reported in the Epistle to the Hebrews, ch. 5: Christ offered up His petitions and pleadings with a strong outcry and with tears. As Christ began His suffering by lamenting about the tribulation of His soul and the agony of His heart [in Gethsemane], so He also now likewise thus concludes [His sufferings] by lamenting that He was forsaken by God, in order to declare that we are not chiefly to view His outward suffering and pain, but rather to contemplate His inner suffering—of how He is crushed by the burden of divine wrath and finds the agony of hell in His heart.

From the foregoing we now [draw several lessons]. **1.** We should perceive what a terribly frightening thing it was that the Lord Christ was crushed with the burden of sin so that He pitiably sighed like a dove and whimpered like a crane, Isa. 38. Indeed, the world regards sin as a minor thing, but we here see how it is regarded in God's judgment. Accordingly, when the Devil, the world, or our flesh wants to entice us to sin, we should call to mind this sad picture of the crucified Christ, of how He lamented being forsaken by God on account of the burden of sin. **2.** Because Christ felt this agony, thinking of nothing else than that He was forsaken by God, behold, from this we may be certain that God will nevermore forsake us. And because God the Lord regarded Christ as black on account of our sin, so is it accomplished for us that He permits His gracious countenance to shine upon us, Num. 6. **3.** In like manner, Christ here laments being forsaken by God; thus does God the Lord also often allow the members of Christ to experience such anguish, so that they think nothing other than that God has forsaken them and will no longer look upon them in grace. We find such examples of temptations especially in David and Job. And with such temptations God more often assails, not the ordinary Christian, but rather the greatest saints, who have increased more than others in the knowledge of God. Just as Christ then no less remains God's Son, even though He was thrust into such great temptation (tribulation), so also such tempted hearts should no less consider that they still are and remain God's children, even though He puts them under such temptations (tribulations) for a long time. Even as Christ in [the] midst of such agony also cried out: **My God, My God**, thereby confessing that in His heart He no less still regards God as His own God and gracious Father, so also such troubled hearts should not cast aside their trust. Instead, they should steadfastly cling to God's promises, for He says in Isa. 49: **Zion says, the Lord has forsaken me; the Lord has forgotten me. Can a mother also forget her child? And even if she does forget it, yet I will never forget you. See I have stamped [branded] you** [your name] into My hands. 4. Finally, since Christ was tempted in everything just like we are, Heb. 5, He will thus always be able to have sympathy for our weaknesses. Therefore we may joyfully step before the throne of grace, since inasmuch as He has suffered and was tempted, He can help those who are tempted, Heb. 2. As St. Peter in his First Epistle, chapter 5, admonishes the believers, they should in their tribulations be comforted, in that precisely the same sufferings are visited upon their brothers in the world. Thus this should rather be our greatest comfort in our tribulations: that such sufferings were also experienced by our Lord and Head, Christ. He will acknowledge us in our need and help us. May He grant us this by grace. Amen.

    O Lord Jesus Christ, let my heart in its final end hear from Your voice these words: Today you will be with Me in Paradise; bind my soul into the bundle of the living. Since You Yourself also for my sake lamented being forsaken by God, so grant me grace that I never forsake You, but instead cling to You with eternal love. Amen.

The Sixth Sermon

Christ complains of His thirst, declares that everything has been accomplished, commends His soul into the hands of His heavenly Father, and thereupon falls calmly asleep.

After this, since Jesus knew that everything had already been accomplished, and so that the Scriptures would be fulfilled, He said: I thirst. A container full of vinegar stood there, and immediately someone ran beneath Him, took a sponge and filled [soaked] it with vinegar and hyssop, stuck it on a reed, held it up to His mouth, gave Him a drink, and said to the others: Wait, let's see if Elias will come and take Him down [from the cross]! When Jesus then had partaken of the vinegar, He said: It is finished. And once more He loudly cried out and said: Father, I commend My spirit into Your hands. And as He said that, He bowed His head and died.

In the 49th chapter of Genesis it is written of the patriarch Jacob, as he was ready to draw up his will and wished to speak [some final words] with his sons and proclaim future things to them, that he began: **Come home and listen, you children of Jacob; listen to your father, Israel.** He wanted thereby to encourage them, so that they would pay diligent attention to his final words and take careful note of what kind of divine mysteries were hidden therein, even as the Holy Spirit moreover regarded them as worthy of recording in great detail. Since the final words of the patriarch Jacob are so justly noted, is it not incumbent upon us even more highly to regard and never to forget the final words of our Lord Christ—One who is much greater than all the patriarchs, and One in whom all the patriarchs had placed their hope? So also for the same reason and in the same manner, the holy evangelists by impulse [i.e., inspiration] of the Holy Spirit diligently recorded the final words [statements] of Christ. In the previous sections [sermons] four of them have been explained. Yet there still remain the final three, namely, of how

I. The Lord Christ complains of His thirst,
II. Immediately thereafter testifies that everything was now finished, and finally
III. Commends His spirit to His heavenly Father, whereupon He gently and willingly gives up His spirit.

I. Since Jesus knew, say the evangelists, **that everything was already accomplished, in order that the Scriptures might be fulfilled, He said: I thirst.** This thirst resulted from exhaustion. For since His holy blood had generously flowed from of His wounds, His strength was exhausted and He had a great thirst. Just as a day laborer, when he has performed hard labor all day long, feels a great thirst, so also a warrior, when he has withstood the slaughter, similarly becomes thirsty. Thus Christ, the righteous Servant of God, had worked the entire previous night and all day for the sake of our salvation; and, as the Prince of Life, He had fought against the forces of hell. His soul had labored, as it is written in Isa. 53; **His strength was dried up like a potsherd, His tongue stuck to His gums**, Psa. 22. For that reason, Christ felt such a thirst upon the cross. The type [of Christ's thirst] was Samson, that precious hero about whom it is recorded in Jdg. 15 that when he had slain the throng of Philistines was afterwards very thirsty. As Christ, the true Nazarene and doubly stalwart Hero, overcame the Devil and all His might on the cross, He experienced such a thirst that it made Him call out with a clear voice: **I thirst.** We should again consider, however, that at that time not merely outward suffering befell Christ. Rather, upon Him was laid the burden of our sins—which He at that moment offered up on the tree, 1 Pet. 2—as well as the wrath of God, on account of which He had earlier lamented of being forsaken by God. Thus, He experienced not only physical thirst, but also spiritual thirst. In Luke 16 the pain of the damned is described as a terrible, fierce thirst, so that they indeed anxiously desire even one small drop of water with which to cool their tongue amidst the great flames.

Furthermore, in the Revelation, chapter 7, it is written of the elect that they will no longer suffer the hunger or thirst which the damned have to fear. We had all deserved this hellish thirst, for since our first parents ate of the fruit of the forbidden tree, they, along with all their descendants, deserved to be delivered into such an eternal thirst. So that we now are rescued and, in contrast, given to drink of the rich blessings of God's House, and to drink with bliss as by a stream, Psa. 36, behold, that is why Christ suffers such a thirst in His suffering (Passion). Beyond that, thus has Christ also thirsted for our salvation and eternal bliss. For since the fire of passionate love burned within His heart, He said: **I thirst**, just as He says to His disciples, Luke 22: **I have heartily desired to eat the Passover lamb with you before I suffer.** He had a desire for us, and thus He said: I thirst. (Take this to mean that [He thirsts] for our salvation.) Thus, this heavenly Bridegroom says in Song of Solomon, chapter 4: You have taken away (or wounded) My heart, My sister and dear Bride.* Since His heart was wounded and burned by love, it thus follows that the resulting thirst and longing were for our salvation. Finally, with His thirst, Christ atoned for the sins that we sometimes commit with our tongue; it is an unruly [instrument of] evil, full of deadly poison, James 4.

---

* Ancient poetry has lovers address each other as sister and brother. Tr.

Since Christ thirsted for us, our soul indeed should in turn rightly thirst for Him, even as David had such a spiritually thirsty soul, Psa. 42: **As the deer cries out for fresh water, so cries out my soul, O God, for You. My soul thirsts for God, for the living God,** as if to say: You are the well of Life, **with You there is a living fountain**, Psa. 36. Thus thirsts also my exhausted soul and languishes for You. Psa. 63: **God, You are my God; my soul thirsts for You. My flesh longs for You in a dry and parched land, where there is no water.** It is as if he means to say: My soul's thirst cannot be satisfied with temporal things; they all are dry and arid. However, the Tree of Life is able to quench it. Psa. 143: **My soul thirsts for You like an arid land.** Whoever, then, will drink this water, which God the Lord gives to a soul that thirsts for Him, such a person will not thirst in eternity, as Christ teaches, John 4. Yea, **He also wants to give the thirsty to drink free of charge from the well of living Water**, Revelation, chapter 21.

As Christ thus complained about thirst, one of the soldiers under the cross took a sponge and filled it with vinegar and hyssop, stuck it onto a reed, and held it to His mouth and gave Him a drink. And he said to the others: **Wait, let's see if Elias comes and takes Him down** [from the cross]. Here we see first of all the immense ingratitude of the Jewish people, whom God led into the promised land, which flowed with milk and honey; and yet they, in turn, give their Creator and Duke to drink of vinegar. Such is still the case with all those who, having received great gifts from God, bring in turn no lovely gifts acceptable to God. Instead they bring the bitter late grapes; that is, all kinds of evil works. Accordingly, we see that Christ's prayer was also perverted. For as He earlier had called out: **Eli, Eli, My God, why have You forsaken Me**, the evil thugs twisted[the words to mean] that He had turned away from God and called upon Elias as a helper in need, [an accusation] which certainly painfully hurt the Lord Christ so that this disgrace (humiliation) broke

His heart. But He bore all this for our sake. We often do not know how to pray, Rom. 8, and frequently pray contrary to God's will. So that such prayers may not cause harm to our salvation, behold, for that reason Christ suffers having His prayer being perverted and interpreted contrary to its meaning.

II. When Jesus then had drunk of the vinegar, He said: **It is finished**, which was also the sixth word from the cross by the Lord Christ. With it He declares that everything has now been accomplished and fulfilled. [That is,] He well knew, upon the completion of His suffering, that He had endured everything that had been required [of Him] for the satisfaction of, and the sacrifice for, our sin. We should then bear in mind that Christ later in His descent into Hell did not suffer anew any agony and pain, in that He here says: **Everything is accomplished.** He had inwardly and outwardly suffered and endured everything that He had to suffer. Rather, it was a victorious descent into Hell, in which He bound the Devil, destroyed [the powers of] Hell, and manifested Himself as a mighty Conqueror of all things. Accordingly, He understood this as the fulfilling of the Scriptures, that now all prophecies about His suffering had been fulfilled, especially also those which testify to His thirst, Psa. 69: **They give Me vinegar to drink in My great thirst.** As Christ preached to His disciples about His impending suffering, He said: **Everything that is written about the Son of Man will be accomplished**, Luke 18. And now [on the cross] He says: **It is accomplished.** Here we see what sort of thoughts Christ was thinking on the cross; namely, that He reflected upon the predictions of the prophets which they had made about His suffering, 1 Pet. 1, so that He indeed might completely fulfill all these things, and that nothing be left out. Finally, He understood [the words "it is accomplished"] to refer to the fullness [adequacy] of His sacrifice, that He now had completely paid for everything of which we were guilty, and had completely won for us that which was required for our salvation. As it says in Heb. 10: **He has with one offering (sacrifice) eternally completed (perfected) those who are being sanctified.** That is why He is justly called by St. Paul in Rom. 10 "**the Law's termination**"; namely, because He fulfilled everything that had been previously proclaimed in the Law and the Prophets, Mat. 11, and also because He accomplished everything that the Law required of us. When the work of creation was then finished, Moses says, Gen. 2, **God completed His work.** Now, as the redemption (the second creation) was finished, Christ again uses the very same word. Thus, we need no other sacrifice, no other payment for sin. His offering (sacrifice) is a complete sacrifice; His payment is a complete payment; He is the Alpha and the Omega of Rev. 1, the Initiator and the One who completes of our faith, and our Salvation, Heb. 12. The high priests of the Old Testament usually daily attended to divine worship and frequently performed various sacrifices. These Levitical sacrifices could never take away sin. However, our High Priest of the New Testament offered up the kind of sacrifice for sin which is effectual forever. Thus, He now sits at the right hand of God and from henceforth waits for the day when His enemies will be laid as a stool under His feet, Heb. 10. Accordingly, whenever the Law accuses us of not having done everything that God has prescribed in it, we can answer: It is accomplished, namely by Christ. He fulfilled it in my stead and gives it to me by grace.

      III. After this Christ shouts out loudly and says: **Father, I commend My spirit into Your hands**, which was the final Word of Christ from the cross. The fact that Christ called out loudly caused one of the ancient teachers to express these thoughts: that death did not overcome Christ in the same way that it overcomes us humans. Death takes away our speech; it stops up our mouth so that no coherent word any longer proceeds from it. However, Christ here dies much differently. He calls out loudly and coherently, and with [the cry] He gives us His spirit. Death, as it were, knew in advance that Christ was going to devour it and conquer it. That's why Death did not want to step up too close. Thus, Christ shouted out so loudly, and His clear voice causes Death to tremble, telling Death that it should step forth and carry out upon Him the right and power that it usually held over the human race.

It is also relevant here that the evangelists say Christ gave up His spirit, thus proving in deed what He said in John 10: **I have the power to relinquish My life, and I have the power to take it again; nobody takes it from Me, unless I Myself relinquish it.** With us humans it is ordained that in death our souls will be taken from us, Luke 12. At that time the soul must leave and vacate the shelter of the body, whether it does so willingly or not. But with Christ it is different; He gives up His spirit, for He is not dying out of necessity or by force. Instead He dies willingly; and certainly no one falls asleep more easily than Christ as He willingly gives up His spirit. That is why Christ's death redounds to our benefit, because He willingly endured Death. It had no claim over Him. As Death takes Him on and kills Him, it thereby loses the power it had over us on account of sin. In Num. 20 and Deu. 10 it is recorded that the high priest Aaron, at God's command, willingly laid aside his high priestly garments, went up on a mountain, and there died. That's what Christ, the High Priest of the New Testament, also does here. He willingly gives up His own life for our sake. Furthermore, that Christ in this last word calls God His Father gives us to understand that now God's wrath is over and done with.

Earlier, when the sun became dark, and Christ understood thereby that God saw Him as black because of the sin of mankind laid upon Him, He cried out wretchedly: **My God, My God, why have You forsaken Me?** However, as Christ now saw that everything was accomplished and that He had fulfilled everything pertaining to the redemption of the human race, He once more addressed God as His own dearly beloved Father and commended His soul into His hands. Just as one dear friend entrusts something to another, turning it over into his hands to protect it, and which he later intends to reclaim, so also Christ does here. He commends His soul to His Father as a precious possession, because He intends soon thereafter on the third day to take it back again. Also, as one receives that which is precious into his hands, so Christ knew that His soul was precious to God. Therefore He commends it into the hands of His heavenly Father.

Since the Lord Christ was also speaking and acting on the cross as our High Priest, it follows therefrom that Christ not only commended His own soul to His heavenly Father, but also the souls of all believers, who are Christ's members. He had, as it were, collected all the souls of believers into a single bundle with His own soul, as Abigail [commends her bundle of gifts to David] in 1 Sam. 25, and commends them into the hands of the heavenly Father. Thus God also says in Isa. 49: **Look, I have branded (inscribed) you** [your name] **into My hands.** And Christ says, John 10, **No one shall rip My sheep out of the hands of My Father.** (Understand by this, into whose hands I have commended them.) Accordingly, the dear Lord, when He intended to enter into His [time of] suffering, inwardly prayed and commended Himself and all believers to the heavenly Father, John 17: **I pray not only for these (the apostles), but rather also for those who will believe on Me by means of their Word.** In the same manner, He now also concludes His suffering with prayer and commends to His heavenly Father, not only His soul, but also the souls of all believers, as those who through the bond of love are united with Christ's soul. So then, when the hour of your death draws near, think on this: Christ already has commended your soul to God. You do likewise; that is, also commend your soul into God's hands. For these are the almighty hands from which you received your soul, Ecc. 12. These are the fatherly hands in which your soul shall encounter no torment, Wisdom of Solomon 7. These are the faithful (trustworthy) hands which on Judgment Day will again give back to you what you have commended to Him, as your body and soul shall once more be reconciled. Thus did Stephen, Acts 7. As the stones flew at him, he was mindful that the soul should be taken care of first, let happen to the body what will. He likewise commends his spirit and soul into God's hands, in which they indeed will be happy and safely kept. He well knew that the hellish birds of prey will ravenously pursue the poor soul when it departs from the body. That is why he commends it into God's hands. In His hands it is indeed kept safe and happy, preserved from all danger, from all misfortune and evil.

After Christ then had spoken all these words from the cross, He thereupon bowed His head and gave up His spirit. This bowing of the head indicated that as a final blessing He wanted to give us a kiss, thereby once more to demonstrate His heartfelt love. Soon thereafter He calmly and quietly departed. In a similar manner, it is written of the patriarch Jacob, Gen. 49: **When Jacob had completed the instructions to his children, he put his feet together on the bed and departed.**

In this passage where it is reported that Christ gave up His spirit, we should remember, first, that Christ truly did die. For the words are clear and distinct: Christ departed and gave up His spirit. Our reason finds this astounding and cannot reconcile itself to it. That God created heaven and earth—that He is righteous, all-knowing, merciful and almighty—[our reason] can comprehend to a certain extent. However, that God's Son actually died on the cross is [to our reason] silly scandal and foolishness. We, however, should believe God's Word more than the judgment of our reason; and of this we should be certain: that Christ, God's Son, truly died. For upon this [fact] rests the foundation of our Christianity, yea, also our salvation.

Accordingly, one must take note of what an occasion we have in the death of Christ; namely, that His sacred soul actually departed the body while at the same time the personal union of the divine and human nature was in no way torn apart, since both body and soul remain united with the person of God's Son. This, then, is a great and (for us humans) an incomprehensible mystery. Even though the soul of Christ was separated from His assumed flesh through death, even so His body in the midst of death still remained a Temple of God in which the fullness of the Godhead resides bodily, John 2, Col. 2. The fact that Christ's body was truly dead, yet remained a Temple of the living God, we, with our thoughts, will never be able to comprehend.

Finally, we must remember why Christ wanted not only to suffer, but rather also to die. For it happened once and for all to fulfill the prophecies and types of the Old Testament, about which St. Paul says in 1 Cor. 15, **Christ died according to the Scriptures.** Thus it is written in Gen. 3 that the hellish snake would pierce the Seed of the woman in His heel; that is to say, even though the hellish snake, the Devil, would have his head crushed underfoot, yet it would not go so badly for the Devil that he would not resist. Rather, it would cost the Lord Christ trouble; He would have to suffer and die because of it. In Psa. 16 Christ says: **You will not leave My soul in hell, nor allow that Your holy One decay** [in the tomb]. You make known to Me the way to life. Thus, then, both Christ's death and resurrection are set side by side; Christ indeed would die and be laid into the grave, yet would once more come forth to life. In Psa. 22 He says that God laid Him into the dust of death. In Isa. 53 it is written that Christ would give His life for a guilt-offering. In Dan. 9 a certain time is designated when Christ would be uprooted, that is, He would be snatched from the land of the living. In Zechariah 9 it is reported that Christ would release the captives through His blood from the pit in which there is no water. That is, it will cost Him His life and blood if He is going to render help to the captives. In Gen. 2 it is written that a deep sleep fell upon Adam, as God intended to craft a wife from his ribs. Thus Christ, the Heavenly Adam, fell asleep into death on the cross, as He wished to acquire for Himself a spiritual Bride and Church. In Exo. 12 it is written that the Passover lamb had to be slaughtered, with whose blood the Israelites were to smear their door posts of their homes. Our Easter/Passover Lamb is Christ, 1 Cor. 5, who also died on the tree, and shed His blood so that we may be safe from the hellish angel of death. Jonah was in the belly of the whale–fish for three days and three nights, Jonah 2. Christ applies [Jonah's experience] to Himself, Mat. 12, and teaches that it, too, was a type of His death. In conclusion, all sacrifices of the Old Testament, which were first [previously] slaughtered, pointed to the death of Christ.

Secondly, Christ chose to die in such a way for our benefit and for our sake, and for many reasons. For since He took our sins upon Himself, He therefore also had to take upon Himself the punishment for our sins, namely death, **for sin's gold (wage) is death**, Rom. 6, so that thereby a satisfaction could take place for the righteousness of God, since God the Lord had said to man in Gen. 2: **The day you eat from the forbidden fruit, you will die the death.** This command of God could not be broken. Accordingly, we should have died the eternal death; thus Christ had to give Himself into death for us, as St. Paul says, Rom. 4, **Christ gave Himself up for the sake of our sin**; and in Heb. 9, **So it is set for man to die one time, but after that the Judgment: Thus Christ offered Himself up one time to take away many sins.** In Mat. 26 Christ says that He sheds His blood for the forgiveness of sins, and once again, Mark 10, that He gives His life for the ransom of many.

Furthermore, Christ chose to overcome death with His death. "By the death of Christ, death is killed" (St. Bernhard). Also regarding this matter it is written in Heb. 2, **that He through death took away the power of him who had the power of** death, that is the Devil. And in Hosea 13 Christ had promised: **I shall redeem you from Hell and rescue you from death; Death, I will be a poison for you; Hell, I will be a pestilence for you.** Moreover, Christ with His death wanted to empower and confirm God's covenant of grace, as it is written in Heb. 9: **Where there is a testament, there the death of the one who made the testament has to occur, for a testament becomes established through that death; otherwise it has no authority if the one who made it is still living.** Accordingly, since Christ is a Mediator and Founder of the New Testament or Covenant of Grace (which consists in this: that God would no longer remember our transgression, Jer. 31), behold, for that reason Christ wanted also to empower such a Testament with His death and the shedding of His blood, just as the Epistle to the Hebrews cited above likens [Christ's acts] to the ratification of the Old Testament, which similarly was done through blood, in that **Moses, having spoken freely to all the people about all the commandments of the Law, took calves' and rams' blood with water and purple wool and hyssop and sprinkled the book [of the Law] and all the people, saying: This is the blood of the Testament that God has given you**, Exo. 24.

Since, however, the New Testament was much more glorious, it therefore had to be ratified with a much nobler and worthier blood, namely, with the blood of Christ, the Son of God. To this St. Paul points when he states, Rom. 5, **that we are reconciled to God through the death of His Son.** That is to say, God established a Covenant of Grace with us which is confirmed through the blood and death of Christ, His Son. For that reason we must not regard Christ's death as merely a human death; rather, God's Son dies! Accordingly, His death has such power that through it we are reconciled with God and are cleansed of our sins. And this power of Christ's death has proved to be also for the believers in the Old Testament, for they had no other sacrifice for sin other than their hope for the death of Christ. Thus it is written, Rev. 13, **that the Lamb of God was slain from the beginning of the world.** Finally, Christ's death should then also work in us the killing off of our flesh, as it is written in Romans 6: **Through Baptism we are buried with Christ, and along with Him are planted into the same death so that the sinful body ceases.**

In conclusion, we must note that the Lord Christ died towards evening around the third hour, as the evangelists testify. This timing serves as a witness that Christ's death had been signified in the sacrifices of the Old Testament. For around the third hour the Jewish people usually assembled themselves in the temple for prayer and for sacrifice, Acts 3. Also God had specifically commanded that the Passover lamb had to be slaughtered towards evening; so also Adam had sinned against God towards evening and thereby brought death into the world. Therefore, Christ chose to die towards evening, thereby fulfilling the significance of the Passover lamb and all the Jewish sacrifices and also announcing with His death that He intended to restore again what Adam had lost through sin. God grant that we acknowledge this with gratitude. Amen.

O Lord Jesus Christ, may Your thirst which You endured on the cross quench the thirst of my soul and protect me from the eternal thirst; may Your perfect atoning sacrifice, which You accomplished on the cross, be a comfort to my soul; give me grace that my soul thirst for You, the Fountain of Life; and, grant that I may commend my soul into Your hands at the hour of death. Amen.

The Seventh Sermon

The miracles that took place after Christ's death.

And behold, the curtain of the temple split into two pieces, from the top to the bottom, and the earth quaked; and the rocks split, and the graves opened themselves, and many of the bodies of the saints who had been sleeping [i.e., were dead] arose and came out of their graves after His resurrection, and came into the holy city and appeared to many. But the centurion who was in charge of Him and standing by, as well as those who were with him and were guarding Jesus, when they saw how He died with such an outcry, and saw the earthquake and what was happening, they were terribly frightened. And, they praised God and said: Truly, this was a pious(godly) Man and the Son of God. And all the people who were nearby and were watching, when they saw what had happened there, smote their breasts and turned back again. However, all of His relatives were standing at a distance; and many women who had been His followers in Galilee saw all this. Among them was Mary Magdalene, and Mary the mother of the lesser James and Joses, and Salome, the mother of the children of Zebedee, who had followed after Him when He was in Galilee and had served Him, and many others who had gone up to Jerusalem with Him.

However, since it was the Day of Preparation, the Jews, [concerned] that the bodies would not remain on the crosses over the Sabbath (for this Sabbath Day was a very important one), petitioned Pilate that their legs (bones) be broken and they be taken down. Then came the soldiers and broke the bones of the first one, and then of the other one of those who had been crucified with Him. As they came to Jesus, however, they saw that He already was dead, and they did not break His bones. Instead, one of the soldiers opened a wound in His side with a spear; and immediately blood and water came out. And he who has seen this, he has testified to this, and his witness is true. And he knows that he is telling the truth, so that you too believe that this took place so that the Scripture would be fulfilled: You shall not break any of His bones. And again, a different Scripture [passage] states: They will look at the One whom they have pierced.

In Isaiah 11 it is prophesied of the Lord Christ **that His rest would be honorable**; that is, after He will have gone to rest on the cross, His honor and glory will continue. For since the death and the burial are the final act, that is, the final part of His humiliation, soon after His death His glory and exaltation begin. Through various miracles in nature, God the Lord publicly declared Christ's innocence, and thereby began to exalt Him. In this lesson we are now instructed about these matters; in it we hear:

I. How after Christ's death, the curtain in the temple was ripped apart, the earth quaked, the rocks split, the graves were opened, and the dead came forth from them.

II. How as a result of these miracles, the centurion acknowledged and confessed Christ to be God's Son; also, how the people out of contrition and sympathy smote their breasts as the Lord Christ's relatives stood alongside at a distance.

III. How Christ's bones (legs) were not broken like those of the two thieves; rather, on the contrary, He was pierced in His side with a spear, from which flowed out blood and water. We shall also hear about what took place after Christ's death 1. in regard to the inanimate creation, 2. with the people, and 3. in Christ's body itself.

What is presented to us in these three parts as helpful and salutary doctrine shall, with the granting of divine grace, be briefly considered.

1. In general, regarding the miracles which occurred in creation (nature) after Christ's death, they were all directed to giving a public testimony to the innocence of Christ, thus manifesting sympathy of creation toward Christ, its Creator. For in a similar manner, just as when a head of the household dies care is taken that the entire household puts on black clothing and mourns, so also here the same occurs at the death of Christ, the Creator of all nature and the Master of the house in this world, Heb. 3. The sun is darkened; she puts on a dark mourning garment. The curtain in the temple rips apart, even as in previous times it was customary with the Jews to rend their garments in mourning. The earth quaked, and the rocks split apart, so that the graves themselves were opened, in the same way that a person quivers and quakes from fear. Of what these miracles specifically consisted, the evangelists report.

In the first place, the curtain in the temple was torn into two pieces, from the top to the bottom. This curtain was a beautiful, thick tapestry of yellow silk, scarlet, and rose red, and twisted white silk, artistically crafted.* It was hung in the Ark of the Covenant (later in the temple) to partition and separate the Holy Place (the part of the temple in which they sacrificed and prayed daily) from the Most Holy Place (the inner place where stood the Ark of the Covenant and the Throne of Grace), Exo. 26. This curtain tore apart after the death of Christ to announce, first, that Christ, the sole High Priest of the New Testament, has now entered into the Most Holy Place and established an eternal redemption by His own blood, Heb. 9. In the ancient

---

* Luther's translation—employed by Gerhard—differs in some details from the Hebrew: "yellow" fabric rather than blue, and twisted "silk" rather than linen. Ed.

times of the Old Testament the priests entered daily into the front part of the Ark and conducted the worship service; but into the Most Holy Place the high priest entered alone only once a year, and not without blood, which he offered for the sin of the people. Accordingly, since Christ had now fulfilled this type with His death—in which He offered Himself up for the sin of mankind—behold, for that reason this very same curtain tore apart.

Secondly, in the same Most Holy Place (which was covered by the curtain, and into which no one other than the high priest dared enter once a year) stood the Ark of the Covenant and the Throne of Grace; therefore, the ripping apart of this curtain announces that by Christ's blood and death we are given access to the Throne of Grace. As St. Paul so gloriously writes to the [Jewish Christians] in Rome: **God had set forth (presented) Christ as a Throne of Grace through faith in His blood so that we may now approach the Throne of Grace with joy, so that we receive mercy, and find grace for the time when help will be required by us**, Heb. 5*.

Thirdly, this ripping apart of the curtain declares that the Levitical ceremonies of the Old Testament have now reached their end. For while these same outward ceremonies all pointed to Christ (but now by His death Christ had concluded the day of His flesh, that is, His outward visible life upon earth), it is easily concluded that through the death of Christ the external, figurative worship service of the Old Testament had now been abolished. That is also the reason, among others, for these words of Christ from the cross: **It is accomplished.** Therefore, as St. Paul, Col. 2, gloriously speaks of the fruits of Christ's death and crucifixion, he concludes this way: **So let no one make it a matter of conscience to you regarding food or drink, or desig-**

---

* I.e., 4—a paraphrase of the final verses of chapter 4. In the German Bible, 4:14–16 are considered the opening thoughts of chapter 5. Ed.

nated festivals, or new moons, or the Sabbath—which is the shadow of Him who was coming; but the body (substance) itself is in Christ.

Fourthly, because the New Testament is confirmed (validated) through Christ's blood and death, the tearing apart of the curtain at the death of Christ is a sign that the mystery of Jewish ceremonies—which previously had been covered and hidden—are now, in the New Testament, clear and revealed. With His works and beneficial acts, Christ gives us the true meaning concerning the obscure (mysterious) figures of the Old Testament. Finally, this ripping apart of the curtain may also be regarded in this way: It shows how the death of Christ shattered the fence or dividing wall which had separated Jew and Gentile through His reconciling of both peoples into one body through the cross; that is, through His own Person He had put this hostility to death.

The second miracle was that the earth quaked. This earthquake was experienced not only in the land of the Jews, but also in other places. For the historians record that in the same earthquake certain cities in Asia and Thracia collapsed.

However, this earthquake was first of all an announcement of the combat which Christ in His death had begun with the Devil and of the assault which He had undertaken against the Devil's palace. For with His death Christ had risen up and begun the battle against the Devil and his hellish palace, which the Devil had in the lowest parts of the earth, Eph. 4. From this battle He emerged on Easter Day as a victorious Conqueror. Thus, the foundation pillars of the earth quaked, both at His death as well as upon Christ's resurrection, Mat. 28. When the blood of innocent Abel was shed, God the Lord cursed the earth for opening its mouth and receiving that blood, Gen. 4. Accordingly, since now the blood of the Son of God was poured out upon the earth, it therefore quaked for fear that it would be cursed anew.

By this earthquake it is also declared that the earth, so to speak, hopped and leapt for joy over the fact that the curse which had befallen it on account of sin had now been averted anew through Christ's death. For in like manner as the mountains skipped like lambs and the hills like young sheep in olden times, Psa. 114, when the children of Israel were led out of Egypt, so also when Christ by His death had won for us rescue from hellish slavery, the earth leapt for joy.

Furthermore, by this earthquake it is announced that through the preaching of the Gospel (which followed upon Christ's death) the entire land, along with its inhabitants, would be set in motion. For just as in ancient times the earth quaked when God gave His Law, Exo. 19, Psa. 68, so also the earth quaked because now the situation was such that the doctrine of the Gospel would soon break forth out of Zion, Isa. 2. When the apostles prayed, Acts 4, that God the Lord would give them the joy to spread abroad the Gospel, the earth quaked. So also then, because Christ by His death had won the very same treasures which are dispensed by the Gospel, the earth quaked after His death.

The third miracle was that the rocks were ripped apart. To some extent this was caused by the earthquake; yet it still was a special miracle, because the hard rocks are not ripped apart in every earthquake. Rather, they are sometimes merely shaken.

However, by this ripping apart of the rocks it is proclaimed, first of all, that the true Rock of our Salvation, the Lord Christ, had died on the cross, thus ripping apart the bond of natural unity of body and soul, Luke 19. When the Pharisees said to Christ that He should forbid His disciples and the people to cry out hosannas to Him, the Lord answered them: **If these were to keep silent, then the rocks would cry out.** That was here fulfilled with the ripping apart of the stony rocks.

Furthermore, this ripping apart of the rocks announces God's wrath, so that the Jewish people, on account of their gruesome evil, might well go under the rocks to hide themselves in the earth for fear of the Lord, Isa. 2. The Jews had a harder countenance than a rock and did not want to mend their ways, Jer. 5. Thus God the Lord let the rocks rip apart, His wrath burn like a fire, and the rocks scatter before Him. We should let this be a warning to us, that we indeed do not harden our hearts like rocks and boulders. Instead, we should allow Christ's suffering to penetrate our hearts, and thereby be moved to true repentance. If we refuse to do so and instead remain in the unrepentance of our rock-hard hearts, then we will experience what is written in the Rev. 6, that in the crevices and rocks the people will try to hide themselves from the wrath of God—a most futile endeavor, for the mountains will melt like wax before the Lord's countenance.

The fourth miracle after Christ's death was that the graves opened, from which many bodies of the saints arose following the resurrection of Christ, went into the city of Jerusalem, and appeared to many. These saints without a doubt were certain of the patriarchs and prophets who had been buried in the area. These arose together with Christ to show that His resurrection had won resurrection to eternal life for believers. They were also, without doubt, in the Lord Christ's train as He triumphantly ascended to heaven. This opening of the graves after Christ's death indeed proceeded in some measure from the shaking and ripping apart of the earth; yet it still was a special miracle, whereby was shown that the opening up of our graves and our resurrection to eternal life were obtained by Christ's death. For in the same manner that the graves of these very saints, who in the Old Testament had fallen asleep in true faith in the Messiah, were opened, so that after Christ's resurrection they came forth from the grave and came into the holy City of Jerusalem . . . so also shall we, who from the heart believe on Christ, who died for us and arose again (I repeat) we believers shall in the same way some day also experience this. That is, our graves will also be opened on Judgment Day, and we shall come forth alive from these same graves into the heavenly Jerusalem, Rev. 21, into the eternal glory of which the earthly Jerusalem was a type.

These, then, are the miracles which happened to creation after Christ's death; and because of them one can rightly say about Christ what Sirach 48 says of Eliseo: **When he was alive, he performed signs; and when he had died, he performed miracles.**

II. In the second part [of the lesson] the evangelists report what resulted from these miracles; namely, that the captain and his soldiers who were standing next to Jesus and guarding Him were frightened because of Him, and they confessed Him to be a godly, innocent man, yea, even confessed Him to be God's Son. Also, all the rest of the people who watched smote their breast in fright, and they returned again to town. Moreover, the holy evangelists also mention the relatives of Christ, and the same women who had followed Christ from Galilee to Jerusalem. They stood at a distance and watched. They did not dare station themselves too close to the cross of Christ, so that they not get themselves into trouble on that account.

Here we have [several lessons]:

1. This glorious confession of Christ which the captain makes signifies that it is also a fruit of Christ's death that He would gather Himself a Church and little flock out of the human race, by which He would be properly acknowledged, confessed and worshiped. This captain and his soldiers no doubt at first also slandered Christ. However, through Christ's preaching from the cross and through the miracles which occurred after His death, their hearts were changed, so that from slanderers they became confessors of Christ. This fruit of Christ's death was previously proclaimed in Isa. 53: **When He gave up His life as a guilt [sin] offering, thus He would have seed.** This is to be understood as the spiritual seed or children, His believing disciples and confessors. These, says the prophet, will then be found mostly when [after] Christ has given His life as a sin offering upon the timber-trunk of the cross. Also, since this captain and his soldiers were Gentiles, [their conversion] signifies the calling of the Gentiles in the New Testament. The Jewish people had rejected Christ and led Him out of Jerusalem. However, God nevertheless sees to it that this heathen captain professes Christ and, as it were, proclaims His praise with a "funeral sermon."

2. The people who were standing and watching beneath Christ's cross smote their breasts. Thus should we, through heartfelt contemplation of the suffering and death of Christ, also be moved to confess our sin and smite our breasts in heartfelt contrition and true humility, even as the repentant publican, Luke 18, smote his breast and said: **God, be merciful to me, a sinner.** But we must not stop with the outward act. Rather, with this outward smiting of the sinner's breast must also be the inward ripping apart of the heart, as Joel says in chapter 2; for the outward without the inward is false and deceitful. When the godly David had allowed the people to be counted, the text in 2 Sam. 24 says: **David smote his heart**; that is, it grieved him, and he smote himself inwardly. The same should also take place with us when we contemplate Christ's death, and out of such contemplation we should come to the acknowledgment of our sin.

3. The relatives of Christ stood here at a distance, thus fulfilling the lament of Christ in Psa. 38: **My loved ones and friends stand against Me [oppose Me] and view My plague, and My neighbors walk afar off.** But even though these relatives of Christ and these women, who had followed Him out from Galilee, had a somewhat stronger faith than the disciples, who had actually forsaken the Lord and fled from Him, yet beneath it all there was a thread of great weakness so that they, for fear, stood far off. Yet Mary and John do step near beneath the cross. Nevertheless, Christ sustained them well in their great weakness and later had an angel preach to them about His resurrection, Mat. 28, and shortly after that showed Himself to them alive, John 20. We should cling to this for our comfort, so that we do not despair because of the weakness of our faith. Rather, we should petition God to strengthen our faith, Luke 17, and to display His power in our weakness, 2 Cor. 12. And should we ever indeed also by God's providence arrive at the point where we lament with David and have to say, Psa. 27, **My father and my mother**, that is my next of kin, **have forsaken me**, we should remember that the Lord Christ also experienced the same thing; and we also should take comfort in David's addendum: **But the Lord uplifts me.**

III. In the third part of this lesson the evangelist John reports to us that the Jews, on account of the imminent Passover Feast, did not want the corpses of the crucified to hang on the cross until evening. Instead, they petitioned Pilate to grant permission for the legs (bones) of the crucified ones to be broken so that they would die sooner and might be taken down from the tree of the cross, not to mention also that God the Lord had given the Jews a law, Deu. 21, that the corpse of one who had been hanged upon a tree was not to be left on it overnight. As they then with the consent of Pilate broke the legs of the two thieves who had been crucified with Christ, they intended to do the same to the Lord Christ; however, they found that He had already died. Therefore, they did not break His legs. Instead one of the roguish knaves ran up and stuck His side with a spear. From this wound flowed out blood and water, which was a great supernatural miracle. For normally the blood of a dead body coagulates, so that it no longer flows. This too was remarkable, that not only blood but instead also water ran out from Christ's side. For that reason, the evangelist John corroborates this account of his and says: **He who has seen this has testified to it, and his testimony is true; and he knows that he is speaking**

the truth, so that you also believe. He also directs us to the Old Testament, that we should unfold the passages and types in which this was previously proclaimed. How are we then to fruitfully contemplate this history?

First of all, that Christ's legs (bones) were not broken fulfills the type of Exo. 12. There God the Lord Himself commands His people to slaughter a little lamb and, along with certain ceremonies, consume it. That, however, such a little lamb points to Christ, the Lamb of God, John 1, St. Paul clearly testifies in 1 Cor. 5; and the entire context of the text points to it. Accordingly, since God the Lord commanded, among other things, that they should not break any bone of the little Passover lamb, such also then had to be fulfilled by the little Lamb of God, by Christ: No bone of His was to be broken or damaged. Furthermore, it was hereby signified that Christ would soon rise again from the dead. Therefore, He wanted to retain His members and bones whole; they were not to be cut up, no matter how much [His enemies] otherwise raged against Him. Finally, Christ did not want any of His bones to be broken because He was the true Serpent–Crusher, who, in accordance with the first promise, was to crush the hellish serpent's head, Gen. 3. Thus He also wanted to keep His bones whole and unbroken, so that He might all the more mightily stomp down and subdue the Devil's power.

Secondly, when Christ's side was opened up with a spear, the prophecy of Zec. 12 was finally fulfilled: **They will look at Me, the One whom they have pierced.** In that very place the prophet announces in the Name of the Lord Christ that the Holy Spirit will be poured out over the believers of the New Testament; that they will look with their eyes of faith at Him whom the godless Jews have stabbed. Furthermore, Christ allowed His side to be opened so that thereby we may look into His tender (benevolent) heart, and so that the burning fire of love may shine forth from His wound. When we truly have good intentions toward someone, we usually say: Oh, if only you could look into my heart! See! So that we now might look into Christ's heart, He has by means of this wound in His side allowed, as it were, a little door to be made. Moreover, by allowing this wound to be opened, Christ intended that we in true faith might hide ourselves from the wrath of God, as has been so beautifully stated in SSo. 2, where the Lord Christ speaks to His spiritual Bride, the Church: **Get up, My lady friend, My beautiful one, and come here, My dove, into the rock holes, into the stonecrevices.** This lady friend of Christ, this dove, is the true Church and each individual believing soul. He graciously beckons them to Himself and desires that they should hide themselves in the rock holes and stone crevices. This Rock and this Stone is the Lord Christ, Mat. 16, Isa. 8. The holes in this Rock are His holy wounds on His hands and feet; the crevice of this Stone is the wound in His side. In it a devoted soul should hide itself in true faith. St. Bernhard also has some thoughts about this text and thus says: "Just as a little bird conceals itself in a hollow tree when it encounters trouble (if the wind is unsteady, [or] if men and cattle frighten it) so also, Lord Christ, my refuge is in the cave of Your wound. If sin and death cause me trouble, I seek shelter within it."

  Finally, we should regard this opening up of Christ's side in this way: The assumed flesh of Christ is a life–producing flesh, John 6, the fountain of eternal spiritual life. So that such life also might flow out to us from this well (fountain) of life, behold, Christ lets His side be opened up. At His curative [soul–saving] birth Christ brought a great treasure along for us. So that this treasure might be distributed, He, in His suffering and death, let His hands and side be opened up. Augustine, *Treatise 120 on John*, here invokes the type of Gen. 6, where it is reported that the Ark of Noah had a door in the middle, through which Noah and his family entered and were kept safe during the Flood. Christ's split side is the true Way, the Door, through which we can enter into secure rest, John 10, and be preserved from the great flood of divine wrath.

 Thirdly, the evangelist John (who alone related this story and diligently took note of the secret interpretations), reports that out of the opened up side of the Lord Christ ran blood and water. As to how we are to view this, John himself shows us in his First Epistle, chapter 5: **Who is it then who overcomes the world, unless it is he who believes that Jesus is God's Son? He it is who came with water and blood, Jesus Christ. Not only with water, but rather with water and blood; and it is the Spirit who testifies to this. He is the Spirit of Truth. For there are three who testify on earth: the Spirit, and the water, and the blood; and the three are together. We accept the witness of man, but God's testimony is even greater; for God's testimony is this, that He has testified about His Son.** In essence, St. John so much as says: God the Lord testified about His Son not only with earthquakes, the ripping apart of rocks and the temple tapestry, and the opening of graves; rather, He also let blood and water run from His opened side; and the Holy Spirit let this be recorded through me in this Gospel. Accordingly, these three parts testify of the Spirit, the blood, and the water of Christ, the Son of God. However, these three parts testified about Christ not only at that time; rather, to this very day they still testify about Him. For the Spirit testifies to Christ in the Word, which Word and pastoral office are called the office of the Spirit in 2 Cor. 3. The water in holy Baptism and the blood in the holy Supper also still today testify about Christ. For these two holy Sacraments are nothing other than witnesses that God, for the sake of Christ, accepts us in grace and washes us from sin. For that reason the beloved ancients [Church fathers] compare this account with the story in Gen. 2. When God the Lord wanted to adjoin a wife to Adam, He let a deep sleep fall upon him, took out of his side a rib, and crafted from it a wife and brought her to Adam, who acknowledged that this was flesh from his flesh and bone from his bones. So also Christ, the second and heavenly Adam, fell asleep into death on the cross; and His side was opened, from which blood and water ran out. Hereby are signified both Sacraments, through which, along with the preaching of the Word, a spiritual Bride is gathered for the Lord Christ, **which is bone of His bone and flesh of His flesh**, as St. Paul says in Eph. 5, directing us with these words to this type.

One can also include here the account in Exo. 17. When the children of Israel themselves were in the barren desert, Moses—at God's command—struck the rock, which gave them water to drink. By this rock is signified the spiritual Rock, Christ, 1 Cor. 10, who was opened up on the cross so that blood and water flowed forth from Him. Whoever will drink of this water which the Lord Christ gives, such a person will eternally never thirst, John 4. For this water and this blood which flowed out of Christ's side does not only quench the thirst of the soul, but it also washes clean from sin and quenches the fire of God's wrath. In the Old Testament, God the Lord ordained the bloody sacrifice and the various cleansings by water to signify the bloody atoning sacrifice of Christ and the washing away of sin through Christ's blood. So that we might see that these types have now been fulfilled by Christ's death, blood and water thus flow from Christ's side. Finally, even as Christ performed His first miracle with water, out of which He made wine, John 2, so also He wanted to perform His last miracle during His days in the flesh in such a manner that clear water flowed out of His side in a miraculous, supernatural way. Water is the first creation; everything else came into being from water. The first world was destroyed by water, and most of the miracles of God occurred on water. God give us grace that we be washed clean of sin through the blood of Christ. Amen.

O Lord Jesus Christ, You who also after Your death, as God's Son and the Lord of all creation, have demonstrated many kinds of miracles, grant me grace that I acknowledge You from my heart to be God's Son, and through such faith overcome the world. Your holy blood, which flowed from Your side on the cross, wash me of my sins. Stretch out Your arms and embrace me in them; hide me in Your wounds. Amen.

THE FIFTH AND FINAL ACT

*Containing within it the history of
the burial of Christ.*

Later, around evening, since it was the Day of Preparation, which is before the Sabbath, came Joseph of Arimathea, the city of the Jews. He was a rich man, a lord of the council, a good and pious man who had not consented in their counsel and action. He also was waiting for the Kingdom of God, for he was a disciple of Jesus, yet secretly for fear of the Jews. He weighed the matter and went into Pilate and asked him if he might not take down the body of Jesus. Pilate, however, was amazed that He was already dead; and he called the captain and asked him if He had been dead for very long. And when he had it verified by the captain, he gave Joseph the body of Christ and directed that Jesus be given to him. And Joseph purchased a linen cloth. However, there came also Nicodemus, who had previously come to Jesus by night, and he brought with him myrrh and aloes mixed together, about a hundred pounds. They then took the body of Jesus, which had been taken down, and wrapped it in a clean linen cloth, and bound Him with linen handkerchiefs and with spices, as the Jews usually took care of their burials.

There was, however, by the place where He was crucified, a garden, and in the garden a grave, which was Joseph's. He had it hewn out of a boulder, and no one had yet been laid in it. There they laid Jesus on account of the Day of Preparation of the Jews, since the Sabbath was about to begin and the grave was nearby. They rolled a huge stone in front of the door of the grave and left. But also there were Mary Magdalene and Mary of Joses; they sat next to the grave. Other women who were also followers of Jesus from Galilee looked on where and how His body was laid. They, however, went back and prepared spices and ointments and then rested on the Sabbath in keeping with the Law. On the next day, which followed the Day of Preparation, the high priests and Pharisees came to Pilate and said: Sir, we have remembered that this seducer said while He was still alive, I will arise again after three days. Therefore, command that someone guard the grave until the third day so that His disciples do not come and steal Him and say to the people that He has arisen from the dead, and the last deception be more offensive than the first. Pilate said to them: Here, you take the guards; go out and guard as best you can. They went out, secured the grave with guards, and sealed the stone.

In Gen. 50 it is reported of the patriarch Jacob that, after he had placed his feet together on his deathbed and died, his son Joseph had him anointed by his servants, the physicians. He also saw to it that Jacob had an honorable and magnificent funeral. In [the death of] Jacob is a type of our Lord Christ, the true Protector or Conqueror. He, on the timber-trunk of the cross (which was His sickbed), carefully put His feet together, handed over His spirit to His heavenly Father, and calmly and quietly died. After His death He experienced this honor: that one of His spiritual sons or disciples, Joseph of Arimathea (along with Nicodemus) prepared an honorable and splendid burial for Him. They purchased a clean linen sheet and brought with them aloes and myrrh of about one hundred pounds. They wrapped Christ's body up into the same linen sheet, bound Him with linen cloths and spices, so that thus everything about the burial of Christ took place honorably and grandly. We now shall be instructed in this lesson, wherein we hear:

I. About the love which Joseph and Nicodemus had for Christ, which they demonstrated with this caring concern for His burial.
II. About the horrible hatred which the high priests and the Pharisees had against Christ, a hatred which had not abated even with the death of Christ; therefore, they requested guards from Pilate to secure the grave.

I. The holy evangelists describe the account of Christ's burial in minute detail. First, they make mention of the time when He was buried; namely, on the evening of the Day of Preparation or Pre-Sabbath, the nearest Friday before the high festival day of the Jewish Passover. It was called the Day of Preparation because on it the Jews worked to prepare what was required of them for a proper Passover celebration. It was also called the Pre-Sabbath because it was the day before the Passover Sabbath. Now just before this Day of Preparation had ended, Christ was buried. For He wanted to rest in the grave for three days because of the prophecies and types of the Old Testament, which in the proper place [sequence] are to be applied here. Just as Christ died before the end of the Day of Preparation, which was the day of His suffering, so also God the Lord sometimes deals with Christ's members. He hastens them out of this life's "Day of Preparation," which is a day of constant suffering, and brings them to rest so that they keep the Sabbath or Day of Rest in their little sleeping-chamber and thereafter, by the power of Christ's resurrection, once again arise with Him to Life. Isa. 26: **Go forth My people into your chamber and lock the door after you; hide yourself for a brief moment until the** [storm of] **wrath blows over.**

Next is mentioned the one who arranged this burial. The disciples of Christ had sneaked into hiding because of fear. Mary the mother of our Lord, because of her tremendous grief, could not undertake the burial herself. The Jews would, without doubt, have buried Jesus in an ignominious manner on the hill of Golgatha like the other two criminals. But, here God awakens two eminent men; namely, Joseph of Arimathea and Nicodemus, so that they undertake this matter and see to an honorable burial for Christ; for **His rest was to be honorable**, Isa. 11. Joseph is here lauded for his honorable stand. Here he was, a lord of the council and a rich man, who, on account of his godliness, in that he was a good, pious man ... who, on account of his uprightness, in that he did not consent with the high priests and elders of the council in their stand against Christ ... who, on account of his confession of faith that he awaited the Kingdom of God, that is, awaited the Messiah ... and who was a secret disciple of Christ ... this person took the risk and went before Pilate and asked if he could take down the dead body of Jesus. To be sure, he had risked daring to go to Pilate to ask for Christ's body. Whatever are you doing, Joseph of Arimathea, that you ask for the very same body which was slain as a murderer and seditionist ... the body over which all the people shouted: **Crucify! Crucify Him!** ... the body which Pilate himself had condemned to death on the cross? Don't you realize that Pilate will deny it to you, that the high priests will kick you off the council, that the people will stone you? However, the love of Christ and the inner motivation of the Spirit moves you in such a way that you, heedless of all danger, not only petition Pilate for the body of Christ, but also purchase a linen sheet or funeral shroud. Therefore, God, who has the hearts of all mankind in His hands, so directs matters that Pilate gives the deceased body of Christ to this Joseph.

The other funeral arranger was Nicodemus, also a secret disciple of Christ, who had previously come to Him in the night and learned the way into the Kingdom of God, John 3, and who had also rebuked his colleagues for desiring, out of envy, to condemn Christ without a hearing, John 7. He brought aloes and myrrh, all together weighing about a hundred pounds, and, along with Joseph, helped arrange Christ's burial. Here we must ponder the miraculous power of the grace of God, which works in believers. At one time, the disciples of Christ had publicly confessed Him during His deeds [ministry]; they also always followed after their Lord and Master. But when Christ entered upon His suffering and death, they fled from Him. However, Joseph and Nicodemus had been secret disciples of Christ up to now, afraid to confess Him publicly. But, as Christ was now hanging on the cross in the very lowest state of His humiliation, forsaken by everyone, these two now find themselves here and arrange Christ's burial. From [their experience and example] we should indeed see that the beginning, the acceptance, and the steadfastness of faith does not stand [depend] upon the power of our nature. Rather, our faith proceeds from the grace of God. This grace often shows itself more powerful in a weak faith than in a strong one, 2 Cor. 12, so that we actually might see that the entire work of our faith and our salvation rests solely in the hands of God, who imparts to each individual the measure of faith as He sees fit, 1 Cor. 12, Eph. 4.

  Thirdly, we call attention to the way in which Christ was buried; namely, with honor and splendor, in keeping with the manner of the Jews who attended to burying. His corpse was wrapped in a clean burial cloth and embalmed with costly spices, specifically with aloes and myrrh. Some would here apply what is written in Isaiah 53: **He was buried like the godless and died like a rich person**; that is, He had a magnificent, expensive burial, just as the rich took care to be buried. However, in the same passage the prophet points to something more encompassing (as will shortly be pointed out) for which we intend to consider a second passage. Psa. 45 prophesies about Christ, even as the context of the text and the Epistle to the Hebrews, ch. 1, clearly testify. It is written in this second passage: **Your garments are sheer (pure) myrrh, aloes, and cacia as you step forth from your ivory palace in all your majestic splendor.** In His burial Christ is similarly clothed with aloes, myrrh and other spices. Also, Christ arises again from His grave with great pomp and splendor—far more gloriously than a king usually comes forth from his ivory palace in splendid array. Just as Christ was honorably and grandly buried, so is it also proper that the members of Christ be honorably buried in the earth, because their bodies have been instruments and temples of the Holy Spirit, 1 Cor. 6, and also because they, like noble kernels [little seeds] of wheat, shall again blossom forth into eternal life, Isa. 66, John 12, and become like unto the transfigured body of Christ, Phi. 3.

Fourthly, we recall the place where Christ was buried: in a garden near the place where He was crucified. Just as Christ desired to begin His suffering in the garden of Mt. Olive, so now He wanted to end it by being buried in a garden, thereby to signify that with His suffering He intended to restore again what the first man had lost in the garden of Paradise. Also, since Christ had made our graves into a soft bed of rest by His burial, He also wanted to be buried in a garden to indicate thereby that not only He (as the fruitful Tree of Life) would soon blossom forth in this garden, but rather that also we, through His power, would sprout up like the grass in a garden, Isa. 66 [:14].

Fifthly, we note that the grave in which the Lord Christ was laid was a new grave, in which no one had previously been buried. The godly Joseph had had this grave made for himself, hewn in a rock, so that by it he might be reminded of his mortality and of the resurrection every time he saw how the trees and grass in the garden dried up in the winter and greened up again in the spring, even as Usa had his grave in a garden, 2 Kings 21. Christ's body was laid in this new grave because it was located nearby and they had to hurry with Christ's burial on account of the Day of Preparation. When we, however, contemplate this grave of Christ, we find that Christ was laid in such a grave because of the extraordinary counsel and direction of God. For, to begin with, it was a new grave, wherein no one had ever been buried, so that one might never think that someone else arose instead of Christ. Also, since Christ had laid Himself into the grave in a novel and extraordinary manner, namely, to rest in it for only a few hours and soon thereafter on His own power to come out again, He also wanted to have a new [unused] grave.

Since had won for us renewal to life by His burial Christ, He wanted also to choose a new grave for Himself. Accordingly, it was the grave of another; for since Christ had no place of His own to lay His head during His life, Mat. 8, so also in His death He did not want to have His own family vault. Abraham had no hereditary portion in the Promised Land—not so much as a foot of land, Acts 7; even so, he purchased for himself a family vault there, Gen. 23. Christ was much poorer. Nor did He want a grave of His own in the Land of Canaan. Through this poverty of Christ we were made rich, 2 Cor. 8. Also, why would Christ have had His own grave, since He, as it were, only wanted to borrow it and use it for a few hours? What use was a grave of His own, in that He obviously was not buried for His own sake, but for the sake of others? Furthermore, Christ's grave was the grave of the godly and righteous Joseph. Christ had died among murderers because He had taken our sins upon Himself. However, He wanted to rest in the grave of the godly and righteous because He soon wanted to arise from the grave again for the sake of our righteousness (justification), Rom. 4. In a spiritual manner, Christ still dies in the hearts of the godless and the evil-doers. However, He has His rest and residence in the heart of the believers and the godly. Why should He have been buried in the grave of a godless person? For He will never again die for sinners. Instead, He makes His residence in the heart of the believers and the righteous.

This, then, is the account of Christ's burial, which the evangelist concludes by announcing that a huge stone was rolled in front of the entrance to the grave, so that the evil knaves might not possibly do any further mischief to Christ's body. But God directs [even this act] in such a way that Christ's resurrection might be that much the more glorious in that no stone is capable of hindering Him.

We should [also] consider the burial of Christ in such a manner that we first compare it with the prophecies and types of the Old Testament, and accordingly take note of their results [fulfillment]. Concerning the prophecies and types of the Old Testament, St. Paul expressly testifies in 1 Cor. 15 that Christ not only died according to the Scriptures, but also according to the Scriptures was buried and arose again from the grave. That is why there must indeed be portrayals about [His burial and resurrection] in the Scriptures passages. Psa. 16: **You will not leave My soul in hell and will not allow Your Holy One to decompose.** This passage is applied to Christ in Acts 2 and 13. Psa. 22: **You lay Me into the dust of death.** Isa. 53: **He is buried like the godless.** Also, as Jonah was in the belly of the whale-fish for three days and three nights, so also would the Son of Man be three days and three nights in the belly of the earth, that is, in a grave, Mat. 12. These prophecies and types the Scriptures themselves clearly apply to Christ. In other respects, one could properly also apply other types to [the burial of Christ]. For example, Joseph lay three years in captivity before he was exalted in glory, Gen. 39; Samson was locked up in the city of Gaza before he lifted the city gates off their hinges, Jdg. 16; Daniel was hurled into the lion pit before he came to glory, Dan. 6. If we then consider the reasons and the benefits for which Christ wanted to be buried, it becomes apparent that Christ's burial was to be not only a testimony that He had truly died, and by His death actually achieved that to which the above references point, but also [an assurance] that He wanted to be buried for the sake of our salvation and for our benefit. For our sake He became man. For our sake He died upon the cross. It follows that He also was buried for our sake. This we can also note attentively.

When God the Lord created heaven and earth, He rested on the seventh day, Gen. 2. Thus, since Christ had now accomplished the redemption of the human race on the cross and had won for us the new creation, the re-birth to eternal life, behold, He thus also wanted to keep His Sabbath in the grave. Christ had not worked quite as hard in the first creation as He did in this second creation, or redemption of mankind. [In the first creation] everything was created through the Word; here Christ had to endure extreme and burdensome suffering. For that reason He indeed rightly rested in the grave. And with this rest in the grave, Christ obtained for us [great benefits]: God the Lord can rest in us and we in Him, so that after death our bodies may rest in the grave and our souls may rest in God's hands, and so that some day we may be able to enter with body and soul into eternal rest. Thus also says Isa. 53: Christ was buried like a godless person. That is, as One who in our place was a condemned, accursed man, He took with Him into the grave all our sin and godless nature and there let them be buried* and covered up so that they never again should be placed into the light before the divine Countenance, Psa. 90—if only we, with true faith, trust in His death, His burial, and His resurrection. He also died as a rich Person, that is, through His death He made us rich, for the Hebrew text may indeed be interpreted: He buried* the godless nature of mankind in His grave; and since He daily suffered and died throughout His entire Life, He has, as St. Paul says, 1 Cor. 15, by His continual suffering thereby made us rich and achieved for us a rich redemption. We should

---

* *Verscharren*, the specific word used here, means to cover something quickly by scraping earth over it.

also remember hereby that our graves are by nature full of dead bones and filth, Mat. 23. Our hearts are fearful about our lying down in such a grave. However, here comes Christ and touches our graves with His Holy Body (which also in the midst of death remained a Temple of the living God). With this touch He turns graves into a resting-place for those who will not always remain dead, but instead shall come forth again to Life. Did not a man come back to life when he touched the dead bones of Elisha, 2 Kings 13? Even more so, should not our graves—touched with the holy body of Christ—be so sanctified and adorned that they no longer are "a box for a body," but rather "a sleeping room for the living"? Christ left behind for us here on earth His burial clothes and His grave, so that we by true faith in a spiritual manner may wrap ourselves in them and bury* ourselves in it and thus, by the power of His death, His burial, and His resurrection, go forth into eternal life.

However, just because we have heard that Christ took our godless nature with Him into the grave and buried it therein, we should nevertheless be on guard that we do not deliberately scratch [dig] it up again. That happens whenever we (against conscience and the witness of our heart) consent to sin and unashamedly [blatantly] continue in it. Not only that, but our Old Man must daily be hastily interred* with Christ and be buried, as St. Paul admonishes us, Rom. 6: **Through Baptism we are indeed buried with Christ into death.** And immediately following: **We know that our Old Man was crucified along with Christ, so that the sinful body ceases to exist.** If our New Man is to arise with Christ and walk in a new life, then obviously our old Adam must die in us daily through contrition and repentance, and his evil lusts must be hastily buried. Truly, anyone who does not then kill the evil lusts and bury the Old Man with Christ, such a person has nothing about which to rejoice in the burial

---

* See note on previous page.

of Christ. Indeed, if there is only a half-hearted attempt in this life to bury the Old Man, he will continually jump back to the forefront and rule in us. Here we must sigh (groan): God does not want to attribute to us our sin and transgression. He wants to help us cover them and suffocate them and finally also to bring us to complete holiness through the resurrection.

  II. In the second part of this lesson, the evangelists instruct us as to what happened after Christ's burial, namely, that the pious women, who had followed Christ out of Galilee, watched where Christ was buried and thereupon considered that they might anoint Christ's body with costly spices and ointments. Nevertheless, they first observed the Sabbath by being quiet and restful. However, to the high priests and scribes the Sabbath was not so important or holy that they were deterred from their evil intentions against Christ. Rather, on the high Passover Feast they hurried to meet together and decided in council to seal the grave of Christ and to keep a watch over it with guards, so that indeed Christ might not, in keeping with His promise, arise again on the third day. For that reason they went to Pilate and petitioned him for guards to watch the grave. They appealed to him that the disciples of Christ might otherwise come and steal His body and then claim He had arisen. Pilate agreed to this request of the Jews, and Christ's grave was thus sealed and well secured with guards. But is this not dreadful jealousy on the part of the high priests and Pharisees, that the innocent death of the Lord Christ could not satisfy it? Is this not an overpowering godlessness, that they so often accused Christ of being a transgressor of the Sabbath when He healed a sick person on that day, and they, on the other hand, upon the High Passover Sabbath rage against a dead Person? Is this not horrible callousness, that they had seen Christ on the previous days demonstrate His innocence with so many miracles, and they nevertheless still persecute Him after His death? Is this not a gross blindness, that with the sealing of the stone and with the watch of the guards, they think that they can keep in the grave Him who through His divine power had already opened the graves of others? Is it not an audacious evil, that they dared to call Christ a seditionist before Pilate, who yet so frequently and often gave them public testimony of His innocence?

However, through such jealous, evil intentions was fulfilled that of which the Son of God had long before lamented, Psa. 41: **They have perpetrated knavery against Me; when He lies down, He shall not rise up again.** The children of Belial have with Belial, as it is written in His language, plotted a godless counsel; they want to seal the grave this way and secure it with guards, so that I should not again come forth from it. We see here, however, the miraculous deeds of divine strength and power. The high priests and Pharisees sealed Christ's grave and secured it with guards so that Christ's resurrection might thereby be prevented. But God saw to it that [their precautions] made the resurrection of Christ even more glorious and majestic. For the heavenly brightness of the angels who appeared at the resurrection of Christ so frightened the guards that they became as pale as dead men. Also, no stone nor steel was able to hold Christ in the grave. Rather, in the face of all the cunning, all the intentions, all the wits of His enemies, Christ comes forth alive out of the grave and through His resurrection enters into His exaltation.

We have an excellent type of this in Joseph, to whom God the Lord clearly revealed his future exaltation in a dream: that his parents and brothers would bow down before him, Gen. 37. His brothers would not allow this to be and instead sold him into Egypt, thinking that, enslaved, he would surely forget about his dream. However, God saw to it that even being sold into Egypt served to exalt and glorify Joseph. And so it goes here for the heavenly Joseph, for the Lord Christ. His enemies wanted to keep Him in the grave forever. Thus, they sealed the stone and secured the grave with guards. However, under the miraculous management of God, even these means a little later had to serve the greater exaltation and resurrection of Christ.

Finally, the sealing of Christ's grave symbolizes that through His death and burial our sins are sealed, just as the angel makes a glorious prophecy about this to the prophet Daniel, ch. 9: **Seventy weeks have been appointed for your people and for your holy city, for the transgressions to be restrained (checked), the sins to be sealed (stopped), and the crimes to be atoned for; and for the eternal righteousness to be brought in, and the visions and the prophecies to be sealed up, and the Most Holy One to be anointed.** From this prophetic foretelling we are able to say that the sealing of Christ's grave symbolizes, once and for all, that our sins have now been sealed up and buried with Christ so that they no longer may condemn us before God's throne. Just as a person dare not rip open a sealed letter, so also now on the Devil must let the guilt–record of our conscience remain sealed and no longer condemn us on account of it. Accordingly, the sealing of Christ's grave also signifies that the visions and prophecies have been sealed, that is, closed up, superseded, and fulfilled, just as one takes care to seal a letter which has been fully composed. For that very reason, when Christ fell asleep on the cross, and directly wanted to lay Himself into the grave to rest, He said: It is finished (accomplished). Therewith, among other things, He intended to signify that through His death and burial the visions and prophecies of the Old Testament had been sealed.

We may also compare this [Passion] account to the story written in Dan. 6. For there it is recorded that King Darius went to great lengths to keep the prophet Daniel alive; however, upon the persistent urging of his council members, he finally was forced to let Daniel be thrown into the lion pit. Then they brought a stone and laid it in front of the door of the grave [i.e., the lion pit, where Daniel was expected to perish]. The king sealed it with his own ring and the rings of his authorities, but God saw to it that Daniel came out of the lion pit again, healthy and alive. This type may be applied to Christ. Pilate, the Gentile judge, at first made a great effort to keep Christ alive; but finally, at the persistent urging of the high priests and elders, he allowed Christ to be ripped apart by those who opened their jaws wide against Him like raging lions, Psa. 22. Yes, indeed, the Lord Christ was finally laid into the pit of the earth, into a grave. Before its door was laid a huge stone. Pilate sealed it with his own ring, and with the rings of the high priests, the scribes, and the Pharisees. Then God saw to it that Christ came forth again from the grave alive and put to shame all His enemies. Thanks be to You, Lord Christ, who died for the sake of our sin, and who arose again for the sake of our righteousness (justification).

O Lord Jesus Christ, You not only died for my sake, but were also entombed so that my sins would be buried from God the Father's sight; and also, through Your interment my own grave was sanctified. Give me grace so that I never again scrape up such sins, but rather let them stay buried. Your holy rest in the grave extends to me the comfort that someday my soul will rest in the loving hands of God, that my body will peacefully rest in the grave, and that on the Last Day I will enter into eternal rest. Amen.

TRANSLATOR'S EPILOGUE

Yet a final note from the translator: I am humbled at how God saw to it that I had the joy and privilege to translate this Passion History by the sainted Dr. Johann Gerhard. It began when my parents had me baptized into the Christian faith as expressed by the Evangelical Lutheran faith at age 5 days on Christmas Day 1930. Not coincidentally, but providentially, it took place in the German language at St. Paul's Lutheran Church (LC—MS), The Grove, Texas. My parents had me join with my older siblings in speaking 18th/19th-century German around our rough-hewn dining table in a humble tenant farm home nestled under a huge live oak, whose trunk could be encircled by three people touching each other's finger-tips. God further saw to it that my parents sang German baroque Lutheran chorales with me at the table after Supper. Though I have never had a formal course in German grammar, this childhood-acquired *Sprachgefuehl* made it possible for me to work on this translation.

Though born into this Lutheran expression of the Christian faith, I, by the grace of God and the power of His Spirit, have remained in this faith by conviction. It truly is an excellent expression of the Christian faith.

God further directed things in that He took me, a Jonah-styled sinful rebel, and confiscated me for His service into the public ministry of The Lutheran Church-Missouri Synod. He graciously saw to it that I was a beneficiary of the most excellent teachers, professors, and pastors at St. John's College, Winfield, Kansas, and at Concordia Seminary, St. Louis. Had I not graduated from this Seminary, I would not have had the necessary theological acumen to translate the works of this brilliant man, Johann Gerhard, who (unlike me) knew, I am convinced, the entire Bible by heart—also in the original languages.

Some of my colleagues, who happen to be very erudite exegetes of the New Testament, have pointed out to me in jocular fashion that some of Gerhard's Old Testament prototype applications to Christ are (in their words) "a bit of a stretch." But in defense of Gerhard (not that he needs it) I strongly assert that though his exegesis may not always be 'textual', it most certainly is always SCRIPTURAL! That is, he always proclaims what *Christus treibt* (what promotes Christ).

In 1989 the Lord saw fit to let me become disabled. After completing this translation, I no longer wonder why He did. May His good and gracious will be done always, also among us.

Yes, God does all things well. He also provided Prof. Richard Dinda, emeritus, to spark my interest in Johann Gerhard. He provided Prof. David O. Berger at our St. Louis Seminary to be the editor for this and for four previous volumes, as well as the instigator of this whole project. 'Twas he who provided me with a copy of this Passion History in German. God also guided things so marvelously that I came in contact with Pastor Burnell Eckardt, of Kewanee, Illinois, who presented me with a precious volume of Gerhard's sermons. And of course, without Pastor James Heiser of Malone, Texas, we would not have had an efficient, faithful, and competent publisher. Finally, I express my appreciation to my family, especially my beloved spouse, Norma Jean. She patiently endured my pain-induced groans which resulted from sitting too long at a time at the word processor keyboard.

I praise the name of the Lord for employing the gifts He gave me so that you, dear reader, may read this *Erklärung der Historie des Leidens und Sterbens unsers Herrn Christi Jesu*. May the same Holy Spirit who so richly endowed Johann Gerhard with spiritual gifts use this volume as a means to awaken in you a renewed faith in and love for your Savior and Lord. May His blessed Name be praised forever.

We yet add a brief postscript in Latin: ***Soli Deo Gloria!***

Index of Citations from the Sacred Scriptures and the Apocryphal Books.

Old Testament

Genesis
2—8, 282, 287, 302, 313
3—7, 10, 134, 140, 167, 195, 225, 242, 267, 286, 300
3:15—273
4—30, 103, 149, 224, 294
6—144, 213, 301
7—239
9—30, 89, 253
14—88
18—68
20—182, 183
22—8, 30, 32, 99, 103, 167, 196, 221, 235
23—151, 311
28—183, 269
31—30, 182, 183
37—8, 129, 223, 316
39—95, 153, 312
40—102
41—183
49—56, 166, 277, 285
50—306

Exodus
4—193
10—38, 273
12—8, 103, 163, 188, 287, 300
14—239
15—34, 239
17—303
19—58, 295
22—261
24—288
26—292
28:36-37—245
34—166

Leviticus
10—129
16—216
17—107
18—202
24—203

Numbers
4—194
6—273, 275
9—153
12—183
14—129
19—224
20—283
21—8, 30, 210, 241
25—88

Deuteronomy
10—283
13—104, 183, 203
19—126
21—214, 238, 299
23—189
25—106, 135
31—131
32—236

Judges
8—195
11—129
15—98, 100, 278
16—8, 30, 312

Ruth
4—135
1 Samuel
17—240
25—101, 284
2 Samuel
1—129
15—45
16—206
24—235, 298
1 Kings
3—75
2 Kings
6—89, 239
13—314
21—310
2 Chronicles
19—212
36—131
Job
1—131
7—150
9—133
16—30, 106
30—135
Psalms
1—117, 232
2—192, 213, 249
4—184, 273
8—196
9—100, 118
10—199
11—178
13—94
16—7, 10, 216, 269, 271, 286, 312
22—7, 62, 140, 141, 193, 199, 201, 210, 238, 244, 250, 263, 274, 278, 286, 312, 318
23—48, 92
25—107
26—214
27—131, 299
31—160, 261, 264
34—46
35—131, 264
36—38, 279, 280
37—83
38—166, 298
39—52, 150
40—31, 82
41—7, 74, 126, 316
42—62, 265, 280
43—140
44—78
45—18, 135, 309
46—225
49—180
51—194
53—199
55—7, 74, 80
59:6—213
63—280
67—273
68—261, 295
69—7, 63, 74, 106, 135, 213, 236, 237, 281
71—60
85—231
87—224
90—313
92—232
95—148, 270
101—173
103—11, 196
106:30—88
109—264
110—129, 233, 248
110:7—48, 240
111-119—46

114—295
116—25, 90, 100, 102, 128
118—107, 177
122—241
143—66, 106, 280
Proverbs
3—184
5—100, 119
6—127
10—212
15—196
18—127
26—169
31—237
Ecclesiasties
12—285
Song of Solomon
1—17, 74
2—78, 79, 301
4—84, 279
4:10-16—58
5—78, 166, 193, 260
7—1
Isaiah
1—191, 194, 240
2—248, 295, 296
5—102, 195, 236
6—47
8—301
9—133, 134, 225, 248
11—242, 248, 291, 308
14—140
26—307
29:45—150
30—87, 94, 168
31—225
31:9—64
33—196, 253
37—129
38—275

43—243
49—33, 76, 276, 284
50—7, 135, 191
53—8, 9, 10, 14, 51, 52, 62, 83, 102, 135, 156, 164, 166, 180, 191, 201, 216, 234, 241, 243, 258, 263, 278, 286, 297, 309, 312, 313
55—242
61—101, 193, 238
63—57, 58, 62, 75, 83, 193, 227
64—172, 194
66—34, 150, 151, 310
66:14—310
Jeremiah
2—272
5—296
8—236
15—272
15:13—207
17—110
17:3—207
18—125, 150
20—125
29—183
31—120, 288
Lamentations
3—192
Ezekiel
3—262
4—102
16—194, 238, 251
18—270
23:46—207
Daniel
2—182
6—312, 317
7—129
9—107, 181, 286, 317

Hosea
10—236
13—101, 218, 242, 288
Joel
2—274, 298
3—64
Amos
8—274
Jonah
2—8, 63, 287
Micah
7—168
Zechariah
6—248
9—100, 101, 183, 223, 286
10—183
11—8, 145
12—8, 300
13—11, 50, 51, 62, 99, 197
Malachi
2—159
4—273

Apocrypha

Sirach
31—184
34—182
48—297
Wisdom of Solomon
3—271
6:3ff—207
7—285
10—239

New Testament

Matthew
1—183
2—98, 183
3—231, 255
4—89, 224, 262
5—48, 88, 91, 107
7—116
8—251, 259, 274, 311
9—60
10—13, 39, 75, 116, 120, 128
11—14, 34, 91, 118, 218, 226, 227, 282
12—8, 30, 116, 153, 287, 312
13—151, 186
15—204
16—33, 114, 227, 301
17—60
18—39, 131
19—88
20—59, 155, 209
21—177
22—10, 100, 133, 167, 274
23—156, 199, 204, 314
24—230
25—39, 274
26—29ff., 223, 287
28—39, 294, 299
Mark
3—60
5—60
7—100
10—253, 287
13—70, 254
14—31
Luke
1—247
2—38, 258
5—255
6—49
8—40, 60
9—46, 86, 116
10—9, 40, 238, 251
11—132, 181, 242

12—157, 191, 283
13—143, 170
14—116
16—161, 279
17—160, 299
18—107, 281, 298
19—213, 295
21—87, 107
22—279
23—10
24—33, 101
John
1—133, 161, 226, 252, 269, 300
2—127, 263, 286, 303
3—8, 18, 80, 92, 155, 210, 241, 308
4—252, 280, 303
5—131, 186, 271
6—259, 301
7—156, 309
7:46—130
8—78, 100, 116, 161, 217
10—51, 55, 76, 90, 228, 250, 283, 284, 302
11—31, 184, 185, 247, 273
12—36, 38, 65, 111, 115, 155, 186, 241, 310
13—77, 116, 257
14—117, 132, 161
15—12, 62, 116, 232
16—93
17—39, 117, 161, 234, 248, 269, 284
17:19—181
18—81
19—8
20—60, 238, 299
21—94, 120, 255
Acts
1—145

2—7, 80, 142, 240, 312
3—289
4—11, 51, 99, 106, 129, 131, 177, 202, 215, 223, 295
5—98, 168, 212
6—231
7—56, 142, 285, 311
9—20, 150
10—46
13—7, 312
14—33, 90, 205
15—98
19—192, 226
20—18
22—232
23—108
25—154
Romans
1—167
2—131, 143, 248
3—133, 167
4—287, 311
5—8, 10, 12, 271, 288
6—149, 287, 289, 314
7—100, 191
8—69, 90, 131, 132, 181, 204, 205, 215, 227, 281
9—150
10—128, 282
11—91
13—88, 208
16—226
1 Corinthians
1—135, 228
2—1, 18
2:8—182
3—132
4—39
5—156, 164, 287, 300
6—52, 218, 310

7—173
10—60, 303
11—47
12—254, 309
13—136
15—7, 140, 188, 286, 312, 313
2 Corinthians
1—227, 260
3—302
3:18—136
4—53, 71, 76, 77, 128, 228
4:6—136
5—216, 252
6—132
8—251, 311
10—89
12—10, 59, 72, 197, 229, 238, 259, 261, 299, 309
Galatians
2—12, 14
3—2, 11, 48, 131, 202, 238
4—203, 215, 260
5—71, 218
6—13, 218, 227
Ephesians
1—20, 161, 254
2—150, 177
3—68, 71
4—254, 255, 294, 309
5—47, 224, 234, 303
6—89, 92, 148
Philippians
2—9, 14, 76, 204
3—310
Colossians
1—13, 161, 274
1:24—227
2—131, 132, 135, 240, 248, 286, 293
3—254

4—102
1 Thessalonians
2—213
5—91
1 Timothy
1—121, 149
3—20
4—47
6—77, 148, 160
2 Timothy
2—100
4—196
Titus
1—116
2—144
Hebrews
1—65, 224, 309
2—276, 287
3—148, 292
4—89, 293
5—107, 233, 234, 274, 276, 293
5:7—67
6—130, 196, 217, 231
7—164
9—8, 151, 287, 288, 292
10—146, 217, 234, 282
11—37, 103
11:13—151
12—192, 225, 282
13—224, 225
James
1—161, 196
4—279
5—131
1 Peter
1—7, 53, 72, 77, 281
2—14, 17ff., 103, 107, 164, 177, 196, 224, 226, 228, 240, 279
2:21—14
5—196, 276

2 Peter
1—133
2—100, 274
3—196

1 John
1—241
2—243
3—39, 131, 136
5—302

Revelation
1—56, 172, 193, 227, 282
3—172, 238, 251
5—172
6—187, 296
7—172, 194, 279
12—131, 273
13—289
14—186, 196, 271
17—78
19—12, 62, 192
21—186, 217, 280, 297
22—131, 225